HOW FREE ARE WE?

HOW FREE ARE WE?

WHAT THE CONSTITUTION SAYS WE CAN AND CANNOT DO

JOHN SEXTON and NAT BRANDT

M. EVANS AND COMPANY, INC. / New York

Library of Congress Cataloging-in-Publication Data

Sexton, John.
  How free are we?

  Bibliography: p. 307
  Includes index.
  Includes text of the Constitution.
  1. United States—Constitutional law—Miscellanea.
I. Brandt, Nat. II. United States. Constitution.
III. Title.
KF4550.Z9S38   1986   342.73   86-4491

ISBN 0-87131-481-9   347.302
ISBN 0-87131-474-6 (pbk.)

M. Evans and Company, Inc.
216 East 49 Street
New York, New York 10017

Design by Lauren Dong

Manufactured in the United States of America

9 8 7 6 5 4 3 2

Contents

Foreword

The constitutional ideas of majority rule, protection of minorities, equality of citizens, diffusion of the powers of government, and desire for a fundamental law are as old as the Magna Charta and as current as the struggle to end apartheid in South Africa.

But few, if any, of the great landmarks in the history of democracy stand taller than the U.S. Constitution, the miracle of 1787. At the time, John Adams called it "the greatest single effort of national deliberation that the world has ever seen." On the occasion of the first centennial, Gladstone called it "the most remarkable work known to me in modern times to have been produced by the human intellect at a single stroke . . . in its application to political affairs."

The genius of the Constitution is that, in Paul Freund's phrase, it is both Newtonian and Darwinian—Newtonian, in the sense of action and reaction, force and counterforce, checks and balances; Darwinian, in the sense that it is organic and evolving.

As a nation we have no hereditary institutions and a minimum of ceremonial symbols. The Constitution itself is our fundamental symbol—the core of our identity and our continuity, our unity and also our diversity.

Originally conceived to repair the flaws in the Articles of Confederation and establish a modest form of national government for widely divergent former colonies, our Constitution has demonstrated a formidable ability to respond to challenges from any source—whether from the militant rivalry of totalitarian governments or from the more friendly competition of parliamentary democracies or even from within, by economic forces that would mire us in depression or by those in high places who violate the public trust on which the Constitution rests.

Again and again over the past two centuries, the Constitution has proved its capacity to protect and expand our freedom, while safeguarding the domestic order and the national security essential for liberty to grow and flourish.

In September 1987, the nation will be celebrating the bicentennial of the Constitution. As we enter this period of commemoration, therefore, I hope that the country as a whole and each of us as individuals will give fresh thought to ways in which our founding document and our present institutions relate to the fundamental freedoms that shape our lives.

In this book, John Sexton and Nat Brandt offer an excellent starting point for such an examination. It is a concise, well-written handbook that makes the Constitution accessible and understandable to every citizen and that enhances our perception of the vital role of the Constitution in our daily lives.

We are proud of our country's past, and our prayer for the future is that the next two hundred years under the Constitution may be even greater than the first.

EDWARD M. KENNEDY
United States Senator

Preface

The Framers of the Constitution would have been surprised at what they had wrought. Even though he signed the Constitution, Alexander Hamilton privately described it as a "weak and worthless fabric" that he was certain would be superseded. Luther Martin saw it as a stab in the back of the Goddess of Liberty. A fellow Marylander, Daniel Carroll, described it as "the Continental Congress in two volumes instead of one." And most delegates to the Constitutional Convention, including James Madison, the "Father of the Constitution," thought—or hoped—that it would last a generation at the longest.

But it has endured, surviving foreign wars, a civil war, the Industrial Revolution, booms and busts, and all the other vagaries of our history and continues to survive into the Nuclear Age. It is still very much alive today—and touches every one of us in uncounted ways. That it does so is best illustrated by the kinds of questions—and answers—that the reader will find here. They address personal issues—to mention a few, women's rights, children's rights, the right of each of us to choose his or her life-style, homosexual rights. Does a woman have the right to have an abortion? Does a child have the same rights that an adult has? How private is your bedroom? Do homosexuals have any rights? Are all the rights in the Bill of Rights equal? The questions also address issues as vital to our national life as the balance of powers among the president, Congress, and the courts: Who decides whether we go to war? What happens if the president is ill? Can the president send Congress home?

In order to put these issues into the proper context, the first part of the book covers the history of the Constitution and the men who wrote it, their motives and intent, the politics that shaped the document, how it has been amended, and explanations of the workings of the different branches of government. That is followed, in the second half of the book, by questions having to do with rights, with special emphasis on individual rights.

However, the book can also be enjoyed as a kind of serendipitous journey into the most fascinating political document ever written. We say fascinating because both of us—one a legal scholar, the other a journalist—have shared, in writing this book, an excitement over the wisdom that permeates the Constitution and its amendments. You won't always agree with a Supreme Court interpretation, but you'll get to appreciate, as we do, the Constitution's flexibility and its paradoxical ability both to withstand terrible political pressures and to bend with the times. It is a living, breathing document in the best sense of those words. And even as this book goes to press—on the eve of the celebration of the bicentennial of the Constitution—the Supreme Court has before it, as it always will, cases that may further clarify, broaden, or even change the way the Constitution is construed in our time. (We've indicated the areas where this is so.)

In summary, the book is intended as a handy guide to the Constitution for the general reader as well as for the college or advanced high-school student. A detailed index lists all the issues covered in the book. In addition, for the student, a compilation of pertinent citations, a brief but helpful bibliography, and the text of the Constitution and its amendments appear in the back of the book. With them appears a calendar of events associated with the bicentennial of the Constitution.

We would be remiss if we did not express our gratitude to several friends and colleagues who helped us in important ways as we prepared this book. Richard B. Bernstein, a historian and attorney who read each draft of the manuscript and who provided us with valuable reactions to it, made an especially important contribution. Daniel Chazin, David Drueding, and Lisa Goldberg, each an experienced attorney who generously took time to evaluate the book as it progressed, helped us immeasurably. Michael Broyde and Frederick Mandler, two New York University Law School students, provided research assistance. And Shirley Gray, whose efficiency and warmth never cease to amaze those who work with her, patiently typed the manuscript and helped to coordinate our efforts. We thank each of you. Our thanks also to Yanna Kroyt Brandt and Past America, Inc., for all their efforts to have this book published.

John Sexton
Nat Brandt

Introduction ══════════════════════════

Growing up, I had a pretty good idea of who our leaders were. I heard FDR on the radio and later watched famous senators like John Kennedy and Richard Nixon on television and still later I met some of the men in the Oval Office. As a boy I was somewhat like the children who, according to psychologists, know two symbols of authority—the corner policeman and the president of the United States. Later, I realized that we had lots of leaders besides presidents and cops.

But I did not know much about what lay behind the actions of the leaders. I knew more about various people who governed than about the government. Somewhere behind all the leaders was some kind of supreme governor that gave them power, limited their actions, and refereed their disputes when they fell to quarreling about who had power to do what.

That supreme governor, of course, is the Constitution. It is also a rather quiet, almost unseen one. To be sure, you can see the Constitution itself on exhibit in its hermetically sealed showcase in the National Archives. But I defy you to read the Constitution without finding your eyes glazing over. Also, it is fearfully complicated, with different branches having power to do different things and having power also to stop other branches from doing other things.

So power lies there quiet and almost unseen. When there is a crisis, however, or a problem that must be solved quickly or a major dispute among leaders over who has power to do what, lo and behold, the Constitution springs into action. Different sides appeal to it, legislators invoke it, the press argues about it, the courts finally—until they may change their minds—interpret and apply it.

Obvious or not, the Constitution is always there governing. When the House of Representatives passes a bill and the Senate does not go along and, in effect, vetoes it—that is the Constitution operating. When the president takes some warlike action and a senator stands up to challenge it—that is the Constitution being invoked. When a president vetoes an act of Congress and when Congress then overrides that veto by a two-thirds vote—that is the Constitution in action. Day after day, in a few dramatic manifestations, but also in a thousand unseen ways, the Constitution is governing, granting power here, checking it there, blocking it entirely somewhere else—as in the case of some official's denying citizens their right to attend the church they prefer, to give the speech they wish, to demonstrate peacefully against the bill they oppose, or to write a newspaper column against the city mayor, the local corporation head, or the town police chief.

It would be nice if, on top of all this, the Constitution were an easily understandable document allotting plain and simple grants of power—perhaps giving the majority total power to govern until the next election and giving the minority the right to oppose. But, as these pages will make clear, the Constitution divides power in complicated ways in order to tame it, to prevent government, public or private, from "ganging up" against the people's liberties. The price we have to pay—and a rather small price it is—for living under a constitution that so nicely balances power is that we have to study the Constitution, learn its habits, understand its needs, know how to make use of it.

The Constitution, someone has said, is like a fine old Swiss watch with all those second and third hands and little windows and stop-and-go buttons. The Constitution, too, has its exquisite balances, springs of power, internal controls: It was not easy to put together; it is quite durable, but it must not be abused. And above all, it is a complex piece of mechanism. Its powers and limitations must be understood; it must not be used for the wrong purposes, such as closing down newspapers or synagogues, any more than a watch should be used to strike a child.

So, we must know our Constitution. The pages that follow might well be subtitled, "What you always wanted to know about the Constitution but were afraid to ask." People should not be embarrassed to show some ignorance of our great charter. As a veteran political scientist, I would not want to have to pass a quiz on some of its provisions! But I do want to know how to find out. So do you—and this work will answer your questions in readable and graphic form.

These days the Constitution is a kind of "growth industry" and for a simple reason—it is approaching its two-hundredth birthday. In fact, we are nearing a "constitutional era" of commemorations—the bicentennials of the drafting of the Constitution in 1787, of the ratification of the Constitution by the states during 1787–1788, of the inauguration of the new federal government in New York City in 1789, of the adoption of the Bill of Rights in 1791.

We will do well to celebrate the birthday of the Constitution, but we must do so with more than parades and fireworks. The Constitution was the work of one of the most intellectually creative groups in Western history. Certainly it was the most brilliant act of constitutional and political planning in the modern era. But no one—certainly not the Framers themselves—believed that the new charter was fixed in its details for all time. Indeed, they provided an amending process that made it possible, though not easy, for later generations to change the Constitution to meet the needs of a changing United States.

Hence we should be willing to "cerebrate" the Constitution as well as to celebrate it. If we really wish to honor the Framers of 1787, we should try to emulate their capacity to stand back from the then-existing government, assess its strengths and weaknesses, and build anew as necessary. Recognizing the external and internal perils that threatened the vulnerable young republic clinging to the shores of the Atlantic, they also saw the great opportunities ahead, such as expansion to the West and the development of commerce.

In short, as the past two hundred years have shown, the Framers planned well. Can *we* wisely use their document for the two centuries that lie ahead—centuries that may produce unimaginable problems and possibilities? We lack the Framers' genius, but perhaps we can imitate their capacity to learn. They had done their "homework," studying and reflecting on Hobbes and Locke, Montesquieu and the Scottish Enlightenment philosophers, and many others. So should we. But we have the great advantage of being able to learn from two centuries of constitutional experience, as reflected so richly in the questions and answers that follow.

James MacGregor Burns
Woodrow Wilson Professor of Government
Department of Political Science
Williams College

How to Use This Book

Inspired by some recent sensationalized news coverage of police who cracked down on pornographic magazines on newsstands—censorship at work—a mutual friend of ours thumbed through our manuscript looking for, as he put it, "the good stuff." What he discovered is what we hope you'll find: "the good stuff" is there—direct answers to questions about how the Constitution touches your life, your home, your work, your marriage, your child—all in the second half of the book. But, in order to appreciate how the Constitution does that, it's also important to understand what led the Framers to decide what they did, and how and why they set up our system of government and certain safeguards and procedures. Their logic and reasoning is fascinating—and pertinent to our lives today in ways the Framers would never have anticipated. Accordingly, we've divided the book into two sections. Dip into the first part, which we call "Our Federal System," and read how the Constitution came to be written, how it's been amended (and can still be amended), how Congress, the president, and the courts interact, and how power is divided between the states and the federal government. The second part of the book—"Our Rights and Liberties"—covers the kinds of questions that can come up almost every day as we react to the news of the day and wonder about the rights involved in subjects as diverse as voting, religion, free speech, equality, criminal justice, our schools, our workplaces, the armed forces. That's where it all comes together. But the book is also designed for times when you just want to browse. All the entries are in question-and-answer form and are written so that you can wander at leisure, stopping to read about topics that interest you without having to read any preceding entry. They make sense on their own. Or—if you're curious about a particular subject—you can locate it in the Index at the back of the book and go immediately to it. In addition, if you want to probe further, you'll also find in the back of the book a list of case citations, a bibliography, the Constitution and its amendments, and a calendar of events associated with the Constitution. So, whether you're reading for pure pleasure and knowledge or are in search of specific data about the Constitution and its workings, you can readily find what you're looking for.

Part One
OUR FEDERAL SYSTEM

The Making of the Constitution

No, not in the strict sense of the word. For most of modern history the word *constitution* has meant the entire legal framework of a nation. For example, the English "constitution" includes the Magna Charta of 1215, which was the first written set of restrictions on kingly power, the Petition of Right of 1628, the English Bill of Rights of 1689, the Reform Bills of 1832 and 1867, many statutes, judicial decisions, and royal pronouncements, as well as common law and established government customs and usages. Thus the English constitution is both much less than and much more than a written constitution such as ours. In fact, a *written* constitution—setting forth a plan of government, establishing its institutions, and proclaiming the rights of citizens—is a relatively new development.

Although claims have been made for the Mayflower Compact of 1620, the 1630 charter of the Massachusetts Bay Colony, and the 1639 Fundamental Orders of Connecticut, many scholars agree that the first written constitution of government was England's 1653 Instrument of Government. The Instrument, which set out a new, republican form of government, and its 1657 successor, the Humble Petition and Advice, were swept away by the Restoration of Charles II in 1660 and had almost no influence on either English or American constitutional development, but they did presage many later reforms in England.

The English colonists in North America regarded themselves as Englishmen possessing all the rights of Englishmen, even though they lived thousands of miles away from the mother country. Each colony had some form of written instrument of government by the eighteenth century, usually a royal charter. Originally, there were three types of colonies: *joint-stock companies,* organized as economic ventures under a charter granted by the Crown conferring certain privileges, as with trade (for example, Virginia and Massachusetts Bay); *compacts,* agreements reached by and among the colonists themselves (Plymouth; Providence, R.I.; Fundamental Orders of Connecticut); and *proprietary colonies,* in which the Crown granted the land composing the colony to one or more landholders known as proprietors. By the mid-eighteenth century, most of the colonies were *royal colonies,* in which the former joint-stock company or compact form had been replaced by direct royal authority residing in the governor. In Maryland, Pennsylvania, and Delaware, the proprietors (not the Crown) appointed the governors; in Connecticut and Rhode Island, the surviving charter colonies, the colonists themselves chose their governors. Each colony also had a two-house, or bicameral, legislature; the lower house was elected by those colonists who could meet qualifications based on the amount of real or personal property they had, while the upper house was selected by the lower house. The upper house, or council, had both legislative and executive powers and duties, in that it also advised the governor on a daily basis. The royal charters that most colonies possessed became the focus of disputes between the colonists and their governments, with the colonials challenging what they saw as arbitrary and unconstitutional exercises of power.

The initial stages of the American Revolution were moves and countermoves in an intricate but fierce struggle to determine the limits of Parliamentary authority. Parliament retained supreme legislative power over the colonies, while at the same time other key agencies, such as the Privy Council, the Secretary of State, the Treasury, the Admiralty, and the Board of Trade, also had responsibility for colonial affairs, with the result that for most of the seventeenth and eighteenth centuries British administration of the colonies was entangled in bureaucratic infighting and prey to incompetence and mismanagement.

In May of 1776, anticipating its action two months later in the Declaration of Independence, the Second Continental Congress passed a resolution calling upon the colonies to prepare new, written constitutions in case it became necessary for them to separate from England. A few colonies merely modified their old charters, deleting all references to the king and England, but within the next few years most prepared entirely new, republican constitutions. These reflected the Americans' concern with arbitrary power, particularly arbitrary executive power. Pennsylvania's constitution of 1776 even did away with a separate executive, establishing instead a Supreme Executive Council chosen by and under the thumb of its one-house legislature. Other states provided for a weak governor and a powerful two-house legislature. Still others, notably New York in 1777 and Massachusetts in 1780, created an independent governor, who was armed with veto power over legislation (although New York's constitution granted only a qualified veto power to a council of revision composed of the governor and several state judges), and a system of checks and balances among the legislative, executive, and judicial branches of government. Massachusetts's most significant contribution to American constitutional thought was a stipulation mandating ratification of its constitution by the people in special conventions called for that purpose. Previous state constitutions merely went into effect after being adopted by their legislatures. The Massachusetts idea recognized the distinction between constitutions and mere statutes. Its constitution—chiefly the work of John Adams—and the New York one—largely that of John Jay—were important models and sources for the subsequent framing of the U.S. Constitution.

◆◆◆ What Kind of Government Did the United States Have before the Constitution?

A loose and often ineffectual confederation.

As early as 1754, Benjamin Franklin had suggested the formation of an intercolonial government, the so-called Albany Plan of Union, but he was generally ignored. It was not until twenty years later, with the summoning of the First Continental Congress, that the American colonists began to experiment with a system of government on a higher level than local or colonial institutions. The First Continental Congress convened in Philadelphia in 1774 to discuss the appropriate response by the colonies to Parliament's repeated assertions of authority to legislate for the colonies even though Americans went unrepresented in Parliament. That Congress, composed of delegates from twelve colonies (Georgia was not represented) chosen by their legislatures, served as the model for the Second Continental Congress, which began meeting in Philadelphia in May 1775.

The Second Continental Congress was originally called to serve only as a deliberative body, but it soon became the chief organ of government of the United States as the pressures of the escalating war with England forced the colonies to delegate to it the power and responsibility of conducting the war and foreign relations. In 1776, in the same week that Congress adopted the Declaration of Independence from England, Congress also appointed a committee to draft a new instrument of government. In 1777, Congress submitted the Articles of Confederation to the states for ratification. The Articles of Confederation were ratified by most states within two years, though Maryland, the last state to ratify the document, did not do so until 1781.

The Articles created a government of severely limited powers. Each state sent a delegation to the Confederation Congress. Voting in it was by state rather than by population, and in order for a law to pass, at least nine of the thirteen states had to vote in favor of it. There was no separate executive, though there was an officer called the "President of the United States in Congress Assembled." There was a separate secretary for foreign affairs, who oversaw the diplomacy of the United States and coordinated the work of the various ambassadors. Congress could request the states to contribute money, arms, and supplies to the United States, but the states could and often did refuse to comply, and Congress had no power to compel them to meet their obligations. Moreover, the Confederation Congress had no power to impose taxes or customs duties. Proposals to give it such authority were consistently defeated by states that were eager to gather money through their own imposts and did not want to surrender these lucrative sources of revenue. In addition, the Congress had no power to regulate interstate commerce. Finally, there was no separate federal court system, though Congress had the power to hear interstate disputes and to establish a committee to hear shipping disputes.

Almost immediately after the Articles of Confederation took their final form there were numerous but unsuccessful attempts to obtain additional powers for Congress. However, unanimous consent was needed to amend the Articles, so one state alone could block a reform agreed to by the other twelve. Congress was frequently unable even to secure a quorum to transact business; at such times, an executive committee composed of one delegate from each state kept the government going until a quorum could be assembled.

It is still a matter of historical controversy just how successful or unsatisfactory a government the Articles created. Although it was true that the Confederation Congress frequently had barely enough resources to maintain the Continental Army, and although states repeatedly flouted congressional authority, the Confederation government deserves credit for several notable achievements. Foremost among these was the winning of American independence. Then, too, to negotiate the Treaty of Paris of 1783, which formally ended the Revolutionary War, Congress chose diplomats who were probably the ablest the United States has ever had: Benjamin Franklin, John Adams, Thomas Jefferson, and John Jay successfully forged alliances with France, Spain, and the Netherlands, and Franklin, Adams, and Jay brilliantly represented the United States in the peace talks in Paris. Furthermore, as a result of the Treaty of Paris, the United States acquired vast new territories stretching to the Mississippi River. In three ordinances passed in 1784, 1785, and 1787, the Confederation Congress established a procedure under which this territory was organized into states, each to be admitted into the Union on an equal footing with the original thirteen. The principle behind these ordinances was later adopted in the Constitution.

◆◆◆ What Prompted the Constitutional Convention?

Almost from the day that Maryland, the last state to do so, ratified the Articles of Confederation on March 1, 1781, leading political figures in a number of states complained that the Articles did not provide a strong enough federal government. They tried repeatedly to get the Articles amended; they were especially eager to give the Confederation Congress authority to levy duties on imports in order to provide the government with its own independent source of revenue. However, every one of their amendments was defeated because of the requirement that amendments to the Articles had to be adopted unanimously.

Then, what began as a meeting between representatives of two states set a model for an even broader conference that blossomed eventually into the Constitutional Convention. The initial meeting came about in 1785, when Maryland and Virginia agreed to settle a long-standing dispute over jurisdictional and navigational rights in coastal waters shared by both states. Commissioners appointed by each of them were scheduled to assemble in Alexandria, Virginia, in March of that year, but George Washington offered the hospitality of his home at Mount Vernon and the commissioners met there instead. The conferees quickly agreed on a compact governing not only water rights but also matters of currency exchange, bills of exchange, and import and export duties. Both states swiftly approved the compact.

As a result of the success of what became known as the Mount Vernon Conference, Virginia proposed a larger conference on commercial measures that would include all thirteen states, to be held at Annapolis, Maryland, in 1786. This meeting proved a mixed bag. Delegates from only five states—Delaware, New Jersey, New York, Pennsylvania, and Virginia—arrived in time. Those from Massachusetts, New Hampshire, North Carolina, and Rhode Island showed up after the conference had already dissolved. And four states—Connecticut, Georgia, South Carolina, and even Maryland—never sent any representatives. Nevertheless, the conferees who were there adopted a resolution, drafted by Alexander Hamilton of New York, calling for a general convention of all states to meet in May 1787, this time in Philadelphia. And, unlike the Annapolis Convention, this meeting would have the authority to discuss all issues having to do with "render[ing] the constitution of the Federal Government adequate to the exigencies of the Union." The resolution was subsequently backed on February 21, 1787, by the Confederation Congress, which officially called upon all the states to send delegates to Philadelphia.

Rhode Island refused, so when the Constitutional Convention convened, it was composed of delegates from twelve states. It took two weeks for enough of them to gather to reach a quorum, but the Convention finally began its work on May 25, 1787. From then through the middle of September, with a recess in midsummer, the delegates deliberated behind closed doors, finally producing the Constitution, in the form we know today, on September 17.

Once the Constitution was written, the Convention sent it to the Confederation Congress with a covering letter from George Washington, who had been the Convention president, recommending that it be forwarded to the states for approval. Article VII of the Constitution provided that the Constitution would go into effect upon ratification by nine states. After a long and bitter contest, the Constitution was ratified by the needed nine states by June 1788. Two more of the original thirteen states ratified it by July 1788. The remaining two, North Carolina and Rhode Island, eventually bowed to pressure from the new federal government and approved it in 1789 and 1790, respectively.

◆◆◆ Who Decided Who Would Write the Constitution?

The state legislatures. They, in consultation with their governors, chose the delegates to the Constitutional Convention, in the same way they had selected representatives to the Second Continental Congress, the Congress under the Articles of Confederation, and other interstate conferences.

All told, fifty-five delegates from twelve states attended all or part of the Convention. More than half had been members of the Confederation Congress, and many others had served in state legislatures. Half were college-educated, three had been or were college professors, and two were college presidents. Many were lawyers, four of whom had attended the Inns of Court in London. Of the most learned and most knowledgeable of American leaders of the period, only John Jay, John Adams, and Thomas Jefferson were not at the Convention.

Although George Washington, Benjamin Franklin, and other elder statesmen such as William Samuel Johnson and Roger Sherman of Connecticut, John Dickinson of Delaware, and George Mason of Virginia did attend, most of the delegates were far younger men. Charles Pinckney of South Carolina, for example, was only twenty-nine years old. The younger men had received their political training under the new state constitutions, which many of them had helped to draft, and under the Articles of Confederation. While sensitive to the needs and peculiarities of their states, they had developed the habit of thinking nationally as Americans rather than as Virginians, Pennsylvanians, or New Hampshirites. The most important of these younger delegates—in addition to Pinckney—were James Madison of Virginia; Gouverneur Morris and James Wilson of Pennsylvania; Oliver Ellsworth of Connecticut; Elbridge Gerry, Rufus King, and Nathaniel Gorham of Massachusetts; and Hugh Williamson of North Carolina. (Alexander Hamilton of New York was present, but despite his efforts to bring about the Convention, and although he later worked to secure ratification of the Constitution, he contributed little of value to most of the Convention's debates.) They formed the core of the Convention—and later of the new government created by the Constitution.

Eighty-one years old and infirm but still mentally alert, Franklin allowed his younger colleagues to do the major substantive work of the Convention. He acted as a voice of conciliation and compromise, seeking to defuse the often-heated debates. Closing out his long career of public service by representing Pennsylvania, Franklin—in a brilliant and widely reprinted speech delivered on the closing day of the Convention—urged all the delegates to put aside their reservations and doubts and sign the Constitution.

Perhaps the one person who was most critical to the Convention's achievement was Washington. He emerged out of formal retirement from public life to serve as a member of the Virginia delegation, persuaded to do so despite personal doubts about the chances for the Convention's success. His services as commander in chief of the Continental Army had convinced him of the weakness of the Articles of Confederation and had prompted his frequent appeals to give the Confederation Congress more power. Keenly aware of his national prestige, Washington shrewdly used his influence to promote his conception of the national interest. Though he gave only one brief speech during the four months of the Convention, his presence alone was assurance that many Americans would find the Constitution palatable. On top of that, he was unanimously elected president of the Convention, at the suggestion of Franklin, his only likely rival. His acceptance of the office, his endorsement of the Constitution, and his signing of that document and the Convention's letter transmitting the Constitution to the Confederation Congress were essential contributions to the ultimate success of the ratification campaign. Furthermore, Washington's silent dignity and reserve in presiding over the Convention's deliberations helped to preserve the delegates' sense of the seriousness of their task and to hold the Convention together.

◆◆◆ Who Actually Wrote the Constitution?

Although James Madison was credited with being the author of the Constitution, he rejected the honor, saying that the document was "not like the fabled goddess of wisdom the offspring of a single brain [but] ought to be regarded as the work of many heads and many hands." Madison himself credited Gouverneur Morris of Pennsylvania for "the finish given to the style and arrangement." And, indeed, the Preamble—"We the People of the United States . . ."—is Morris's doing.

Madison's name is so closely connected with the Constitution because of a set of resolutions he drafted, later called collectively the Virginia Plan. (It was only after his death and the publication of the journal he kept during the Constitutional Convention that Madison became known as the "Father of the Constitution.") The resolutions were offered by Edmund Randolph, governor of Virginia and spokesman for its delegation, when the Convention began the actual business of revising the Articles of Confederation on May 29, 1787. These resolutions, which called for a completely new form of government, formed the basis of the Convention's deliberations and, ultimately, of the Constitution itself.

Madison's resolutions were a major departure from the structure of the Articles of Confederation. They called for the creation of a national government having legislative, executive, and judicial branches. The Articles had only created a Congress, which itself could create some executive departments and quasi-judicial bodies with drastically limited jurisdiction. Madison's national legislature would have two branches, the first to be elected by the people, the second to be elected by the first from nominees chosen by state legislatures. A state's representation in each chamber was to be based on its population. The national body would have power to legislate in all areas in which the individual states would not be competent and in which national uniformity was necessary. The national judiciary would include at least one supreme tribunal. It and the national executive would be chosen by the national legislature. The executive and some members of the national judiciary would constitute a council of revision, with an unconditional veto power over all legislation.

Although the Virginia Plan was the focus of the debates at the Constitutional Convention, it was not the only plan offered. In response to the bias
in favor of large states inherent in that plan, most notably in the Virginia
Plan's provision that both houses of the legislature be apportioned among
the states on the basis of the population, William Paterson of New Jersey
acted as spokesman for the small states in offering a series of proposals later
known as the New Jersey Plan. The critical difference between the two
plans was that the New Jersey Plan preserved the form of representation of
the Articles of Confederation—that is to say, each state, no matter how
large or small, would receive an equal vote in each house of the national
legislature. The dispute over representation dragged on for weeks. Although the Convention rejected the New Jersey Plan on June 19, the
Convention did not find a way out of the representation dilemma until July
16, when it adopted the Great (or Connecticut) Compromise. This compromise, in which the delegates from Connecticut played the role of
brokers and conciliators, provided that the lower house be apportioned on
the basis of population and direct taxation, although slaves were to be
counted as three-fifths of free persons for both purposes, and that each
state would have equal representation in the upper house.

Two other delegates offered their own plans. Charles Pinckney of South
Carolina offered his on the same day that Randolph presented the Virginia
Plan; although the original version has disappeared, historians who have
managed to reconstruct it from the notes of other delegates have shown
that it resembled the original Virginia Plan in most respects. In the midst
of the debate over the Virginia and New Jersey Plans, Alexander Hamilton
of New York offered a proposal for a truly consolidated national government. His plan would have reduced the states to mere administrative
districts, created a bicameral legislature in which the members of the
upper house would serve "during good behavior" (this meant for life unless
removed by impeachment), and provided for an executive who would also
serve during good behavior. Hamilton's plan, offered in a six-hour speech
delivered on June 18, the day before the New Jersey Plan was rejected, was
never seriously considered by the Convention.

During the deliberations, the various resolutions, proposals, and drafts
were referred to committees for recasting. Each revised and rewritten draft
then formed the basis for the next stage of the Convention's discussions.
The committees considered not only formally adopted resolutions but also
individual delegates' memoranda as well as informal drafts. All the proposals served as raw material from which the committees prepared the next
draft for general discussion.

After more than three months, the Convention, on September 8, created a Committee of Style and Arrangement and appointed to it Madison, Morris, Hamilton, Dr. William Samuel Johnson of Connecticut, and Rufus King of Massachusetts. In five days, the committee produced a nearly final draft almost identical to the text of the Constitution that was subsequently approved.

With the assistance of the other members of the committee, Morris completely reorganized and rephrased the previous drafts, giving the wording of the Constitution terse dignity and power, especially in the Preamble. His choice of certain phrases was made in a conscious effort to emphasize two major points: that it was the people of the United States, not the states, who were creating the Constitution and empowering the new government, and that the focus of the Constitution was on the centralization of power in a national government. For example, in previous versions the preamble merely listed the states constituting the United States without setting forth purposes and goals. Rather than listing them by name, Morris's Preamble begins, "We the People of the United States." Morris hoped that such a turn of phrase would protect the new government from embarrassment if a state chose not to ratify the Constitution. But those who have studied the Convention's work—and, indeed, Morris, Madison, and James Wilson themselves—also knew that those opening words underscored the nationalist thrust of the Constitution, that the new government would not be another mere confederation of states.

One final note: The man who actually penned the original copy of the Constitution—now on display in the National Archives in Washington, D.C.—was Jacob Shallus, a Pennsylvanian who was assistant clerk to that state's legislature, which met in Philadelphia in the building now known as Independence Hall. He was paid the equivalent of thirty dollars for the job.

◆◆◆ Who Are "We the People"?

Originally, "We the People of the United States" referred to little more than the ratifiers of the Constitution. But in the nearly two centuries since 1787, numerous amendments have given the phrase new meaning, so that now it signifies all Americans.

In the draft of the Constitution first proposed, the Preamble—closely modeled on the introductory statement of the Articles of Confederation—included no statement of purposes and carefully identified each state in the new Union:

> We the People of the States of New Hampshire, Massachusetts, Rhode-Island and Providence Plantations, Connecticut, New-York, New-Jersey, Pennsylvania, Delaware, Maryland, Virginia, North-Carolina, South-Carolina, and Georgia, do ordain, declare, and establish the following Constitution for the Government of Ourselves and our Posterity.

However, because the Constitutional Convention had decided that the Constitution would go into effect upon being ratified by nine states, rather than all thirteen, it seemed foolish to list all the states. Anyway, it was by no means clear which states would accept or reject the new charter. So Gouverneur Morris of Pennsylvania artfully evaded the issue by using the shorthand designation "We the People of the United States." Although Patrick Henry of Virginia subsequently denounced the wording of the Preamble in his state's ratifying convention, demanding to know who the people of the United States were, no delegate to the Convention found fault with the revised wording:

> We the People of the United States, in Order to form a more perfect Union, establish Justice, insure domestic Tranquility, provide for the common defence, promote the general Welfare, and secure the blessings of Liberty to ourselves and our Posterity, do ordain and establish this Constitution for the United States of America.

At the time the Constitution was being written, each state had adopted qualifications for voting that excluded many Americans from the political process. The qualifications limited the right to vote to those who could show that they had sufficient property—either in cash or real property—to entitle them to vote. Many states also restricted voting to those who took an oath subscribing to certain religious doctrines, such as a belief in God, or in God and Jesus Christ, or in the Christian religion. Almost nobody even conceived that anyone but sufficiently wealthy white men would vote, and restrictions on who could hold office in the states were even more stringent. The Framers of the Constitution refused to impose similar religious "test oaths" or property qualifications for holding federal positions such as member of the House of Representatives. But they provided that voting qualifications for election to the House would be the same as those set by the states for electing the "popular" branch of their legislatures. Even this provision—which made the Constitution the most liberal and democratic government charter in the world—nevertheless excluded many Americans.

As the Constitution settled into use over the next two hundred years and amendments were added, Americans whom the Framers never dreamed would take part in American politics were included in the national political community. For example, the Fifteenth Amendment, ratified in 1870, guaranteed blacks, most of whom were newly freed slaves, the right to vote. Under the Nineteenth Amendment, ratified in 1920, the Constitution finally recognized women's right to vote—a right that had been recognized in twelve states by 1914.

In 1961, the Twenty-third Amendment extended the right to vote in presidential elections to residents of the District of Columbia—which would have amazed the Framers, who never anticipated that the seat of government would grow to become one of the ten largest cities in the nation, with hundreds of thousands of residents who were effectively disenfranchised because they did not live in a state. In 1964, the Twenty-fourth Amendment—by abolishing the poll tax—rejected once and for all the old doctrine that a person had to demonstrate some "stake" to be allowed to vote.

Finally, in 1971, the Twenty-sixth Amendment guaranteed the right of eighteen-year-olds to vote in federal, state, and local elections. Before this amendment was passed, each state was free to establish its own minimum voting age because the federal Constitution did not do so. Thus, before 1971, while eighteen-year-olds could vote in Georgia and Kentucky, nineteen-year-olds in Alaska and twenty-year-olds in Hawaii, most states had set their minimum voting age at 21.

Thus, two centuries later, "We the People of the United States" means far more than it did in 1787—and the United States is far more than ever a democracy.

◆◆◆ Why Did Some of the Founding Fathers Not Attend the Constitutional Convention?

For a variety of reasons, including doubts over its purpose. And one state refused to send any delegates at all.

Several noted patriots were unable to attend. Thomas Jefferson was our minister plenipotentiary to France, and John Adams, our minister in Great Britain; neither man, it was felt, could be spared from his important diplomatic duties. Actually Adams spent all of 1786 and most of the next year writing his three-volume work, "A Defence of the Constitutions of Government of the United States of America," amassing in it the accumulated thinking and experience of Western civilization on federal and republican governments. The first volume appeared in Philadelphia just as the Convention began and had some influence on the delegates and later on the public debates over the new Constitution. Jefferson read the Constitution with close attention and, in several long letters to his friend James Madison, identified what he believed to be the key defects of the new form of government, namely the lack of a bill of individual rights and of a limit on the number of terms a president could serve. Jefferson helped persuade Madison to endorse publicly the demand of many opponents of the Constitution that a bill of rights be added to the document as soon as possible after ratification.

Although he was not abroad, John Jay never made it to Philadelphia either. His nomination to the New York delegation was effectively opposed by a faction loyal to Governor George Clinton, who preferred a weak national government so that New York could continue to reap the benefits of regulating its own trade. Besides, Jay could not be spared from his work as the Confederation government's secretary of foreign affairs. Indeed, to all intents and purposes, Jay *was* the nation's government at many times during the Confederation period. Nonetheless, he stayed in close touch with George Washington and other delegates to the Constitutional Convention and made several useful suggestions that found their way into the Constitution. One such suggestion was the Supremacy Clause (Article VI), which says that federal law takes precedence over state law.

The most famous individual who chose not to attend was Patrick Henry of Virginia, who had defied the Crown in 1765, denouncing the Stamp Act and saying, "If this be treason, make the most of it." Henry later claimed that he did not attend the Convention because "I smelt a rat." Maybe so, but more likely he, Richard Henry Lee of Virginia, and William Findlay of Pennsylvania—as well as others like them who had been chosen by their state legislatures—did not attend because they believed that the most important theater of politics was at the state level. Many leading citizens had already disdained service in the Confederation Congress, and often Congress had to implore members to attend in order to make up a quorum so that it could function. No doubt prompted in part by the disappointing results of the Annapolis Conference in 1786, these men refused to participate in the Confederation Congress or the Constitutional Convention in Philadelphia in 1787—an indication that they believed that nothing significant or valuable would come of the Philadelphia meeting.

Alone of the thirteen states, Rhode Island would not send any delegates, though several merchants from Providence and Newport assured those who did go that they would support any stronger frame of government that the Convention might produce.

◆◆◆ Did the Constitutional Convention Overstep Its Mandate?

On the surface it would seem so—and that's one reason why now, two centuries later, some lawmakers are concerned about the potential of a "runaway" convention should a convention be called to consider a constitutional amendment for a balanced federal budget.

The resolution drafted by Alexander Hamilton of New York that the Annapolis Convention of 1786 adopted recommended that the states should appoint delegates to meet in Philadelphia in May 1787 "to devise such further provisions as shall appear to them necessary to render the Constitution of the Federal Government adequate to the exigencies of the Union." However, the word *Constitution* referred at that time to the whole structure and arrangement of institutions making up the government of a society. It did not mean a written document setting forth the system of institutions of government and their several powers and limits. Had it been adopted unchanged, this recommendation would have given the Constitutional Convention unlimited discretion to propose not merely amendments to the Articles of Confederation, but an entirely new constitution as well. Several states followed the recommendation of the Annapolis Convention and appointed delegates to what would become the Constitutional Convention. Other states chose to wait for the Confederation Congress to act on the Annapolis Convention's recommendations.

On February 21, 1787, the New York delegates to the Confederation Congress proposed a resolution calling for a convention in terms almost identical to those urged by the Annapolis Convention. That set off a debate during which the Massachusetts delegates, Rufus King and Nathan Dane, proposed the resolutions ultimately adopted, among them:

> That in the opinion of Congress, it is expedient, that on the second Monday in May next, a Convention of delegates, who shall have been appointed by the several States, be held at Philadelphia, for the sole purpose of revising the Articles of Confederation, and reporting to Congress and the several Legislatures, such alterations and provisions therein, as shall, when agreed to in Congress, and confirmed by the States, render the Federal Government adequate to the exigencies of Government, and the preservation of the Union.

A purely literal reading of this resolution and of the Articles of Confederation amendment provisions suggests that the writing of a new constitution fell far outside the mandate of the Convention.

Once the Constitutional Convention got under way in earnest in late

May 1787, Governor Edmund Randolph of Virginia proposed a set of resolutions written by James Madison later known collectively as the Virginia Plan. They called for a completely new government to replace, not just to amend, the Articles. The next day the Convention resolved itself into the more informal organization called the Committee of the Whole to discuss the Virginia Plan and, to begin with, faced the question of the Convention's powers under the congressional resolution. Yet the delegates no sooner raised the issue than they settled it almost without debate. Of chief concern was the first of Randolph's resolutions: "That a National Government ought to be established consisting of a supreme Legislative, Executive and Judiciary." This immediately raised the question whether the delegates should create a national government that would absorb the states or merely a stronger federal government with the power to operate directly on the American people, unlike the Confederation Congress, which had no such power. Even the most outspoken nationalists at the Convention argued for the preservation of the states. Thus, almost without dissent about their mandate from Congress, the delegates to the Convention proceeded without qualms as to their authority to frame a new form of federal government to replace the Articles. And they adopted Randolph's resolution.

◆◆◆ Why Were the Debates at the Constitutional Convention Kept under Wraps?

Because the delegates didn't want everyone looking over their shoulders—and, anyway, legislative debates then were held in private almost without exception.

On May 29, 1787, the delegates to the Convention adopted a rule "[t]hat no copy be taken of any entry on the journal [of the Convention] during the sitting of the House, without leave of the House . . . [and] That nothing spoken in the House be printed, or otherwise published or communicated without leave." This rule of secrecy apparently had the approval of nearly every delegate and was strictly observed. As George Mason of Virginia wrote to his son:

> This, I think, myself, a proper precaution to prevent mistakes and misrepresentation until the business shall have been completed, when the whole may have a very different complexion from that in which the several crude and undigested parts might, in their first shape, appear if submitted to the public eye.

One of the few who objected was Thomas Jefferson, then the American minister to France. He complained to John Adams, the American minister to Great Britain:

> I am sorry they began their deliberations by so abominable a precedent as that of tying up the tongues of their members. Nothing can justify this example but the innocence of their intentions, and ignorance of the value of public discussions.

The idea to keep the discussions secret was not surprising in the eighteenth century. Both legislative debates and proceedings were only rarely, if ever, open to the public in Britain and America, and legislatures did not hesitate to prosecute printers for publishing reports of debates and votes without permission. Such reports, it was widely and justly believed, frequently contained gross inaccuracies and should not benefit from even an implied legislative endorsement. Only rarely in the ratification process did opponents of the new Constitution criticize the rule of secrecy. And neither the Anti-Federalists nor the few published criticisms of and comments on the rule during the Convention appealed to any notion whatsoever about the public's "right to know."

What is known about the actual workings of the Convention has been pieced together from surviving notes, committee drafts, and members' private journals. The first account of the Convention that came out was Luther Martin's *Genuine Information,* a pamphlet published in 1788 by this Maryland delegate who became one of the bitterest opponents of the Constitution. The official *Journal* of the Convention, kept by its secretary, Major William Jackson, was published in 1819; it is a skeletal and error-riddled document. In 1821 appeared *Secret Proceedings,* a pamphlet reprinting John Lansing's transcript of the diary of the Convention kept by Robert Yates. Yates and Lansing were two delegates from New York who opposed strengthening the Confederation government; they left Philadelphia on July 10. Thus, Yates's notes, though pungent and informative, break off a little less than halfway through the Convention. Lansing's own more fragmentary notes were not discovered and published until 1939.

Several delegates kept notes of the Convention's proceedings, but by far the most complete and important was James Madison's *Notes of the Debates in the Federal Convention of 1787.* Madison, the architect of the Virginia Plan, which formed the basis of the Convention's deliberations, set out to be its informal chronicler as well. Each day—and he never missed a session—Madison kept a shorthand journal that he laboriously copied out each night. He remembered in his old age that this self-imposed chore nearly killed him, but his fellow delegates occasionally assisted him by providing him with their notes or speeches. Madison was able to keep his record secret until his death, allowing only his close friend and political ally, Thomas Jefferson, to read it. And he resolved not to permit publica-tion of the *Notes* until the death of all delegates to the Convention, in order to spare any delegate the embarrassment that disclosure of his remarks at the Convention might cause him. As it turned out, Madison himself outlived all the other delegates. When he died in 1836, his widow followed his instructions and sold the *Notes* and his other papers to the federal government. Attorney General Henry D. Gilpin published a three-volume edition of Madison's papers, including the *Notes*, in 1840, and the *Notes* have been frequently reprinted. It was because of his *Notes* and his extraordinary contribution to the work of the Convention that Madison came to be called the "Father of the Constitution."

Madison's *Notes* are the most important source for historians, legal scholars, litigants, and judges in trying to determine the intent of the Framers of the Constitution. The problem, however, is that, even with the *Notes* and all the other sources available, there frequently is not enough information to arrive at a definitive answer. Moreover, even if a definitive understanding of what the Framers meant by a given provision could be determined, it is by no means evident that that single interpretation should be considered binding through the centuries. As Chief Justice John Marshall declared in 1819, the Constitution is "intended to endure for ages to come and, consequently, to be adapted to the various crises of human affairs."

◆◆◆ Why Did Some Delegates to the Constitutional Convention Fail to Sign the Constitution?

For a number of reasons, but perhaps the most common was that most of those who did not sign had left the Convention long before the Constitu-tion was completed. In all, of the fifty-five delegates from twelve states who attended, only thirty-nine actually signed the completed document.

George Wythe of Virginia, a staunch supporter of the movement for a stronger national government, left the Convention a few weeks after it opened because his wife was gravely ill and dying. Other delegates left because of the pressure of other personal affairs, among them such impor-tant contributors as William Paterson of New Jersey and Oliver Ellsworth of Connecticut. Still others arrived late and left early, feeling little com-mitment to the work of the Convention.

John Lansing and Robert Yates of New York left in disgust in early July, concluding that the Convention was bent upon creating a powerful national government and submerging the states to the level of mere administrative units. Their departure deprived the New York delegation of a quorum. Alexander Hamilton, the state's sole remaining delegate, left the Convention to return to his law practice for several weeks in the summer of 1787, but he returned for the final few weeks of deliberations. At the signing of the Constitution on September 17, 1787, Hamilton carefully wrote the name of each state opposite its delegates' signatures and signed the document himself on behalf of New York despite some question whether he had the authority to represent the state on his own.

Three delegates who stayed to the end—Edmund Randolph and George Mason of Virginia and Elbridge Gerry of Massachusetts—refused to sign the Constitution. Randolph, Virginia's governor and one of the state's most popular politicians, had begun the Convention by proposing the Virginia Plan—the resolutions, drafted by James Madison and offered by the Virginia delegation, which became the basis of the Convention's deliberations. Randolph was, at the outset anyway, a major advocate of scrapping the Articles of Confederation in favor of a more powerful and "dignified" government. But almost immediately he began to waver, opposing various proposals to strengthen Congress, to create a powerful executive, and to grant general rather than enumerated powers to the new government. Although he carried some of his points, Randolph's fears that the new Constitution would prove unpopular led him finally to announce a neutral stance: he would not sign the Constitution, but he would not oppose it either. Instead, he said he would keep his judgment open during at least the first stages of the controversy over whether it should be ratified by the thirteen states. By the time Randolph did endorse the Constitution, his indecisiveness proved an embarrassment and he had to write a public letter explaining his vacillation. Virginia did ratify the Constitution, but by a close vote.

George Mason, who also initially supported the move for a stronger national government, was later moved by his loyalty to Virginia to emphasize the interests of the states and could not accept many of the compromises incorporated into the final version. He believed that the government established by the Constitution would be too powerful and aristocratic. He said it would pose a threat to liberty because, for one thing, the Convention had rejected his proposal to attach a declaration of rights to it. Mason, who said, "I would sooner chop off my right hand" than sign the Constitution, became a leading opponent of ratification in his state.

Elbridge Gerry feared democracy—"the worst," he said, "of all political evils." He had resisted various proposals to give the people a greater role in government; he opposed the election of members of the House of Representatives by citizens and advocated a president chosen for a term of fifteen years by the governors of the states. Gerry claimed that, by giving encouragement to the unstable forces of democracy, the Constitution would plunge the nation into civil war.

Of the nonsigners, only Mason later refused office under the new Constitution. Randolph became Washington's attorney general and succeeded Thomas Jefferson as secretary of state. Gerry served as a senator during the 1790s and died as Madison's vice president.

◆◆◆ Was There Significant Opposition to Ratification of the Constitution?

Yes, and at times it seemed that all thirteen states might not ratify it.

When the Constitutional Convention sent the Constitution to the Confederation Congress in late September 1787, controversy immediately broke out about whether Congress should recommend it to the states. Several members argued that the Convention had gone far beyond its assigned task and that the Constitution was a threat to liberty and to republican government; consequently, they said, either Congress should not transmit the Constitution at all or it should recommend against its adoption. James Madison, who was not only a member of the Confederation Congress from Virginia but also a just-returned delegate from the Constitutional Convention, successfully argued that Congress should merely send the Constitution to the states without comment, thus leaving to the people the decision whether or not to adopt the new form of government.

The Convention had provided in Article VII that the Constitution should be ratified by the people of each state in conventions specially called for that purpose. The alternative would have been ratification by state legislatures. But the Convention delegates shrewdly recognized that the legislatures would probably reject the Constitution out of hand. So they adopted an idea first put forward in the Massachusetts Constitution of 1780: the constitutional ratifying convention—an affirmation of faith in the general public's judgment.

At the time there were no clearly organized political parties, though loose networks of like-thinking politicians existed across state boundaries. Supporters of the new Constitution quickly seized on the name Federalists and stigmatized their opponents by referring to them as Anti-Federalists—the implication being that many of them wanted to break up the Union into several regional confederacies. Though they fought back, the Anti-Federalists could never rid themselves of the label.

The ratification debates were marked by high-minded intellectual argument and no-holds-barred political maneuvers. In Pennsylvania, for example, there were not enough Anti-Federal members of the state legislature to block the calling of a ratifying convention directly, but there were enough to deprive the legislature of a quorum if they all stayed home. The Federalist legislators angrily directed the sergeant at arms to locate and apprehend two Anti-Federal legislators, the minimum number needed to complete the quorum. Accompanied by a cheering mob, the sergeant at arms broke into a locked rooming house and seized the two men, who were held until their votes against calling a convention could be recorded.

The ratification battle was conducted in the press, through broadsides and by pamphlets setting forth the arguments of both sides. *The Letters of the Federal Farmer* by Richard Henry Lee of Virginia was the most important Anti-Federalist publication. The most significant of the Federalist publications was *The Federalist*, a series of eighty-five newspaper essays written by John Jay, who was forced by illness to withdraw after only five essays, Alexander Hamilton, who wrote fifty-one of them, and James Madison, who wrote twenty-six. (The remaining three were written jointly by Hamilton and Madison.) Nearly all these publications appeared anonymously under pen names derived from classical literature such as Brutus, Caesar, and most famous of all, Publius of *The Federalist*. This was typical of the late eighteenth century both in England and in America.

The first five states to ratify—Delaware, Pennsylvania, New Jersey, Georgia, and Connecticut—did so unanimously or by overwhelming majorities. Massachusetts proved far more difficult; the final vote for ratification (187 to 168) came about only after the Federalists suggested that their opponents prepare a series of proposed amendments to be affixed to the Constitution for consideration should it actually be ratified. Soon thereafter, Maryland and South Carolina ratified by wide margins. New Hampshire, on June 21, 1788, became the ninth state to ratify, thus putting the new Constitution into operation under the terms of Article VII. But Virginia and New York, the largest and richest of all the states, had not yet taken action, and a nation without either or both could not survive.

James Madison and Edmund Randolph led the fight for ratification in the Virginia convention. Opposing them were George Mason, who had refused to sign the Constitution, Richard Henry Lee, and above all,

Patrick Henry, the leading orator of his time. Henry and Madison battled for weeks, until Virginia finally was persuaded by the cogency of Madison rather than by the sometimes incoherent remarks of Henry. On June 25, before word of New Hampshire's ratification arrived—but after adopting a twenty-article declaration of rights and twenty other amendments—Virginia's ratifying convention adopted the Constitution by a vote of 89 to 79.

Alexander Hamilton led the fight for ratification in New York, with the assistance of John Jay, the most respected Federalist political figure in the state. They wisely delayed the vote on ratification until news arrived of the ratifications of New Hampshire and Virginia. The Federalists then carried the day by a vote of 30 to 27, though New York's ratification was conditional on the consideration of proposed amendments by the new Congress.

◆◆◆ Which States Failed at First to Ratify the Constitution?

North Carolina and Rhode Island. North Carolina's first ratifying convention chose to keep the state in a kind of limbo, and Rhode Island refused even to authorize the election of such a convention.

The impasse in North Carolina was the work of Willie Jones, a wealthy political leader who had been elected to but refused to attend the Constitutional Convention. Jones, the leader of the state's Anti-Federalists, represented residents of North Carolina's back country against the mostly Federalist coastal and urban regions at the state's first ratifying convention in Raleigh in July 1788. Elections to it had been marred by violence and bitter invective, and Jones's faction controlled nearly two out of every three delegates. Jones believed that North Carolina and any other states that rejected the Constitution could force through concessions by amending the new charter. So in the face of the oratorical and forensic brilliance of James Iredell, the state's leading Federalist and later an associate justice of the U.S. Supreme Court, Jones proposed that North Carolina hold itself in abeyance. The convention adopted his motion by a vote of 183 to 84, and Anti-Federalists felt assured that this would pressure the new national government into adopting a bill of rights, or perhaps even calling a second constitutional convention.

Rhode Island had long taken a contrary, stubbornly independent course in American politics ever since the colony was founded in the 1630s by Roger Williams, a refugee from religious persecution in Massachusetts. The state had repeatedly vetoed amendments to the Articles of Confederation, and its several statutes protecting Rhode Island debtors from the claims of out-of-state creditors made the state a byword for reproach throughout the nation. One Massachusetts Federalist even welcomed Rhode Island's refusal to send delegates to the Constitutional Convention; he proposed that Massachusetts and Connecticut divide the state between them. Other Federalists would have been content with expelling the state from the Union or with allowing Rhode Island to go its own way. Rhode Island's governor, John Collins, explained the state's refusal to send delegates to Philadelphia by charging that the Convention violated the Articles of Confederation. When asked to ratify the new Constitution, the state government responded in March 1788, by issuing a call to town meetings to vote on it. Infuriated by the legislature's evasion of the ratification procedures specified by the Constitutional Convention, Federalists boycotted the meetings. The result was a lopsided vote of 2,708 to 237 to reject the Constitution. The Federalists were equally distressed when the legislature rejected further calls for a ratifying convention.

When the new national government began operations, North Carolina and Rhode Island occupied a strange position. Anti-Federalists in both states joined forces with die-hard opponents of the Constitution in Pennsylvania, New York, and elsewhere in a fruitless campaign for a second convention to rewrite or propose amendments to the Constitution. Meanwhile, the new government gingerly tried to accommodate itself to this embarrassing situation by refraining from assuming some functions—such as that of the post office—while assuming others—such as making payments to invalid pensioners. In trying to woo the "wayward sisters," Congress at first declined to impose federal tariffs and other customs duties on goods entering the United States from Rhode Island and North Carolina. As their recalcitrance persisted, however, congressional and executive patience frayed, and customs restrictions on goods from those states were passed in the summer and fall of 1789—though only some minor restrictions were actually imposed, as a moratorium on imposing the others was adopted to encourage the two states to come into line.

North Carolina was the first to relent; the state had always been less rigidly Anti-Federalist than had Rhode Island. In fact, North Carolina had sent a delegation to the Constitutional Convention and had appointed commissioners to observe closely the actions of the new government. Despite the expectations of Jones and his allies, the United States seemed all too able to do without the two holdout states, and the campaign for a second constitutional convention failed. Eventually Iredell and his colleagues succeeded in calling a second ratifying convention, which met in November 1789. Its delegates adopted the Constitution, 194 to 77, after vehemently rejecting a last-ditch attempt to tack on to it amendments such as a declaration of rights and restrictions on the federal government's powers to tax and regulate commerce.

Rhode Island proved far more stubborn, using excuses and delaying tactics. Congress's implied threat to remove its moratorium on major trade barriers against the state gave impetus to the Rhode Island Federalists' campaign to call a state ratifying convention. By then, the proposal to attach a bill of rights to the Constitution had removed one of Rhode Island's main objections. The ratifying convention was finally scheduled to meet in May 1790—though, worried that the convention might reject the Constitution, Providence and Newport, the state's largest cities, threatened to secede if that did happen. The convention, however, did ratify the Constitution, by the narrow vote of 34 to 32. And so Rhode Island, one of the first states to declare its independence from England in 1776, became the last of the original states to ratify the Constitution.

◆◆◆ How Was Our Government Set Up Once the Constitution Was Ratified?

Only after a great deal of frustrating delay and political maneuvering. It took the better part of a year, once New Hampshire became the critical ninth state to ratify the Constitution in June 1788, before the new government began to become a reality.

First of all, the Confederation Congress, still in existence and meeting in New York's City Hall, had to set dates for the election of representatives and for the state legislatures to choose presidential electors. Then it had to select a new national capital, make sure senators were elected by the state legislatures, and finally, see that a president and vice president were selected by the electors. These formidable tasks were set out by the Constitutional Convention in a resolution adopted and sent to the Confederation Congress together with the completed Constitution. They were made complicated by the Anti-Federalist campaign for a second constitutional convention and by the "wayward sisters," North Carolina and Rhode Island, which did not ratify the Constitution until well after the various branches of government began operating.

One of the earliest disputes centered on where the new national capital should be located. First, should the temporary capital, in New York, be moved, and if so, where to? And second, where should the permanent capital be? The debate raged between northern states that wanted to retain

New York as the capital and southern states that wanted it moved south, preferably to at least Philadelphia. Eventually, a compromise was worked out. New York, the nation's capital since 1785, would continue as the temporary capital. A site to be determined later but located on the Potomac River between Maryland and Virginia would become the probable location of the permanent capital.

As for the elections to be held under the Constitution, the problem was complicated. It was up to the state legislatures to call for elections for the House, but there was no uniformity in how they went about it. Some did it by a general at-large vote, others by district voting.

The states also chose presidential electors in their own individual ways—several by popular vote, some through their legislatures, some by a combination of both. And because of delays caused by Anti-Federalist opposition to the Constitution, New York never did pick electors for the first presidential election.

The choice of senators was as varied: by joint ballot of both houses in the legislatures of Virginia, Maryland, New Jersey, and Delaware; by ballot in each house in New Hampshire, Massachusetts, and New York; and by the vote of the one-house legislature in Pennsylvania. The methods used in Connecticut, South Carolina, and Georgia are not known—no records were kept.

George Washington was the unanimous choice of the electors as the first president, but he had been a far from aggressive candidate for the office. In fact, he served only because he saw it as his duty. But controversy did surround who would be the first vice president. Washington was a Virginian, so clearly a northerner was needed for balance. The choice narrowed to two men from Massachusetts—John Hancock and John Adams, both signers of the Declaration of Independence in 1776. At first it appeared that Adams would probably be named chief justice of the Supreme Court, leaving the vice presidency to Hancock. However, Hancock's vacillations in support of the new Constitution and his attitude favoring amendments to it began to turn supporters against him. Adams, who enjoyed a reputation for integrity and ability, became the favored choice. But it was far from smooth sailing. Alexander Hamilton and other Federalists tried to keep him from getting elected by too great a vote. For one thing, they wanted to solidify their influence with Washington and to block Adams because he envisioned that the vice president would be a sort of "prime minister" of the Senate. Their campaign was successful: Adams failed to get a majority of second-place votes and his feelings were deeply hurt. However, he did win a plurality and thus became the first vice president.

It took weeks for the new House of Representatives and the Senate to form quorums needed to open business, count the electoral votes, and get the new government under way. In the meantime, the old executive departments of the Confederation Congress continued in existence. The new Congress was scheduled to begin March 4, 1789, but each house continued to adjourn from day to day until the House finally convened on April 1 and the Senate on April 6. On April 6 the electoral votes were counted by both houses and the Senate elected John Langdon of New Hampshire president pro tempore—that is, for the time being—until John Adams could reach New York to head the Senate.

Washington, meanwhile, had to borrow money to pay for his trip from his plantation at Mount Vernon to New York. He arrived in time to be sworn into office on April 30, 1789. The oath was administered by Robert R. Livingston, chancellor of the state of New York. (Washington finally paid off the debt of £600 to a merchant of Alexandria, Virginia, in December 1790.)

The business of the new Congress next focused on creating a system of customs duties and establishing new departments of State, the Treasury, and War, each to be headed by a secretary. Then it enacted, and Washington signed into law, the Judiciary Act of 1789, one of the oldest and most important laws in American history. It created a Supreme Court with a chief justice and five associate justices, a system of district courts, and a system of circuit courts. The act also provided that in certain instances litigants could appeal from a state's highest court to the U.S. Supreme Court—a provision that gave the Court ultimate authority to enforce the Constitution against the states.

The first chief justice—chosen by Washington—was John Jay of New York, who had been secretary for Foreign Affairs under the Articles of Confederation. His colleagues on this first Court—all of whom Washington also named—were James Wilson of Pennsylvania, William Cushing of Maryland, John Blair of Virginia, John Rutledge of South Carolina, and James Iredell of North Carolina (which by then had ratified the Constitution). Wilson, Blair, and Rutledge had all served at the Constitutional Convention. Cushing and Iredell were leaders of the ratification forces in their states. (Iredell was chosen after Robert Hanson Harrison, a respected Maryland judge who had been an aide to Washington during the Revolution, declined to serve because he had just become chancellor of Maryland and was also in ill health. Harrison died a few months after the Court first convened.) The justices met for the Court's first session on February 2, 1790.

◆◆◆ Is There Any Source for My Rights Other Than the Constitution?

Yes. There are five other sources: the constitutions of the fifty states, the laws of the United States, the laws of the fifty states, common law, and treaties.

In recent years state constitutions have been used more and more to expand individual rights because of what was seen to be the unwillingness of the Supreme Court to extend, through its interpretations, the scope of rights guaranteed under the federal Constitution. For example, many state constitutions now have an equal-rights amendment prohibiting discrimination based on sex.

Frequently, state constitutions, like the federal Constitution, limit only the abridgement of rights by government. For example, your First Amendment right to speak freely does not prevent your employer from firing you for saying something he or she didn't like, any more than your Fourth Amendment protection against invasions of your privacy prevents your boss from opening your attaché case. Those guarantees protect you only from the government and its agents. Important relationships between you and other persons—perhaps the most important relationships in your life—are generally unaffected by either your state or federal constitution, though they may be governed by state or federal statutes.

Federal and state statutes are an important source of your rights. Sometimes, they add to the rights that the Constitution provides against the government. For example, several statutes passed just after the Fourteenth Amendment was ratified in 1868 give citizens the right to sue for money damages government officials who deprive them of the rights guaranteed in the amendment.

Other times, federal and state statutes may give you rights in your relationships with other persons. In 1964, for example, Congress passed the Civil Rights Act, which, among other things, outlaws racial discrimination in employment and housing. Nothing in the Constitution protects a black worker from being refused a job by a company in private industry because he or she is black, but the Civil Rights Act does.

So also, state statutes can expand your rights. For example, some states have laws that ban discrimination against homosexuals—a type of discrimination not presently covered by federal law.

Common law, the system of judge-made law originating in medieval England and still in use and being expanded upon by modern courts, also gives you certain rights. In fact, common law provides most of your basic rights against other persons. For example, there is a common-law right to privacy. If your neighbor bugs your telephone or an advertiser uses your photograph without your permission, you can sue, alleging a violation of common law.

Finally, treaties may be a source of some of your rights, though rarely do treaties that our nation signs provide greater rights for individuals than are found in our federal and state constitutions, statutes, and common-law rules. It is true, however, that you could invoke a treaty if it conferred a right not otherwise available to you. For example, because of a clause in the Treaty of Paris of 1783 between Great Britain and the United States, Loyalists who were exiled during the American Revolution were able to sue Americans who owed them money before the Revolution. And treaties are certainly an important source of rights against foreign governments for Americans who travel abroad or otherwise deal with those governments and their citizens.

There is a hierarchy among the sources of your rights. The U.S. Constitution is supreme. No treaty, state constitution, federal or state statute, or common-law rule may lessen the rights bestowed by the Constitution. So also, by virtue of the Supremacy Clause of the Constitution (in Article VI), no state constitution, statute, or common-law rule may reduce a federal right, no matter what the source of that federal right. Finally, a treaty and a federal statute are of equal force; neither is superior to the other. Therefore, if a treaty and a federal statute are inconsistent, the one that became effective most recently controls the other.

Amending the Constitution ═══════

Formally by amendment, but in practice also by the evolving interpretations of the Constitution by the Supreme Court and other courts and by the development of informal customs and usages.

The amending procedure spelled out by Article V of the Constitution is a difficult and drawn-out process, as recent proponents of an equal-rights amendment for women have discovered. There are two steps to amending the Constitution: first, proposing an amendment; second, ratifying it. An amendment may be proposed in two ways: Either two-thirds of the members of each house of Congress propose the amendment, which is then sent to the states, or Congress complies with the "Application" of the legislatures of two-thirds of the states and calls a convention for proposing an amendment, which is then sent to all the states for ratification. No matter how it is proposed, three-fourths of the states must *ratify* an amendment for it to become part of the Constitution. Congress can decide that this ratification be done either by the legislatures or by specially elected state ratifying conventions. Congress can also set a time limit for ratification: usually seven years, a limit first set when the Eighteenth Amendment, outlawing liquor, was proposed in 1917.

The amendment procedure raises several constitutional issues. For example, can a state rescind its ratification of an amendment, as some have tried as the result of political shifts in their legislatures? Or can a state legislature require that its ratification vote be by more than a simple majority? In a 1975 case, a three-judge federal district court ruled that the Illinois legislature could require a three-fifths vote for the equal-rights amendment. However, the issue has never been decided definitively. The Supreme Court indicated in 1939 that the issue may be one of a number of "political questions" that are best left to the political branches of government to resolve.

So far, all the amendments that have been proposed and adopted have originated in Congress. However, for some years there has been a growing movement to call a convention to consider an amendment that would make a balanced federal budget mandatory. The proposal is at present two states short of the two-thirds needed.

Of thirty-three amendments proposed by Congress, only seven have failed to win ratification by the states. They were a limitation on when congressional salary increases become effective (proposed in 1789), a set of guidelines for apportioning House seats (1789), a proposal to revoke the citizenship of anyone accepting a foreign title or honor (1810), the so-called Corwin amendment to prevent future amendments that would interfere with the institution of slavery in any state (1861), a ban on child labor (1924), the equal-rights amendment for women (1972), and statehood for the District of Columbia (1978).

Although an amendment is the most formal, sweeping, and visible way to revise the Constitution, most changes have actually taken place as the result of interpretations by the Supreme Court and lower federal courts. Here the major issues are twofold: First, does the Constitution mean what it always meant or does its meaning change with time and context? Second, are the courts bound solely to interpret the existing language of the Constitution or can they go beyond it and deduce other constitutional rights from, for example, its structure and purpose? Each of these issues has spawned bitter legal and scholarly quarrels over the original intent of the Framers of this or that constitutional provision. For example, can the court deduce a "right of privacy" from various provisions of the Constitution? It did so in 1965 in a case involving the use of contraceptives by married couples.

American constitutional thought has swung back and forth between two views about interpretation that were best stated by two chief justices, John Marshall in 1819 and Roger B. Taney in 1857. Marshall, in the case of *McCulloch v. Maryland*, declared:

> The subject is the execution of those great powers on which the welfare of a nation essentially depends. . . . This provision is made in a Constitution intended to endure for ages to come and, consequently, to be adapted to the various crises of human affairs. . . . We must never forget that it is a *constitution* that we are expounding.

Taney took the opposing view in the *Dred Scott* case:

> [The Constitution] speaks not only in the same words, but with the same meaning and intent with which it spoke when it came from

the hands of its framers, and was voted on and adopted by the people of the United States. Any other rule of construction would abrogate the judicial character of this Court and make it the mere reflex of the popular opinion or passion of the day.

The third way in which the Constitution changes, by informal custom and practice, is perhaps best illustrated by the institution of the cabinet. Nowhere is it mentioned in the Constitution except for a glancing reference—in Article II, Section 2—to the president's power to "require the Opinion in writing, of the principal Officer in each of the executive Departments, upon any subject relating to the Duties of their respective Offices." Similarly, not only was our system of political parties not contemplated by the Framers, but parties were actually distrusted.

However, often so-called extraconstitutional practices provoke controversies that find their way into cases brought before federal courts and produce new interpretations of the Constitution—as did the controversy that culminated in 1974 in *United States* v. *Nixon.* At the time, President Richard M. Nixon—as had nearly every president since George Washington—refused to divulge private conversations he had had with aides. At specific issue were a number of tape recordings that a grand jury investigating the Watergate scandal had subpoenaed. Citing executive privilege, Nixon refused to turn over the tapes. However, the Supreme Court, in a unanimous ruling, ordered him to do so. The Court said it was up to the judge of the court issuing the subpoena to decide whether a claim of executive privilege was justified.

◆◆◆ Has There Ever Been an Attempt to Call a Second Constitutional Convention?

Yes, many, starting even before the Constitution was completed and for purposes as diverse as considering amendments to ban polygamy and to limit federal taxing power. There's even a current effort—two votes shy of adoption—to call a convention to consider an amendment requiring a balanced federal budget. But no attempt has yet been successful, in part because of a number of unresolved questions growing out of the Constitution's provision calling for such a convention.

Article V of the Constitution sets forth two ways to propose an amendment to the Constitution: the familiar route—by which Congress, by a two-thirds vote of each house, proposes amendments for ratification by the states—and the convention route. The latter procedure, according to

Article V, provides that "[t]he Congress . . . on the Application of the Legislatures of two-thirds of the several States, shall call a Convention for proposing Amendments." However an amendment is proposed, it must be ratified by three-fourths of the states, either by state legislatures or by the vote of specially elected state ratifying conventions. That choice is left to Congress.

All authorities agree that if Congress receives the "magic number" of state applications—now thirty-four—it must call a convention. But what they cannot agree on are the answers to a number of questions: What if state applications are ten years old—as some of those calling for a balanced-budget amendment are? Are they still valid? Does each state application have to be worded in precisely the same way? Can Congress limit a convention to the subject proposed in the applications or can the convention ignore any limitation on its scope? Who decides how delegates to a convention will be chosen? Can a state withdraw its application for a convention? Who resolves disputes that might arise at any stage in the process, the courts or the political branches of government?

Even before the men who wrote the Constitution finished their work at the Constitutional Convention in Philadelphia, Edmund Randolph of Virginia proposed that they ask Congress to call a second convention to review and revise the proposed Constitution before submitting it to the states. The delegates rejected the idea, though Anti-Federalists opposed to ratification of the Constitution subsequently echoed the proposal and both Virginia and New York applied to Congress in 1789 to have a second convention.

Ever since, Congress has received hundreds of state applications for a second convention. In 1833, after South Carolina lost a struggle with the federal government over tariffs and Georgia had lost a Supreme Court decision concerning sovereignty over Indian lands, both states unsuccessfully called for a convention. In 1861, Illinois, Kentucky, Ohio, and New Jersey applied for one "to take into consideration the propriety of amending the Constitution, so that its meaning may be definitely understood in all sections of the Union"—a proposal, designed to avert the impending Civil War, that got nowhere.

Between 1893 and 1929, thirty-five states filed applications with Congress—some seeking specific amendments, others seeking a convention with no limitation. In 1929, Wisconsin insisted that Congress had to summon a convention because it had received three more than the then-required thirty-two state applications. But the applications covered a potpourri of different purposes, some were twenty and thirty years old, and at least eleven specifically sought the direct election of senators, which the

Seventeenth Amendment, ratified in 1913, had already accomplished. So Congress decided against calling one.

From 1941 to the mid-1950s, more than twenty-five states applied for a convention to consider an amendment to limit the rate on federal income, inheritance, and gift taxes to 25 percent, but the movement ran out of steam. Similarly, in 1967, Congress received applications from thirty-two of the now-needed thirty-four states (Alaska and Hawaii having joined the Union in 1959) for a convention to consider various amendments designed to reverse reapportionment decisions made by the Supreme Court. But the required two additional state applications never materialized.

The success of the current proposal for a convention to consider a balanced-budget amendment may well hinge on the answers to the unresolved questions. Realizing that situation, the Subcommittee on Civil and Constitutional Rights of the House Judiciary Committee decided, in July 1985, to conduct hearings on these and other issues raised by the movement for another constitutional convention. Legislation is already pending in the Senate to establish procedures for such a convention. Over all this hovers the warning of Charles Pinckney of South Carolina, who in the last days of the Constitutional Convention in 1787 rejected Edmund Randolph's plea for a second convention. "Conventions," Pinckney declared, "are serious things and ought not to be repeated."

◆◆◆ Why Wasn't a Bill of Rights Included in the Constitution to Begin With?

Mainly because, when the topic was brought up in the closing weeks of the Constitutional Convention, the delegates were too exhausted to frame one. Moreover, they had a ready excuse for not writing one: Most state constitutions contained declarations or bills of rights, and these were the primary guarantees of individual rights in the United States until the Bill of Rights was adopted. No such declaration, for example, was included in the Articles of Confederation—and nobody complained about that omission—because the Articles dealt directly with the states, not with the people as such.

Neither of the competing original models presented to the Convention—the Virginia Plan or the New Jersey Plan—included any declaration of rights. It wasn't until nearly the end of the Convention that Elbridge Gerry of Massachusetts and George Mason of Virginia proposed the appointment of a committee to draft a declaration of rights for the new Constitution. Mason was the primary author of his state's Declaration of

Rights of 1776, the model for all later bills of rights, but his and Gerry's proposal to appoint a committee to consider such a provision for the federal Constitution was voted down by all the states at the Convention almost without debate. Gerry was treated similarly when he and Charles Pinckney of South Carolina proposed a constitutional guarantee of freedom of the press. In fact, Roger Sherman of Connecticut said that "the Power of Congress does not extend to the Press." This offhand rejection of the need for guarantees of individual rights such as freedom of the press was one reason why Mason refused to sign the Constitution.

The omission of a bill of rights prompted vigorous criticism even from supporters of the Constitution such as John Adams and Thomas Jefferson. Alexander Hamilton had argued in No. 84 of the *Federalist* papers that a bill of rights was unnecessary, that the Constitution itself, without saying so, was nevertheless a bulwark of individual liberty. But Jefferson believed otherwise, and he was able to win the grudging support of James Madison, who pledged in the Virginia ratifying convention that he would work in Congress for the preparation and adoption of a declaration of rights should the Constitution be adopted. As if to remind him and his fellow Federalists of their promises, several states attached to their ratification agreements as many as twenty proposed amendments to the Constitution, most of which were the raw material that later gave rise to the first ten amendments.

Madison was unable to get his fellow members of the new House of Representatives to consider a proposed bill of rights until two months after the convening of the first Congress. In June 1789, he announced to the House that he had prepared a draft declaration and presented it for their consideration. The draft included guarantees of religious liberty, freedom of speech and press, the right of conscientious objectors to refuse military service, and many other provisions that emerged in the final amendments presented to the states for ratification. Of perhaps greater importance was Madison's proposal that states as well as the federal government be barred from infringing on religious freedom, freedom of the press, or trial by jury in criminal cases. This proposal went far beyond even the most radical recommendations sent to Congress by the states. Madison regarded it as the keystone to all his proposals and was deeply disappointed when Congress rejected it.

It was only at the end of September of 1789, after numerous conferences and revisions, that the House and Senate agreed on the wording of the amendments to be submitted to the states for their approval. And so, despite the supposed urgency of adding a list of rights to the Constitution, it was not until December 1791 that the first ten amendments were ratified by enough states to secure their addition to the Constitution.

◆◆◆ Did All the States Ratify the Bill of Rights?

No, not until 1939, when Connecticut, Georgia, and Massachusetts finally did as a symbolic gesture to commemorate the 150th anniversary of the proposal of the first ten amendments. The first time around, the amendments were adopted before they had a chance to act.

The writing of the amendments—actually twelve of them at the outset—took up several months in the middle of 1789. James Madison of Virginia began the process in late April by announcing that moderate Federalists like himself would follow up on their promise to propose amendments if the Constitution itself was ratified. He ran into trouble from two quarters: militant Federalists such as Fisher Ames of Massachusetts, who believed such amendments were completely unnecessary and just a sop to public opinion, and extreme Anti-Federalists such as Patrick Henry, a fellow Virginian, who believed the amendments did not go far enough in limiting the powers of the federal government with respect to individuals. Despite the opposition, however, Congress proposed the twelve amendments and sent them to the states on September 24, 1789.

The campaign for their ratification by state legislatures was uneventful. On December 15, 1791, Virginia—the eleventh state to do so—ratified ten of the twelve amendments. (The two that failed related to the apportionment of representatives and their compensation.) Virginia's deciding vote occurred before Connecticut, Georgia, or Massachusetts had a chance to act.

◆◆◆ Has the Constitution Been Changed Frequently?

Considering that the document is nearly two hundred years old, no. The Constitution has been amended only twenty-six times since it was ratified in 1788—and the reasons have varied widely.

The first ten amendments, known as the Bill of Rights, were part of a package of amendments adopted by Congress and sent to the states. They were offered in fulfillment of the pledge of moderate Federalists such as James Madison to work for certain additions to the Constitution in exchange for their states' ratification. These amendments were adopted in 1791.

The Constitution was next amended in 1798. The Eleventh Amendment was a reaction to the Supreme Court's decision in *Chisholm* v.

Georgia in 1793. Executors of the estate of a South Carolina citizen, who at his death was owed nearly $70,000 for supplies provided to Georgia to support the Revolution, brought a lawsuit against Georgia to recover the debt. The Court permitted them to do so, but its ruling provoked a nationwide furor because the decision—that states could be sued without their consent—was seen as an attack on their sovereignty. The decision, many believed, would also allow Loyalists (colonists who had sided with England) whose property had been seized by the states during the Revolution to sue in federal courts to regain their property. Nearly every state had taken such punitive measures against Loyalists. To counter the Court's decision, Congress passed, and the states ratified, an amendment that deprives federal courts of any power to hear civil suits against a state by citizens of another nation or state.

The Twelfth Amendment, ratified in 1804, repaired a defect in the electoral college system that did not become apparent until thirteen years after the Constitutional Convention. Under the Constitution's provision for electing the president and the vice president (Article II), the electors were not bound to designate which candidate they preferred for the presidency. As a result, both Thomas Jefferson and Aaron Burr received an equal number of electoral votes in 1800, even though everyone knew that Jefferson was the Republican party's candidate for president and Burr the candidate for vice president. The Twelfth Amendment established the system of separate voting for the two offices that we still employ today.

The genesis of the Thirteenth, Fourteenth, and Fifteenth Amendments harks back to the issues that divided the nation before and during the Civil War. Of particular concern was the controversial *Dred Scott* case in 1857. Writing for the Court in that case, Chief Justice Roger B. Taney legitimized slavery wherever it existed in the United States and its territories and denied that black Americans had any rights that white Americans were "bound to respect." The Thirteenth Amendment, ratified shortly before the war ended in 1865, abolished slavery or "involuntary servitude" except as punishment for a crime. The Fourteenth Amendment, ratified in 1868, revised the constitutional distribution of power between the states and the federal government, assuring the primacy of the federal government and making some of the guarantees of the Bill of Rights applicable to the states. The Fifteenth Amendment, ratified two years later, guaranteed black Americans the right to vote—although southern whites quickly found ways to block them. Each of these amendments was designed to give teeth to laws passed by Congress after the war to create constitutional and legal protections for the freed slaves.

Forty-three years elapsed before the next two amendments, the Sixteenth and the Seventeenth, were added to the Constitution. Like the Eleventh, the Sixteenth Amendment was a direct reaction to a Supreme Court decision. Ratified in 1913, it grants Congress the right to levy an income tax. The amendment overturned a Supreme Court decision declaring a 2 percent federal income tax enacted in 1894 unconstitutional.

The Seventeenth Amendment, also ratified in 1913, changed the method of electing senators to direct election by the people of a state rather than by state legislatures. The effort to establish such direct election was an outgrowth of reform campaigns aimed at breaking up the corrupt influences of special interests and business trusts. The amendment stymied these interests' ability to control senatorial elections through bribery or blackmail of state lawmakers and by striking deals with political bosses.

The Eighteenth Amendment, ratified in 1919, established Prohibition, the so-called noble experiment. This constitutional ban on the making, the selling, and the transporting of alcoholic beverages was designed to provide constitutional authority for the enactment of the Volstead Act, which set up a national program to enforce Prohibition.

The Nineteenth Amendment, ratified the following year, guarantees women the right to vote. Universal suffrage was unheard of when the Constitution was framed. Voting then was limited to male property owners, and women later only enjoyed the franchise in certain states at certain times.

The Twentieth Amendment, ratified in 1933, eliminated the so-called lame duck sessions of Congress. Previously, because the Constitution provided that the president be inaugurated on March 4, there was a period of some four months between election day and inauguration day during which an outgoing president and Congress could enact laws opposed by a newly elected president and Congress. By moving inauguration day back to January 20, and by moving the opening of the new Congress to the first week in January, the Twentieth Amendment deprives lame duck officeholders of the opportunity to quickly make laws.

That same year, 1933, the Twenty-first Amendment, which repealed the Eighteenth Amendment and national Prohibition, was ratified. A major political issue during the 1920s, repeal is considered a principal factor in President Herbert Hoover's failure to win reelection in 1932. His party, the Republican, refused to support repeal, while the Democratic party made repeal a major plank in its political platform.

The Twenty-second Amendment, ratified in 1951, limits to two the number of terms a president can serve. It was adopted in reaction to the four consecutive terms in office won by Franklin D. Roosevelt.

The Twenty-third Amendment, ratified in 1961, grants citizens of the District of Columbia the right to vote in presidential elections. Until then, residents of the nation's capital had no voice in national voting.

The Twenty-fourth Amendment, ratified in 1964, abolished the poll tax—a tax that had to be paid in order to vote—which some southern states had used effectively to disenfranchise poor blacks.

The Twenty-fifth Amendment, ratified in 1967, deals with the possibility of a president's illness or incapacity. It establishes the way the office of vice president is filled if the vice president must assume the presidency. The immediate stimulus for the amendment was the assassination of John F. Kennedy in 1963. However, the subject had been of concern since the illnesses suffered by Dwight D. Eisenhower when he was president in the 1950s.

The last amendment that has been adopted, the Twenty-sixth, ratified in 1971, guarantees eighteen-year-olds the right to vote. It was a response to a Supreme Court decision that struck down a federal statute granting this right in state elections. The Court held that only a constitutional amendment could require states to allow eighteen-year-olds to vote.

◆◆◆ **Are All the Guarantees of the Bill of Rights Applicable to the States as Well as to the Federal Government?**

No. The right to bear arms, for one, doesn't apply to the states, nor do several other provisions of the first ten amendments. Moreover, although most of the guarantees do apply now to the states—through the Due Process Clause of the Fourteenth Amendment—the way in which they have come to be applied has been slow, uncertain, and sometimes confusing.

In 1789, when James Madison introduced a draft of a bill of rights in the House of Representatives, he thought its most important provision was one forbidding states from infringing freedom of speech and of the press, rights of conscience, and the right of trial by jury in criminal cases. But, to Madison's disappointment, his proposal did not pass. Instead, the Bill of Rights that was submitted to and ratified by the states expressly limited only the power of the federal government.

Forty-four years later, in the case of *Barron* v. *Baltimore*, the Supreme Court made it clear that states were not bound by the Bill of Rights, which had finally been ratified in 1791. The city of Baltimore had diverted some streams in laying out and constructing new streets. The diverted streams dumped "large masses of sand and earth" around John Barron's wharf, raising the bottom of the harbor so high that most ships could not use it. Barron sued Baltimore in Maryland state court, arguing that the resulting damage to the wharf's usefulness deprived him of his property without compensation and thus violated the Fifth Amendment. Barron won a $45,000 judgment, but this was overturned by a state appellate court. He appealed that decision to the United States Supreme Court, but the Court refused to help him. Writing for a unanimous Court in his last major constitutional opinion, Chief Justice John Marshall held that the issue was one of jurisdiction. The case, he said, could be heard in a federal court only if it dealt with a federal right. But, Marshall held, no federal right had been violated because the Fifth Amendment does not restrain the states. Marshall said that if the framers of the Bill of Rights had intended it to apply to the states, they would have said so specifically. The justices realized that the framers had thought of the document only as a restraint on national powers.

The decision in *Barron* v. *Baltimore* dramatically affected the development of civil rights in America. Because of it, for over thirty years, citizens could not invoke the protections of the Bill of Rights against state or local governments. Then, in 1868, the Fourteenth Amendment was adopted. That amendment contains the Due Process Clause, which provides that states shall not "deprive any person of life, liberty, or property, without due process of law." Those words prompted an ongoing debate, focusing on the words "due process of law," over whether the amendment made the Bill of Rights applicable to the states. Some, such as Justice John Marshall Harlan in 1884, argued that because all the rights contained in the Bill of Rights were fundamental and essential to due process of law, they were incorporated—that is, absorbed or included—in the language of the clause. However, a majority of the Court rejected his view, reasoning that if those who wrote the clause had intended it to include the Bill of Rights, they would have written it that way.

In the early twentieth century, the application of the Bill of Rights to the states seemed a lost cause until the case of *Gitlow* v. *New York* in 1925. Even though it ruled against the civil liberties claim before it—the Court rejected a claim by Benjamin Gitlow, a Communist party official, that his conviction under New York's "criminal syndicalism" law violated his First Amendment rights—the Supreme Court for the first time recognized that at least some of the protections contained in the first ten amendments were applicable to the states through the Due Process Clause. The Court said:

For present purposes we may and do assume that freedom of speech and of the press—which are protected by the First Amendment from abridgment by Congress—are among the fundamental personal rights and "liberties" protected by the due process clause of the Fourteenth Amendment from impairment by the States.

Within two decades, the other fundamental protections in the First Amendment—freedom of religion and assembly—were applied to the states, again under the Due Process Clause.

Meanwhile, the Court moved beyond the realm of the First Amendment to make other parts of the Bill of Rights applicable to the states. For example, in 1932, in *Powell v. Alabama*, the Court applied the Sixth Amendment guarantee of a fair trial, in general, and counsel in capital criminal cases, in particular, to the states, once again citing the Due Process Clause.

The Court did not develop a concrete and coherent theoretical framework to explain why certain rights and not others should be applied everywhere until 1937, when Justice Benjamin N. Cardozo wrote a landmark opinion for the Court in *Palko v. Connecticut*. Cardozo acknowledged that there were, and must be, some federal constitutional rights fundamental enough that they had to be "incorporated" into the Due Process Clause and hence made applicable to the states. To identify the parts of the Bill of Rights that had to be incorporated, he distinguished between, on the one hand, basic rights that are "implicit in the concept of ordered liberty" and part of "those fundamental principles of liberty and justice which lie at the base of all our civil and political institutions," and on the other hand, those rights without which justice would not perish. Recognizing the difficulty in deciding which rights are fundamental, Cardozo cited the First Amendment freedoms of thought and speech as rights so "implicit in the concept of ordered liberty . . . that a fair and enlightened system of justice would be impossible without them."

During the quarter century after Cardozo's opinion in the *Palko* case, the list of "incorporated" rights was expanded only twice—to include the concept of separation of church and state (First Amendment) and to require a speedy and public trial (Sixth Amendment). Justice Hugo L. Black's attempt to expand it further in 1947 failed. Dissenting that year in *Adamson v. California*, Black presented a lengthy historical argument that the framers of the Fourteenth Amendment intended the Due Process Clause to incorporate the entire Bill of Rights as restrictions on the states. But Black, like John Marshall Harlan in 1884, was not able to persuade a majority on the Court to accept his view. Rather, the Court continued the practice of "selective incorporation," sorting through the Bill of Rights and incorporating some rights while refusing to incorporate others.

With the advent of the 1960s, the process of selective incorporation accelerated dramatically, as the "Warren Court"—headed by Chief Justice Earl Warren—led a civil liberties "revolution." In its decision in *Mapp v. Ohio* in 1961, the Court incorporated the Fourth Amendment's guarantee against unreasonable searches and seizures into the Due Process Clause. By 1969, the Court had incorporated virtually all the guarantees of the first eight amendments into the Due Process Clause except for four provisions: the right to bear arms (Second Amendment); the involuntary quartering of soldiers in private homes (Third Amendment); grand-jury indictment as the only way to begin a criminal prosecution (Fifth Amendment); and trial by jury in civil cases (Seventh Amendment). Some of these four protections are provided in some states by state constitutions or laws.

◆◆◆ How Did the Fourteenth Amendment Fundamentally Alter the Scope of Our Constitutional Rights?

By giving the federal government major responsibility in enforcing individual rights and ensuring equal protection under the law for all citizens. Until this dramatic reshaping of constitutional law took place—a change that took decades to evolve after the ratification of the Fourteenth Amendment in 1868—state governments exercised almost unrestricted authority over their citizens, and the federal government was virtually powerless to protect individuals from them.

The Fourteenth Amendment, adopted primarily to provide blacks who had once been slaves with all the rights of other Americans, has become over the years one of the most important parts of the Constitution. Its critical portion is its first section:

> All persons born or naturalized in the United States, and subject to the jurisdiction thereof, are citizens of the United States and of the State wherein they reside. No State shall make or enforce any law which shall abridge the privileges or immunities of citizens of the United States; nor shall any State deprive any person of life, liberty, or property, without due process of law; nor deny to any person within its jurisdiction the equal protection of the laws.

This section gives the national government primary responsibility for guaranteeing individual rights. The second sentence establishes specific prohibitions on the power of the states to infringe upon or violate individual rights. The three clauses of the sentence—the "privileges or immunities," the "due process," and the "equal protection" clauses—have generated a long and complex line of cases and interpretations trying to fix the exact meaning of the language of the amendment.

Of these, the Privileges or Immunities Clause has had the most confused history and the least influence on constitutional law. In no part of the congressional debates on the Fourteenth Amendment is there more vagueness and inconsistency than in the discussions of this clause. Representative John Bingham of Ohio, one of the Republican architects of the Fourteenth Amendment, saw in the clause a "euphony and indefiniteness of meaning" that was a "charm." And even though the clause speaks in language that seems more concrete than "due process" or "equal protection," the Supreme Court has never given the concept of national "privileges or immunities" much content.

Although on its face the Due Process Clause appears to be concerned with procedure—that is, *how* things are done—the clause has been read to impose substantive limits on government as well—at first, limits on state economic regulation. In the early part of this century, the Supreme Court used the Due Process Clause in this way to strike down state laws establishing standards for minimum wages and maximum hours on the ground that such laws deprived individual workers of their liberty to enter into contracts with their employers. That line of thinking was finally abandoned in the late 1930s (on the ground that workers didn't really *freely* accept oppressive working conditions), but a new kind of "substantive due process" has arisen, in which the Court has linked the clause with significant nonproperty rights, such as the right to privacy involved in the use of contraceptives and a woman's right to have an abortion.

Of course, the Due Process Clause does have a procedural side as well as a substantive one. For example, the Supreme Court has said that a state may not deprive a poor person of welfare benefits without giving him or her a hearing. This kind of protection, designed to guard against mistakes and ensure fairness, places an important limitation on state and local governments.

Recent decades have witnessed the rapid expansion of the number of rights protected by the Due Process Clause—either as substantive due process or procedural due process. Today, nearly all of the Bill of Rights, which originally applied only to the federal government, has been held to apply to the state governments as a result of the Due Process Clause.

The Equal Protection Clause imposes additional limits on the states. It comes into play when a state treats groups of people differently based upon such factors as race, religion, or sex; or when a state deprives one group of a fundamental right provided to others, such as the right to vote; or when the action of a state discriminates between groups irrationally. Classic examples of statutes that the Court has struck down as violations of the Equal Protection Clause include a Virginia law forbidding marriage between persons of different races, the school segregation laws overturned in the famous case of *Brown v. Board of Education,* and an Alabama law that permitted judges to make husbands—but not wives—pay alimony.

Taken together, the Due Process Clause and the Equal Protection Clause of the Fourteenth Amendment create a new charter of federal rights applicable to the states for the protection of all citizens. And the federal Constitution has become a bulwark, protecting individuals from violations of their rights by state and local governments.

◆◆◆ Are All the Rights in the Bill of Rights Equal?

No. For one thing, some—like the right to speak or to petition the government—are considered more fundamental than others because they are the keys to making our system of democracy work. Then, too, two freedoms guaranteed in the Bill of Rights will occasionally conflict with each other, as when the press wants to cover a trial in a way that will compromise the defendant's right to a fair trial, forcing a choice between the rights. And, finally, some of the first ten amendments—which were ratified in 1791—have almost no practical importance today.

The men who wrote the Bill of Rights did not assign priorities to them, but later interpreters of the guarantees have concluded that some values or concerns must be preferred to others. It was often not a simple task, but in 1938 the Supreme Court suggested a general principle for deciding which rights should receive "preferred" status. In *United States v. Carolene Products Co.,* the Court noted how it had usually deferred to a legislative body's findings that certain facts existed that posed problems that the legislature then tried to correct by passing a law. In most cases challenging such a statute as unconstitutional, the Court said, it would presume the statute was valid, leaving it up to the challenger to prove otherwise. However, in the now-famous Footnote 4 to the Court's opinion, Justice Harlan Fiske Stone indicated that the Court would not follow this presumption in all cases. "There may be," he said, "narrower scope for operation of the presumption of constitutionality when legislation appears on its face to be within a specific prohibition of the Constitution, such as those of the first ten amendments, which are deemed equally specific when held to be embraced within the Fourteenth."

Stone went on to suggest that if a government does something that makes it difficult to repeal "undesirable legislation" or that otherwise restricts the operation of the democratic process, its action would be examined with "more exacting judicial scrutiny." As such examples, he gave restrictions upon the right to vote, restraints upon dissemination of information, interferences with political organizations, and prohibitions on peaceable assembly.

What is interesting about this footnote—which has influenced the Court's decisions under the Bill of Rights for nearly fifty years—is Stone's implied argument that "economic" or "property" rights do not merit the strict protection he prescribed for the rights he listed. Thus, it can be argued that some guarantees of the Bill of Rights are more important than others, that the First Amendment's right to free speech, for example, is more important than the Fifth Amendment's guarantee that your property may not be taken without due process of the law.

There is another way in which one right might be more important than another. Sometimes two fundamental rights may come into conflict, forcing a choice between them. For example, the Sixth Amendment right of a defendant to a fair trial might conflict with the First Amendment right of the press to cover the trial. The Supreme Court has held that in some cases the defendant's right to an impartial jury might require the judge to exclude the public, including the press, from important pretrial proceedings on the suppression of evidence—proceedings necessarily considering information that, if widely publicized, would make it impossible to find jurors who had not already formed an opinion on the case.

Finally, some of the amendments just are not as important to us as they were to the framers. Although it is the subject of continued controversy, the Second Amendment, which guarantees "the right of the people to keep and bear Arms," is one of those amendments that are important for the most part only for their symbolic value. The amendment has little meaning at present because it has been interpreted to refer only to state militias and does not bar the federal government or any state from regulating the sale, transportation, and use of guns. Of even less import is the Third Amendment, which precludes the quartering of soldiers in the homes of civilians without their consent. It arose from circumstances common both before and during the Revolutionary War. The Third has been invoked successfully only once since it was added to the Constitution nearly two hundred years ago—in a 1982 suit brought by striking prison guards against the governor of New York, who had called out the National Guard to staff state prisons and whose subordinates had the National Guard quartered in homes on the prison grounds in which the striking prison guards lived.

Although it is sometimes suggested that the First Amendment is paramount among the amendments because it precedes the others, there is no support for this view in the text of the Bill of Rights, and the Court has never embraced it.

◆◆◆ Can a Constitutional Amendment Be Repealed?

Yes. The Eighteenth Amendment was. It was ratified in 1919 but repealed fourteen years later by the Twenty-first Amendment. These two amendments, taken together, mark the rise and fall of Prohibition in the United States.

American politicians have crusaded against liquor ever since the country was founded. For example, in a document dating from the 1820s or 1830s that was recently auctioned in New York, John Quincy Adams, Andrew Jackson, and James Madison jointly declared:

> Being satisfied from observation and experience, as well as from Medical testimony that ardent spirit, as a drink, is not only needless, but hurtful; and that the entire disuse of it would tend to promote the health, the virtue, and the happiness of the community, We hereby express our conviction that should the citizens of the United States, and especially all *young men*, discontinue entirely the use of it, they would not only promote their own personal benefit but the good of our country and the world.

Most of the time, opponents of alcohol, like the Women's Christian Temperance Union, concentrated on urging moderation or abstinence from hard liquor. But in the late 1800s the tenor of the movement changed, became more strident, and expanded into a campaign to outlaw all alcoholic beverages. The Eighteenth Amendment, proposed in December 1917 and ratified in January 1919, provided constitutional backing for the Volstead Act, a federal law that banned alcoholic beverages from interstate commerce. The amendment specifically prohibited "the manufacture, sale, or transportation of intoxicating liquors within, the importation thereof into, or the exportation thereof from the United States and all territory subject to the jurisdiction thereof for beverage purposes." The amendment also granted concurrent power to both Congress and the states to enforce the amendment.

The Prohibition amendment, as it came to be called, was a dismal failure. It resulted in a thriving illegal industry devoted to the making and sale of "bootleg" liquor and stimulated a wave of organized violence and general disrespect for law that proved powerful arguments for its repeal.

American politics throughout the 1920s was dominated by arguments between "wets" who favored repeal and "drys" who opposed it. The humorist Will Rogers complained that the Democrats spent all too much time at their national convention in 1932 fighting about getting a drink instead of dealing with the Great Depression. Nevertheless, the Democrats' endorsement of repeal contributed significantly to Franklin D. Roosevelt's victory over incumbent Herbert Hoover.

During its brief and controversial life the Eighteenth Amendment sparked many criminal-procedure issues under the Fourth and Fifth amendments. The most notable, *Olmstead* v. *United States* in 1928, dealt with the still hotly debated issue of wiretapping. In it, the Supreme Court upheld the conviction of bootleggers based on wiretap evidence obtained without a warrant on the ground that a wiretap was not a search or seizure within the meaning of the Fourth Amendment. However, Justice Louis D. Brandeis dissented, roundly criticizing the government for breaking the law in order to enforce it. The Brandeis view—that the Fourth Amendment's ban against unreasonable search and seizure should follow the development of science and technology—was adopted by the Court four decades later in another wiretapping case, *Katz* v. *United States,* in which the federal government tapped a telephone in a public phone booth.

The Twenty-first Amendment is unique in that it specifically provided that it had to be adopted by state ratifying conventions rather than by state legislatures. This was done to minimize the efforts of powerful Prohibition lobbies to block repeal, as well as to ensure that the will of the people, rather than political considerations, was expressed. The amendment was proposed by Congress on February 20, 1933, and, after thirty-six of the then forty-eight states had ratified it, declared in effect on December 5, 1933. At the time, this was a record for the shortest period between submission of an amendment to the states and its ratification.

Though the Twenty-first Amendment repealed the Eighteenth, it preserves state authority to regulate or prohibit the sale of liquor. It is under the authority of this provision that some parts of the nation have been—and still are—"dry."

Congress ═══════════════════════════════

◆◆◆ **Why Are Representatives Elected for Only Two Years While Senators Are Elected for Six?**

Because the Framers of the Constitution intended the two houses of Congress to represent different groups, perform different functions, and be subject to different degrees of restraint.

The Framers followed the practice common to most of the original thirteen states and to the legislature they knew best—the English Parliament. They adopted a bicameral (two-house) legislature, with a "democratic" or "popular" branch, like the House of Commons, and an "aristocratic" branch, like the House of Lords. The House of Representatives was intended to represent the people of the United States, and its members have always been elected directly by the people. On the other hand, the Senate was to represent the states, and its members were chosen by state legislatures until the adoption of the Seventeenth Amendment in 1913, which made senators also directly elected by the people.

The Framers—motivated perhaps by a maxim that dominated colonial and early state politics: "Where annual elections end, tyranny begins"—believed that the representatives ought to be accountable to the voters at frequent intervals. Some, such as Alexander Hamilton of New York, initially favored a three-year term, but a two-year one was finally decided upon.

The Framers also believed that the Senate should be a check on the House, and they provided for senators to serve a far longer term. How much longer bounced from four years to seven and even longer before a six-year term was settled upon. This freedom from having to stand for reelection at short intervals, the Framers argued, would enable senators to develop detachment and independence of thought. They would be able to exercise their legislative functions without having to worry about politicking so frequently and would be able to consider the long-term effects of legislation, treaties, presidential appointments, and impeachment trials.

In fact, the Senate was given exclusive power to approve, or disapprove, treaties and executive and judicial appointments, and the responsibility for hearing trials of impeachment precisely because it was thought that those responsibilities called for qualities far more likely to be found in the Senate (whose members were elected by state legislatures for terms of six years) than in the House (whose members are popularly elected every two years). On the other hand, the Framers gave the House exclusive power to originate money bills because they wanted initial decisions on taxation and appropriations to be made by a body closer to, and directly accountable to, the people.

◆◆◆ Must My Representative Live in My District?

No. As far as a representative's place of residence is concerned, all the Constitution requires—in Article I, Section 2—is that a representative "be an Inhabitant of that State in which he shall be chosen."

When the Constitution was adopted, each state was left free to decide its own approach to electing representatives to sit in the House. Some states experimented with district voting, others with at-large voting, and still others tried a hybrid approach in which all the state's voters cast ballots for candidates to represent each part of the state. Ultimately, all the states adopted the congressional district system.

Asher C. Hinds, author of *Precedents of the House of Representatives*, which was published in 1907 and is still perhaps the leading treatise on the rules and procedure of the House, argued that custom is the only source of the "rule" that a representative must live in his district. In any event, it is a custom with which representatives have found it politically advisable to comply. For example, John F. Kennedy lived in Hyannisport, Massachusetts, but rented an apartment at 122 Tremont Street in Boston in the heart of the district he represented in the House from 1947 to 1952.

◆◆◆ Can I Lose My Congressional District?

Yes, because a state may redraw the boundaries of congressional districts so that you find yourself in another district. But you cannot lose your right to vote for a candidate for the U.S. House of Representatives.

Districts are rearranged or new ones formed every ten years following a census, when states reapportion them to reflect changes in population. This occurs because the Supreme Court has mandated that in a congressional election every citizen's vote has to be worth as much as another citizen's—the "one person, one vote" principle. The Court's position is based on its interpretation of Article I, Section 2, of the Constitution, which says that representatives will be "chosen every second Year by the People of the several States." This means, the Court declared in 1964, that for the "people" to choose the Congress, each person must have an equal voice in the choice. A single vote in a congressional district within a state cannot weigh substantially more or substantially less than a single vote in a different district within the same state. Thus, state legislatures—in setting the boundaries for congressional districts—must include, as far as possible, equal numbers of residents in each district.

The Constitution provides that every state have at least one representative, hence at least one congressional district. The total number of representatives from a single state is based on that state's population in proportion to the total number of Americans living in all fifty states. Some states gain representatives, some lose some every ten years—as has happened, for example, in the last twenty years as a growing number of Americans have moved from the eastern seaboard to the Southwest. When New York State lost 683,000 residents in the 1970s, it also lost two representatives (and their congressional districts) and had to redraw the boundaries of the congressional districts within the state to reflect the new, lower number of representatives.

As a result of the Court's decisions, there is general conformity in the size of congressional districts within the nation; as of the 1980 census, the average one contained 519,000 persons. The only significant deviation from that figure occurs in states that have only one representative, because their total population is so small. Alaska's single congressional district contains 438,000 people, South Dakota's 686,000.

And what is true for congressional districts—voter equality—must also be true for legislative districts within states and even cities, whose boundaries frequently vary from congressional districts. The Supreme Court ruled in 1964 that the Equal Protection Clause of the Fourteenth Amendment requires such districts to be drawn so as to provide equal representation for equal numbers of people. That decision ruled out any bicameral (two-house) state legislatures patterned after Congress if the upper house, like the U.S. Senate, was based on geographical representation—for example, two senators from each state senate district no matter how many people lived within each such district.

However, even in a districting system where the districts have equal populations, the boundaries may be redrawn to favor one political party at the expense of another or to favor one group at the expense of another.

This is called *gerrymandering*—a term derived from the name of a noted Massachusetts political leader, Elbridge Gerry, who, while governor of that state in the early 1800s, supervised the drawing of legislative district lines to favor the Jeffersonian-Republican Party. One of the districts he drew was so oddly shaped that it looked like a salamander, so Gerry's Federalist opponents called it a Gerry-mander—and the name stuck. The Supreme Court has held that gerrymandering to minimize the voice of racial minorities is unconstitutional. It has yet to rule on the constitutionality of gerrymandering to favor one party over another, though the Court now has before it a case in which a group of Indiana Democrats have challenged a Republican legislative redistricting plan on the ground that the plan unconstitutionally discriminates against Democrats.

◆◆◆ Did Anyone Who Heard the Lincoln-Douglas Debates Actually Vote for Either Man?

No, because until 1913 senators were not elected directly by voters. They were chosen by state legislatures.

The election of 1858, during which the Lincoln-Douglas debates took place, was actually an election for a state legislature. Although Abraham Lincoln and Stephen A. Douglas were the candidates for the U.S. Senate and the focus of popular attention, the citizens who heard them argue contemporary issues could only vote for party choices running for the Illinois legislature. The Democrats won a majority in it and sent Douglas to Washington, D.C.

The Framers of the Constitution were faced with a difficult dilemma when structuring Congress. Should it be elected by the states, as the delegates to the Confederation Congress had been chosen by state legislatures under the Articles of Confederation? Or should it be elected directly by the people? In one of the major compromises that held the Constitutional Convention together, the Framers agreed that the House, the "lower" branch, would be elected directly by the people of the states, while the Senate, representing the states themselves, would be picked by the state legislatures. (Interestingly, however, the Framers specified in Article I, Section 3, that each senator would have one vote, thus abandoning the system under the Articles that gave an entire state's delegation only one vote altogether.)

Gradually, the development of political parties made the election of senators more predictable simply because the party that controlled a state legislature controlled the choice of senators as well. In the late nineteenth century, many reformers charged that large corporations and trusts were "buying" state legislatures, and thus the Senate, making sure in the process that no laws to regulate their abuses would be enacted by Congress. Members of the Progressive movement, which fought for the direct election of senators, also cited the problems created when contested Senate elections tied up state legislatures for weeks or months at a stretch. In time, twenty-nine states adopted methods of polling voters to determine their choice. The model was Nebraska, which required its state legislature to abide by the choice of voters in selecting who would represent the state in the Senate.

Finally, in 1913, the Seventeenth Amendment was ratified. It eliminated the old system and made members of both houses of Congress elected directly by the people.

◆◆◆ Have Americans Always Had a Right to Know What Their Legislators Do and Say?

Not at all. Article I, Section 5, of the Constitution does require each house of Congress to keep "a Journal of its Proceedings," to publish it— "excepting such Parts as may in their Judgment require Secrecy"—and to enter "the Yeas and Nays" on the record "at the Desire of one fifth of those Present." But even the limited terms of this provision represented a departure from the history of legislative debates and record keeping. And after the Constitution was adopted and the House and Senate began work, only the House held open sessions and published a record of its proceedings. The Senate only began open sessions in 1795.

The Framers of the Constitution, and their colonial predecessors, all looked to the English Parliament as the model for their rules, procedures, and legislative customs. Dating back to the reign of Henry VIII, when it was first struggling for power, the House of Commons jealously guarded what was known as the doctrine of parliamentary privilege. This doctrine, which was designed to protect the House of Commons from the Crown and the House of Lords, held that only the House itself could punish members or otherwise call them to account for what they said on the floor of the House—a doctrine that is preserved today in the "Speech and Debate" Clause of the Constitution (Article I, Section 6). During the English Civil War (1641–1649), the House of Commons tentatively experimented with publishing its votes and fragments of debates and even allowing those who were not members to attend its sessions. But even after the Glorious Revolution of 1688, in which King James II was forced to abdicate, Parliament was quick to punish those who published unauthorized accounts of debates and statutes. And, apparently, such measures were necessary. Members of rival factions frequently published false and misleading accounts and even phony legislation. It was only in the mid-1700s that Parliament eased its restrictions on attendance at its sessions and publication of its debates, votes, and enactments.

The American colonies followed the English model without any question whatever being raised about the public's "right to know." It was James Franklin, Benjamin Franklin's older brother and the publisher of the *New-England Courant*, who became the first man in the history of the English-speaking world to publish an officially recorded vote of a legislature. The vote, of the Massachusetts General Court on January 15, 1726, was on the question whether that colony would accept interpretations made by the Privy Council in England of the colony's charter of 1691, a power previously jealously guarded by the colony's legislatures. However, Franklin's bold venture did not create a general practice. For the most part, colonial legislatures kept their debates and votes secret, publishing "division lists" only when the minority insisted that their dissents from decisions be made public.

It was the intensification of disputes between colonists and their governments in the days leading to the Revolution that stimulated public interest in what their representatives were up to behind closed doors. Pamphleteers and politicians complained increasingly about the lack of information from colonial, and later state, legislatures and the Continental and Confederation Congresses. Although Charles Thomson, the long-serving secretary of Congress, kept the local press supplied with information about its doings and occasionally published sketchy *Journals* of the work of Congress, for the most part there was little departure from the long-standing custom of keeping legislative business within the legislatures. This is why, for example, the decision of the Constitutional Convention of 1787 to close its deliberations to the public sparked almost no immediate controversy. (Anti-Federalists later complained about this secrecy only as another way to attack the proposed Constitution.) Later, ratification debates in Massachusetts, New York, Pennsylvania, and Virginia were taken down by stenographers hired by publishers who hoped to tap public interest in the debates by publishing them, but this was a new development.

At the same time, one enterprising printer, Mathew Carey of Philadelphia, managed in 1786 to persuade some state legislatures to permit him to take down and publish accounts of their proceedings. In part in response to this practice, when the House of Representatives first met in New York in 1789, the fact that its proceedings would be open to the public was taken for granted, and the only question was where to seat the reporters so that they could hear and record the debates accurately. The Senate, however, clung to tradition, perhaps because its members regarded themselves as representatives of the states rather than of the people. It was not until 1795, when a controversy developed over the election of Swiss-born Albert Gallatin as a senator from Pennsylvania, that the Senate agreed to open its doors to the public and the press, in order to avoid charges that it was a small and exclusive oligarchy seeking to close its membership to representatives of the people. The debates over Gallatin were reported without comment, and Gallatin failed in his bid to become a senator on the ground that he had not been a citizen of the United States long enough to qualify under the Constitution for the office of senator. (Article I, Section 3, requires that a person be a citizen of the United States for at least nine years before election to the Senate.)

The *Annals of Congress*, begun in 1789, was the first compilation of the debates of Congress and was published until 1834, when it was succeeded by the *Congressional Globe*. (During that time the *Congressional Debates* began publishing in 1821, lasting until 1837.) The *Globe* in turn was succeeded in 1873 by the *Congressional Record*, which is still published today. However, the *Record* is not a completely accurate account of the doings of the House and Senate. Members may speak for only a moment and then enter a 10,000-word speech in the *Record*, giving a misleading sense of what actually took place on the floor. Sometimes this practice can have ludicrous results, as when the *Record* in 1972 published New Year's greetings from Representative Hale Boggs of Louisiana, the majority whip, who had been lost in a plane crash in Alaska some weeks before. Boggs's staff had arranged for the publication before he left for Alaska. Furthermore, at times the House or Senate may vote to delete "unseemly" debates between members as not befitting the dignity of Congress. And the Constitution permits both the House and Senate to keep debates and committee reports secret, as the House did in 1976 with the report of the so-called Pike committee on alleged violations of law by the Central Intelligence Agency. When a CBS News reporter, Daniel Schorr, and Aaron Latham of the *Village Voice* collaborated on a story for the *Voice* reporting and quoting extensively from the report, the House leadership threatened to hold them in contempt of Congress, a charge that carries with it the possibility of incarceration in the jail kept by the Capitol police in the basement of the Capitol. However, the House leadership gave the idea up.

Two major federal laws now exist to give the public a broad right to information about our government. The Freedom of Information Act, enacted in 1967 and revised extensively in 1974, 1976, 1978, and 1984, is designed expressly to let Americans know what the government and its agencies are doing, and in particular to compel the government to open its records to public scrutiny. The Sunshine Act, passed in 1976, seeks to ensure that government agencies conduct their decision-making processes as much in public as possible. However, many people believe that often the government is still not as forthcoming as it could be with information.

◆◆◆ Whose Job Is It to Balance the Budget?

Nobody's. Although there has been some talk of amending the Constitution to require a balanced budget, it does not now demand that the government take in as much as it spends. As to who shapes the budget, the men who wrote the Constitution expected Congress to be its primary architect. James Madison, for one, believed that Congress's power over the nation's purse strings was its most potent weapon in the checks and balances among the three branches of government. Today, Congress still makes the final decisions about the shape of the budget, but the president plays a primary role in the process.

Although the Framers intended that Congress be the primary actor in the budgetary process, Congress became less able to play that role as the new government's responsibilities multiplied. The congressional budgeting process came to consist of endless negotiations among the various House and Senate committees, each of which had its own ideas about how to raise taxes and spend appropriations. In 1921, Congress itself recognized the need for more centralized decision making and passed a law turning over the chief responsibility for developing the budget to the president. Administrative agencies henceforth submitted their budget requests to what is now the Office of Management and Budget. The president then submitted this "executive" budget to Congress, which could approve or disapprove its provisions and also audit expenditures.

For the next fifty years, Congress tended to give the president most of what he asked for. This was hardly surprising because its members were not trained financial analysts and had little time each year to scrutinize a budget that was easily a thousand pages long. But in 1973 President Richard M. Nixon's attempt to set a ceiling on spending prompted Congress to reform the entire process. Nixon had submitted to Congress a budget that placed a $250 billion limit on expenditures, but Congress refused to set such a limit on what its members wanted to spend. Nixon was able to override their rejection by simply refusing to spend the funds that Congress then appropriated. In doing so, he cited an interpretation of Article II, Section 1, of the Constitution that says the president has the power to impound such funds. Congress responded by enacting a law that requires that the president spend any funds it appropriates.

This act, passed in 1974, also entailed a major reorganization of the budgetary process. It added budget committees to both the House and Senate and gave Congress its own think tank to analyze the president's budget. It also postponed the start of the fiscal year from July 1 to October 1; as a result, Congress now has nine months rather than six months after the president submits his budget in late January each year to review and revise it.

Presidents since Nixon have taken it upon themselves to work toward balancing the budget, with varying degrees of success. Jimmy Carter set as his goal a balanced budget for fiscal 1980. Ronald W. Reagan claimed to be seeking to achieve the same goal through a combination of spending and tax cuts, and actually succeeded in signing into law in 1981 the largest and most far-reaching cuts ever approved by Congress. But neither Carter nor Reagan has come close to balancing the budget. They, like their predecessors, still have reason to echo the words of Herbert Hoover: "Bless the young, for they shall inherit the national debt."

The budget—and the national debt—have continued to grow. The book containing today's budget is the size of a large phone book, and the government now spends $1 trillion each year—as much money every two minutes as was spent during George Washington's eight years in office.

Although the Constitution does not require Congress to adopt a balanced budget, a movement is afoot to adopt a constitutional amendment to require one. Opponents, however, say that the proposed amendment would, among other things, deprive the federal government of flexibility in responding to changing needs and circumstances, foster competition for scarce funds among regions of the country, special-interest groups, and political factions, and pressure state and city governments to assume a greater share of the burden of paying for government programs.

In December 1985, Congress passed the Gramm-Rudman Act, a bill that imposes tax increases or mandatory, automatic spending cuts should the federal budget deficit exceed targets set for each year by the legislation, targets that would result in a balanced budget by 1991. Such spending cuts would eventually be defined and implemented by the Comptroller General. Social Security and several other domestic programs are exempt from the cuts.

President Reagan signed the bill on December 12, 1985. Four hours later, the Public Citizen Litigation Group, a Washington-based public-interest law firm, filed suit on behalf of a Democratic congressman, challenging the constitutionality of the law on the ground that it improperly delegated legislative power to unelected officials. A special three-judge court agreed, and struck down key provisions of the act in February 1986. The Supreme Court is now considering the case.

◆◆◆ Does My Tax Money Always Go Where Congress Sends It?

Generally, yes, although this has sometimes been a sore point between the president and Congress. In practice, Congress usually deals with broad expenditures and not individual items. This leaves the president a fair amount of control over how tax money is actually spent.

The Constitution specifically assigns to Congress the powers of the purse: "All Bills for raising Revenue" must "originate in the House of Representatives" (Article I, Section 7). Congress also has the exclusive "Power To lay and collect Taxes, Duties, Imposts and Excises, to pay the Debts and provide for the common Defence and general Welfare," to "borrow money on the credit of the United States," and to "coin Money" (Article I, Section 8). Moreover, the Constitution provides that "[n]o Money shall be drawn from the Treasury, but in Consequence of Appropriations made by Law" (Article I, Section 9). This combination of powers prompted James Madison to believe that "the legislative department alone has access to the pockets of the people."

Despite Congress's constitutional authority over the purse, presidents at various times in our history have asserted a controversial power known as impoundment, refusing to spend money that Congress appropriated. The first such incident occurred in 1803, when Thomas Jefferson delayed for one year spending $50,000 voted by Congress for gunboats. Jefferson felt the Louisiana Purchase made the use of gunboats on the Mississippi River unnecessary. By the same token, in 1876, Ulysses S. Grant ignored the protests of representatives and refused to spend more than half of the $5 million Congress appropriated for river and harbor improvements. Grant called them "works of purely private or local interest, in no sense national" and was able to hold up the expenditures for about a year.

The impoundment controversy broke out again during the administration of Richard M. Nixon. In 1973 he impounded $14.7 billion in funds approved by Congress for a wide variety of projects, including weapons systems and social programs. In doing so, Nixon pointed to both Jefferson's and Grant's impoundments of funds. He cited what he called his inherent executive authority as president and commander in chief. (Although the Supreme Court never considered Nixon's claim that the Constitution gave him this power, several lower federal courts rejected it.)

In response to Nixon's action, Congress passed the Impoundment Control Act of 1974, which, among other things, gives Congress control over any presidential decisions to delay or refuse to spend appropriated funds. However, because its appropriations bills involve such large sums of money and cover millions of different items, it is still very difficult for Congress to control funding for a specific expenditure.

◆◆◆ Why Are Appropriations for the Army Limited to Two Years?

Because American patriots were afraid that standing armies—that is, a permanent military establishment—threatened the chances of the young nation's survival. They wanted to ensure civilian supremacy over the armed forces. To do so, they wrote into the Constitution provisions to give Congress and the president authority over the military.

The Framers' fear of standing armies sprang from colonial experience, when the British army was used to suppress the protests of Massachusetts colonists against the Crown's colonial policies. Among the offenses that Thomas Jefferson charged King George III with in the Declaration of Independence in 1776 was that he had attempted to "render the Military independent of and superior to the Civil power." The specter of such military rule continued to haunt many Americans even after the Revolution, when both former and present Continental army officers formed an organization called the Society of the Cincinnati.

The devices incorporated into the Constitution to establish civilian control of the military included giving Congress the power to declare war, to regulate and support the army and navy, and to call out military forces when domestic or international conflicts warrant it (Article I, Section 8). In addition, the president was named commander in chief of the army and the navy (Article II, Section 2).

Another control was the limit on appropriations for the army: "The Congress shall have Power . . . To raise and support Armies, but no Appropriation of Money to that Use shall be for a longer Term than two

Years" (Article I, Section 8). Actually, that limit exceeded the British practice of setting a one-year limit on army appropriations, but it was chosen in order to tie funding to the two-year term of members of the House of Representatives, which has the power to originate money bills.

According to the wording in the Constitution, the limit only applies to the army and not to other branches of the armed forces, and even this limit has been eroded over the years. For example, as the result of a dispute with a contractor, the U.S. attorney general in 1904 issued an opinion that said that the constitutional two-year limit on appropriations for the army did not apply to the payment of royalties for the construction of artillery pieces for military fortifications. The opinion distinguished between laws for raising and supporting the army itself and laws for obtaining military supplies, which are not covered by the limit. Similarly, in 1948, the U.S. attorney general ruled that the two-year limit applied only to funding for the army. Thus, appropriations for the navy and air force could be for longer periods and Congress could appropriate funds to the air force to buy planes and equipment without requiring that the money be spent within two years. And, in 1971, the U.S. Court of Appeals for the District of Columbia Circuit held that the Selective Service Act calling for a national draft was not a money bill and thus not subject to any two-year limit on its life.

◆◆◆ What Gives the Federal Government the Right to Break Up AT&T?

Article I, Section 8, of the Constitution, which gives Congress the power to regulate interstate commerce. In 1890 it exercised this authority when it enacted the Sherman Antitrust Act, which made illegal "Every contract, combination in the form of trust or otherwise, or conspiracy, in restraint of trade or commerce among the several States." The act was designed to combat the growing merger of businesses into large entities called trusts. The trusts often controlled an entire industry, stifling economic competition.

The scope of the Sherman Antitrust Act has grown as the Supreme Court's view and the importance of interstate commerce to the national economy have expanded. Originally, the Court followed a very narrow reading of the power of the Interstate Commerce Clause. In 1895, in the first case involving the act, the Court held that a stock purchase that gave a company control over 98 percent of the sugar refining in the United

States did not violate the law. The Court reasoned that the purchase occurred only within one state and that the effects upon interstate commerce that might result were secondary because manufacturing was not "commerce" under the Constitution.

The 1895 opinion led to an increase in corporate mergers and combinations. But nine years later the Court ruled against the merger of two large railroad corporations, finding that the combination of competing railroads restrained interstate commerce and therefore was illegal.

In 1914, Congress added two more laws to fight monopoly power: the Clayton Act and legislation establishing the Federal Trade Commission (FTC). The Clayton Act—and the Robinson-Patman Act of 1936, which amended it—among other things forbids certain price discriminations and exclusive contracts as well as certain corporate mergers. The FTC, along with the courts, has jurisdiction to enforce many antitrust provisions and establishes restrictions against unfair methods of competition.

The AT&T antitrust case involved elements of all these statutes. The original suit was filed by the government in January 1949. It began as an antitrust action aimed at breaking up the company's monopoly of the telephone-equipment market, but as it developed in the ensuing years the suit expanded to include long-distance service as well. Like four of five such cases, this one ended seven years later in a *consent decree*—that is, a binding agreement entered into by both parties in a lawsuit and enforceable by the courts. The decree essentially allowed the Bell System to continue to dominate the telephone market as long as its parent corporation, AT&T, refrained from expanding into the manufacturing and service industries.

Indicating that the 1956 consent decree was inadequate, the government in 1974 filed another antitrust action against AT&T. This lawsuit ended in 1982 in the now-famous decree that divested the corporation of its local phone-operating companies. Before approving this decree, the U.S. District Court for the District of Columbia examined the reasoning behind the antitrust statutes to determine if the agreement was in the public interest:

> The need to safeguard free competition is a direct result of the fundamental premise of our economic system that "unrestrained" interaction of competitive forces will yield the best allocation of our economic resources, the lowest prices, the highest quality and the greatest material progress, while at the same time providing an environment conducive to the preservation of our democratic political and social institutions.

The decision was summarily affirmed by the Supreme Court—that is, the Court decided it without oral argument based only on the initial briefs submitted by both sides in the case. As is often so with a summary affirmance, the Court issued no opinion, indicating only that it agreed with the lower court's decision.

◆◆◆ What Gives Congress the Right to Enact Laws to Protect the Environment?

The Commerce Clause of the Constitution (in Article I, Section 8). The theory is that the way the environment is treated—even within a state—has an impact on other states and, in a sense sufficient to justify federal action, on "interstate commerce."

It may be surprising that the burning of garbage can be regulated as part of interstate commerce under amendments to the Clean Air Act in 1983. But, beginning with cases that had nothing to do with the environment, the Supreme Court has made it clear that Congress's powers under the Commerce Clause extend not only to matters directly affecting interstate commerce but also to activities that at first glance might appear to be entirely local.

As early as 1942, the Court made a far-reaching decision in a case involving an Ohio farmer who, to feed his family, grew more wheat than a federal marketing quota allowed. The Court ruled that Congress could forbid this extra production. It said that actions that might seem local in nature, and thus beyond Congress's authority, are in reality small pieces in a larger puzzle. Because Congress could regulate the puzzle as a whole, the Court continued, it could also regulate each piece of the puzzle, no matter how small. In fact, within broad limits, it was for Congress to decide whether it is necessary to regulate local activities in order to regulate interstate commerce effectively. In the case of the Ohio farmer, the Court reasoned that because the farmer had produced food for his family, he would purchase less food from the interstate stream of commerce.

Almost forty years later, in a 1981 case involving the environment—*Hodel v. Virginia Surface Mining Ass'n*—the Court upheld federal regulations regarding strip mining. It said that once Congress decides that an activity affects interstate commerce, it may regulate, or prohibit, that activity under its constitutional power to regulate such commerce. The ruling made clear that the broad range of federal laws regulating the environment has a solid basis in the Commerce Clause.

◆◆◆ Can Congress Pass a Law Punishing Only Me?

No. That kind of bill—called a bill of attainder—is specifically banned by the Constitution.

The ban was a response to abuses that were common in English history in the sixteenth and seventeenth centuries and, like other English traditions, found their way into American practice as well. Parliament often asserted the power to punish its foes by enacting laws imposing punishments on those persons by name. Such bills of attainder usually ordered that the person be executed, that his descendants be "attainted" (that is, penalties were imposed on them simply because they were related to him), and that his estate be confiscated. A more lenient form of statute, called a bill of pains and penalties, imposed a prison term or some lesser form of physical punishment on the person.

Similar abuses occurred in America. Many states used bills of attainder to confiscate the property of Loyalists during the Revolution.

Clauses in Sections 9 and 10 of Article I of the Constitution specifically prohibit the federal government and the states from enacting bills of attainder. Both provisions were written with almost no debate and without dissent. The Supreme Court has interpreted these bans as barring bills of pains and penalties as well.

The first major case under the prohibitions occurred in 1867, when the Court struck down a Missouri constitutional provision that required clergymen, among others practicing certain professions, to swear an oath of allegiance to the United States and to disavow acts of disloyalty to the United States during the Civil War. The Reverend John Cummings, a Roman Catholic priest, disobeyed the requirement on principle. He was subsequently jailed when he refused to pay a fine. The Court concluded that, because the Missouri provision deprived Cummings of his rights and punished him without judicial process, it was both a bill of attainder and an *ex post facto* law, each of which the Constitution forbids. In a similar case that same year, the Court struck down a federal law requiring an identical oath from lawyers practicing in a federal court.

In more recent times, an attempt by Congress to deny pay to three government workers who had been investigated by the House Committee on Un-American Activities on charges of subversive activities was struck down by the Court in 1946. And in 1965 the Court invalidated a federal law that singled out members of the Communist party and made it a crime for them to serve as an officer or to work for a labor union in any capacity except a clerical or custodial position.

Critical to the Court's position in such cases is whether a statute denies a privilege or takes away a person's right, and whether such action is intended to be a punishment. Thus, in 1977, the Court rejected former President Richard M. Nixon's challenge to a federal law giving custody of his presidential papers and tape recordings to the government. Nixon claimed that the bill was a bill of attainder. The Court, however, held that it wasn't, inasmuch as Congress did not intend to punish Nixon or to deprive him of a right or privilege. This was clear because the law provided that Nixon be compensated for the property.

◆◆◆ Can Congress Pass a Law Making Illegal Something I've Already Done?

No. As with a bill of attainder, clauses in Sections 9 and 10 of Article I of the Constitution forbid the federal government or a state from enacting what are known as *ex post facto* laws (from the Latin phrase meaning "after the fact"). Nevertheless, the issue has surfaced from time to time, most notably after World War II, when Nazi German and Japanese officers and leaders were tried for war crimes.

Americans in the eighteenth century were familiar with English cases involving *ex post facto* laws, which frequently were used by the British government to punish as treason actions that were legal when they took place. The most famous one involved William Prynne, a Puritan lawyer who was tried on charges arising from a book he had written in 1630 against the theater that included a chapter entitled "Women Actors notorious whores." Unfortunately for Prynne, his book was published in 1634, only six weeks before Queen Marie Henrietta, the wife of Charles I, was to appear in an amateur theatrical production. The dreaded Court of Star Chamber charged Prynne with libel and sentenced him to stand successively in two pillories, losing one ear in each, to pay a fine of £5,000, and to be imprisoned for life.

The Framers wrote the ban on *ex post facto* laws into the Constitution almost without debate. The only objection was that it would be a reflection on the national legislature even to include such a ban.

The best definition of an *ex post facto* law was given by Justice Samuel Chase back in 1798 in *Calder* v. *Bull,* a case involving a Connecticut statute that dealt with a probate decree. Chase wrote:

> 1st. Every law that makes an action done before the passing of the law, and which was innocent when done, criminal; and punishes such action. 2d. Every law that aggravates a crime, or makes it

greater than it was, when committed. 3d. Every law that changes the punishment, and inflicts a greater punishment, than the law annexed to the crime, when committed. 4th. Every law that alters the legal rules of evidence, and receives less, or different testimony than that law required at the time of the commission of the offence, in order to convict the offender.

In *Calder* v. *Bull*, the Supreme Court held that the ban on *ex post facto* laws applied only to criminal law. Civil cases were excluded. For example, in 1855 the Court upheld a Pennsylvania statute that imposed a special tax on bequests left by persons who had died before the act was passed. Similarly, the Court has upheld statutes disqualifying convicted felons from holding certain jobs or professions, even though the laws applied to persons convicted before they were passed. It did this in 1898 in a case involving a New York law that barred convicted felons from practicing medicine and, in 1960, in a case involving another New York law that barred convicted felons from serving as union officials.

Perhaps the most controversial issue raised concerning *ex post facto* arose in 1946, when the Senate Republican leader, Robert A. Taft, and others denounced the Nuremberg and Tokyo War Crimes Trials. Taft argued that, although the German and Japanese leaders on trial had indeed committed acts repugnant to civilization, they had not violated any laws except, perhaps, those of their own countries. Therefore, he said, any trial for alleged "crimes against humanity" defined after the war was a violation of the constitutional ban on *ex post facto* laws. The issue reached the Supreme Court that same year after a military commission trying Japanese officers condemned to death General Tomoyuki Yamashita for failing to prevent atrocities by soldiers under his command during the American invasion of Luzon in the Philippines. The Court upheld the sentence by a vote of 7 to 2, but one of the dissenters, Justice Wiley B. Rutledge, argued that the trial clearly violated the *ex post facto* provisions. The charges against Yamashita, Rutledge said, though vaguely grounded in the laws of war, did nothing more than define offenses and order their punishment after the allegedly criminal conduct had been committed.

The Presidency

◆◆◆ **Can a Presidential Candidate and His Running Mate Be from the Same State?**

Possibly. The Constitution has never been tested on this point. But, practically speaking, the situation is not likely to arise.

What the Constitution does say on this point has been debated for a long time. Both the original portion of Article II, Section 1, and the Twelfth Amendment that superseded it say only one thing about the issue: that the electors in the electoral college will vote for president and vice president, "of whom," to use the Constitution's original phrasing, "one at least shall not be an Inhabitant of the same State with themselves."

Some scholars maintain that the proper interpretation of the constitutional wording is that the candidates must be from different states, that the Framers of the Constitution—eager to promote national unity—did not want electors voting solely along state lines for favorite sons.

Be that as it may, no political party has ever nominated presidential and vice presidential candidates from the same state. It just isn't politically wise. Instead, parties choose their candidates not only from different states, but frequently also from different regions. For example, in 1960, John F. Kennedy of Massachusetts ran with Lyndon B. Johnson of Texas against Richard M. Nixon of California and Henry Cabot Lodge of Massachusetts. In 1964, Johnson selected Hubert H. Humphrey of Minnesota as his running mate to oppose Barry Goldwater of Arizona and William Miller of New York. In 1968, Humphrey chose Edmund S. Muskie of Maine as his running mate against Nixon (now moved to New York) and Spiro T. Agnew of Maryland. Ronald W. Reagan of California and George Bush of Texas have run against Jimmy Carter of Georgia and Walter F. Mondale of Minnesota in 1980 and against Mondale and Geraldine Ferraro of New York in 1984.

◆◆◆ **Can You Win the Presidency Even If You Lose the Popular Vote?**

Yes. It happened in 1876. And presidents have been elected without getting a majority. That was true of a number of presidents including John Quincy Adams, Abraham Lincoln, Woodrow Wilson, Harry S Truman, John F. Kennedy, and Richard M. Nixon. A candidate does not need to get a majority of the popular vote or even a plurality—more votes than any other candidate—to be elected president. That's because the president is chosen by the electoral college.

The Framers of the Constitution decided against relying solely on direct popular voting to elect a president because they feared that regionalism and alliances between larger states would dominate national elections. So they established the electoral college in which each state is given votes equal to the number of its representatives in both the House and the Senate. (As a result, the strength of smaller states was slightly increased; currently the five smallest states contain 1.2 percent of the population but control 2.7 percent of the votes in the electoral college.)In order to be elected president, a candidate must receive a majority of votes in the electoral college. By tradition, all electoral votes of a state go to the candidate with the greatest number of popular votes in that state. In the past, sometimes maverick electors have gone against the voters' will; as a result, a number of states have passed laws making the electors' unanimous vote mandatory.

However, when the Founding Fathers first set up the procedure for electing the president and vice president, they did not separate the two elections; there was only one electoral college election and each elector had two votes. The person who received the most votes became president (assuming he received a majority), and the second leading vote getter became vice president. If no one received a majority, the House of Representatives chose the president from the five leading candidates. This system worked well in the elections of both George Washington and John Adams. However, in 1800 there was a tie in the electoral college between Thomas Jefferson and Aaron Burr, his running mate. After thirty-six ballots, the House finally elected Jefferson president; Burr then automatically became vice president.

The 1800 election forced Congress to rethink the method of electing presidents. The result was the Twelfth Amendment, ratified in 1804, which provides for separate elections for president and vice president by the electoral college. If no presidential candidate receives a majority of electoral votes, the House chooses the winner from the top three candidates. Unlike any other vote in the House, this election allows only one vote for each state. If no vice presidential candidate receives an electoral college majority, the Senate selects the winner from the top two candidates.

The chief result of these provisions is to encourage two-party politics, with both opposing candidates having broad national support. In all but three presidential elections, the person elected did in fact receive the largest number of popular votes. Yet in more than a third of them candidates who did not receive a majority of the popular vote were elected.

In 1824, five candidates ran for president and no single one received a majority of either the electoral or popular vote. The House of Representatives chose John Quincy Adams as president, even though Andrew Jackson had a plurality of both the popular and electoral votes. In the elections of 1844, 1848, and 1856, Presidents James K. Polk, Zachary Taylor, and James Buchanan, respectively, received less than a majority of the popular vote because of the presence of third-party candidates. Each did, however, receive a plurality of the popular vote and a majority in the electoral college.

Abraham Lincoln was elected president in 1860 with less than 40 percent of the popular vote. However, there were three other contenders for office, and Lincoln was the most popular of the candidates with the broadest base of national rather than regional support.

Rutherford B. Hayes was elected president in 1876, even though Samuel Tilden received a narrow majority of the popular vote. Hayes was elected because he carried twenty-one of the thirty-eight states as well as a bare majority of the electoral votes, 185 to Tilden's 184 votes. Initially, it appeared that Tilden had won a majority in the electoral college, but an electoral commission appointed by Congress to settle contested southern tallies reversed the votes of three states, shifting them from Tilden to Hayes.

In 1880, James A. Garfield won election, not by a majority of the popular vote but by a plurality because of the presence of a third-party candidate. The same thing happened to Grover Cleveland when he first ran in 1884 and again in 1892, when he won a second term. Oddly enough, in Cleveland's first bid for a second term in 1888 he was defeated by Benjamin Harrison, even though Cleveland received a majority of the popular vote. His support, however, was sectional and concentrated in the South. Harrison carried states with the greater number of electoral votes.

The most successful third-party candidacy in American politics occurred in 1912, when former President Theodore Roosevelt, a one-time

Republican, ran as a Progressive. He outpolled the Republican nominee, President William Howard Taft, but Woodrow Wilson, a Democrat, defeated both of them and won an overwhelming 81 percent of the votes of the electoral college.

Harry S Truman was elected president in 1948, getting the most but not a majority of the popular vote—yet a majority of the electoral vote. Four candidates ran in that election. In 1960, John F. Kennedy was also elected president without a popular-vote majority. He defeated Richard M. Nixon in a very close election in which Senator Harry S. Byrd of Virginia was a third-party candidate. Similarly, in 1968, Nixon won only a plurality of the popular vote over Democrat Hubert H. Humphrey because of the third-party candidacy of former Governor George A. Wallace of Alabama.

There is an additional quirk sometimes associated with the electoral college. The vice president, as president of the Senate, counts the electoral votes before a joint session of Congress and announces the result. Occasionally, this has meant that a vice president who has just unsuccessfully run for the presidency is put in the position of announcing his own defeat. Thus, in 1960, Richard M. Nixon announced John F. Kennedy's victory over him, and in 1968 Hubert H. Humphrey announced Nixon's triumph. In 1980, Vice President Walter F. Mondale announced the defeat of the Carter-Mondale ticket by Ronald W. Reagan and George Bush.

◆◆◆ Can You Become President Without Anyone Ever Voting for You?

Yes. Gerald R. Ford did, though he was, of course, an elected representative from Michigan.

Seven presidents have died in office. This century alone has seen the deaths of Presidents Franklin D. Roosevelt and Warren G. Harding and the assassination of John F. Kennedy, and it has witnessed the resignation of Richard M. Nixon, whom Ford succeeded.

The Framers of the Constitution anticipated the chaos that might result from an interruption in the exercise of executive authority. They tried to avoid discontinuity by providing that in the case of the president's "Removal . . . from Office, or of his Death, Resignation, or Inability to discharge the Powers and Duties of the said office" the vice president would succeed him.

It is only in cases of a president's death, removal, or resignation that the question of who becomes president is relevant. When there is no president—as, for example, when a president dies—the vice president is first in the line of succession. But what if there is no vice president? The United States has been without one no less than fifteen times. Both vice presidents under James Madison, who served two terms, died in office. Eight other presidents lost their vice president for the same reason. In recent times, both Harry S Truman and Lyndon B. Johnson, who succeeded to the presidency upon the deaths of Franklin D. Roosevelt and John F. Kennedy, respectively, then served without a vice president at their side.

The Constitution gives to Congress the power to decide the appropriate line of succession to the presidency in the event that both the president and vice president are unable to discharge the duties of the presidency (Article II, Section 1). Congress first formulated an official line of succession in 1792 after George Washington suffered two serious illnesses during his first term. (It took him forty days to recover from the removal of a growth on his leg in the spring of 1789, and in May of the following year he had a severe case of pneumonia.) The plan was revised by Congress in 1886, five years after the assassination of James A. Garfield and eighteen years after the impeachment of Andrew Johnson, who was vice president when Abraham Lincoln was assassinated. Congress drew up a new line of succession yet again in 1947, after the sudden death of Franklin D. Roosevelt in 1945.

Under the 1947 act that is now in effect, if both the presidency and vice presidency are vacated for whatever reason, the office of president passes first to the Speaker of the House of Representatives and then to the president pro tempore of the Senate, both of whom are members of Congress. Thereafter, the line of succession passes to members of the cabinet, all of whom are appointed officials who may never have run for any elected office whatsoever. The line follows the order in which the cabinet department was created: the Departments of State, Treasury, Defense, Interior, Justice, Agriculture, Commerce, Labor, Health and Human Services, Housing and Urban Development, Transportation, Energy, and Education.

Today, it is not likely that there will be a vacancy in the vice presidency for long. This is so because the Twenty-fifth Amendment, ratified in 1967, empowers the president to nominate a new vice president, subject to confirmation by a majority of both houses of Congress. That is what happened in 1973 after Vice President Spiro T. Agnew pleaded "no contest" to charges of income-tax fraud and resigned. President Nixon nominated Ford, then House minority whip, to replace Agnew—the first use of the procedure set out in the Twenty-fifth Amendment. When Ford became president himself in 1974, he became the first president to hold that post without ever having been elected to national office. Nobody outside his congressional district had ever voted for him. As soon as Ford became president, there was again no vice president. Ford then appointed Nelson Rockefeller as vice president, and the Congress agreed to that. So from 1974 until 1977, the United States was headed by both a president and vice president who had not been elected to their office.

◆◆◆ Why Are Presidents Limited to Two Terms?

The Twenty-second Amendment, ratified in 1951, sets that limit. But before that, George Washington's example of serving for only two terms set a tradition that withstood challenge until 1940 when Franklin D. Roosevelt broke it.

The issue—how long should a president be allowed to serve—was a major point of dispute at the Constitutional Convention in 1787. After weeks of fruitless talks, the delegates chose to set the term at four years and rejected proposals to limit the number of terms a president could serve. Many opponents of the new Constitution—and even some of its supporters, such as Thomas Jefferson—found this feature repugnant. They charged that the president could well become a king, securing reelection after reelection for life.

Virtually every delegate to the Convention, as well as other knowledgeable Americans, knew that Washington would undoubtedly become the nation's first president if the Constitution was adopted—which is what happened. Washington was the unanimous first choice of the electors in the electoral college in the first election. He is still the only president ever to have been elected unanimously by the electoral college. Actually, he only wanted to serve one term; he said he was exhausted from trying to calm the growing division between Federalists and Republicans. But all the members of his cabinet, including both Alexander Hamilton and Thomas Jefferson, who were leaders of the emerging Federalist and Republican parties, as well as key members of both houses of Congress persuaded Washington to accept a second term. However, he firmly resisted similar efforts to persuade him to stand for a third term in 1796.

Washington's decision not to seek reelection again created what came to be known as the "two-term tradition." Although John Adams was defeated in his bid for a second term, the next three presidents—Jefferson, James Madison, and James Monroe—served two terms apiece, then chose not to run again, citing Washington's example. Andrew Jackson decided similarly in 1836 after two terms.

By 1876, when Ulysses S. Grant declined a third chance at the presidency, the two-term tradition had almost taken on constitutional significance. Grant's subsequent attempt to run a third time in 1880 was widely denounced as a betrayal of the Constitution, and he failed even to secure the nomination of his party. After him, no president seriously considered the possibility of serving longer than eight years until 1912, when Theodore Roosevelt—who had served for nearly eight years—sought the Republican nomination and then, after losing it to the incumbent president, William Howard Taft, formed the Progressive party. Roosevelt argued that he was not violating the two-term tradition because his "first" term was actually William McKinley's second term, which Roosevelt completed when McKinley was assassinated in 1901. But strong feelings against Roosevelt's apparent challenge to Washington's example helped to secure his defeat by Democrat Woodrow Wilson.

The issue rose again in 1940 when Franklin D. Roosevelt stunned the nation by announcing that he would seek a third term. Roosevelt had spent the spring and summer keeping the nation guessing as to which of half a dozen potential successors he would endorse. But he decided that none was sufficiently able or politically skilled to lead the United States during the probable war that was coming. Furthermore, the possible successors were either unfriendly to his New Deal policies or, in his view, could not have defended them against conservative attacks. Despite howls of outrage from Republicans and from traditionalists of both parties, Roosevelt won the election, though his margin of victory over Wendell L. Willkie was far smaller than that of either of his previous two victories. By the time Roosevelt ran for a fourth term in 1944, the controversy over his flouting of Washington's example had pretty much abated. His decision this time was based on his belief that he could not abandon the presidency during the middle of World War II. He faced no serious opposition, even though he was already in poor health and stood a poor chance of surviving a fourth term.

After Roosevelt's death in 1945—a few months after his inaugural—Republicans were determined never to permit another president to serve more than two terms. In 1946, they quickly framed the Twenty-second Amendment, which restricted all future presidents to two, full elected terms. (The amendment also bars any person who succeeds a president and finishes an unexpired term longer than two years from being elected to more than one subsequent full term. It thus set an absolute ten-year limit that any person may serve in the presidency.) The amendment did not apply to then-President Harry S Truman, who had succeeded Roosevelt. Truman stood for election in 1948 but declined to run in 1952. The

Republicans then discovered that they had hobbled themselves because their own candidate, Dwight D. Eisenhower, the popular commander of Allied forces in Europe during World War II, was constitutionally ineligible for a third term in 1960. Many political observers believed he could have been reelected for as many terms as he wanted.

◆◆◆ What Happens If the President Gets Sick?

A president who is sick is still president, but if his illness is serious, the Twenty-fifth Amendment, ratified in 1967, may come into play. It provides for the vice president to assume the president's duties until the president is better.

The question, of course, is, Who decides how serious the sickness is? The Twenty-fifth Amendment offers two alternatives, but possible problems still remain. For one thing, the president himself can step down temporarily from office by informing in writing the Speaker of the House and the president pro tempore of the Senate that he is "unable to discharge the powers and duties of his office." (Later, after his recovery, he can resume his office by writing those same leaders that he is better.) Alternatively, the vice president and a majority of the members of the cabinet or of some committee appointed by Congress can determine that the president is in no condition to serve.

Throughout American history, presidents have been loath to admit they were ill. They, their families, and their advisers often felt that the administration's programs, if not the national security itself, would be vulnerable if they admitted that they had a grave illness. And presidents certainly have not been immune to serious medical problems. George Washington had an anthrax tumor removed from his leg in 1789 and nearly died of pneumonia in 1790. He also suffered from chronic rheumatism. Andrew Jackson, famous for his stamina and courage, suffered from malaria, dysentery, osteomyelitis, and bronchiectasis; six feet tall, he weighed only 125 pounds.

In the 1890s, at a time when press coverage of the presidency was still in its infancy, Grover Cleveland was able to feign being on vacation while he had a serious cancer growth removed from his mouth while aboard a boat on the Hudson River.

Perhaps the most significant cover-up of a president's illness occurred in 1919 when Woodrow Wilson was struck by a paralyzing embolism while on a national tour to promote ratification of the Treaty of Versailles. He recovered briefly, only to suffer a second and irreversible stroke. During the last seventeen months of his second term the United States was actually governed by a triumvirate consisting of Wilson's second wife, Edith; Joseph Tumulty, the White House secretary; and Dr. Cary Grayson, the White House physician. Wilson's condition was carefully kept not only from the public but even from his vice president, Thomas R. Marshall. He was never hospitalized, but his wife kept watch over his door, barring all but the most necessary visitors.

Although he was crippled by polio, Franklin D. Roosevelt maintained an image of a vigorous and active leader even during his last year of life, when he apparently did not know how sick he was. Either his physicians did not tell him or they were unwilling to admit that he was fatally ill from circulatory ailments that eventually culminated in a fatal cerebral hemorrhage. Among those who were not informed of Roosevelt's deteriorating condition was Vice President Harry S Truman. Not surprisingly, when Roosevelt died on April 12, 1945, Truman felt "as if the sun, the moon, the stars, and all the planets had fallen in on me."

It was during Dwight D. Eisenhower's convalescence from a heart attack and a bout of ileitis, an intestinal disorder, that the tradition of issuing health bulletins about a president was established. When Eisenhower won the presidency in 1952, he was sixty-two years old—one of the oldest men ever elected to the office. Determined to avoid the examples of Wilson and Roosevelt, Eisenhower and his vice president, Richard M. Nixon, exchanged confidential letters early in his administration setting forth an agreement as to when Nixon would assume the responsibilities of the presidency if Eisenhower found himself too ill to carry them out. (This practice has been followed by all subsequent presidents and vice presidents.) Eisenhower actually contemplated resigning when, in his second term in office, he suffered a small stroke that panicked Wall Street investors, prompting stock-market prices to plummet $4.5 billion in value within a half hour. However, he recovered within a week and resumed full control over the government.

It was both Eisenhower's record of illnesses and the assassination of John F. Kennedy in 1963 that spurred the adoption of the Twenty-fifth Amendment. But eight months after its ratification in 1967, Lyndon B. Johnson—despite the tradition of issuing health bulletins that began with Eisenhower—was able to keep secret the removal of a skin cancer from his ankle.

The first application of the Twenty-fifth Amendment's provisions dealing with presidential disability did not occur until 1985, when President

Ronald W. Reagan underwent surgery for the removal of a large intestinal polyp. He wrote a letter to the Speaker of the House and the president pro tempore of the Senate, turning over presidential power to Vice President George Bush before being put under anesthesia. The letter was a deliberately vague attempt to accomplish the purpose of the Twenty-fifth Amendment without formally invoking it. But for all practical purposes, the amendment was in effect once Bush was made acting president. The informal process was carried out by White House aides because they did not want to unduly alarm the nation. They also felt they were in uncharted legal waters. They believed that the Twenty-fifth Amendment was designed for a longer, more debilitating illness than this one appeared to be. (Reagan resumed his duties and responsibilities, by a second letter, eight hours later.) The aides said they were concerned about setting a precedent that might pressure future presidents into using the Twenty-fifth Amendment on inconsequential occasions such as when a president is under anesthesia to have a tooth pulled.

Earlier, in 1981, when the President was shot and wounded by John W. Hinckley, Jr., no one in the government moved to invoke the Twenty-fifth Amendment.

◆◆◆ What President Was Impeached?

Andrew Johnson, who succeeded to the presidency when Abraham Lincoln was assassinated as the Civil War drew to a close in 1865. He was impeached but not convicted—and thus not removed from office.

Impeachment is the method the Framers wrote into the Constitution to start the process of removing a president from office (by the authority of a clause in Article I, Section 2). The House of Representatives impeaches— that is, accuses—the president of specified charges called articles of impeachment. According to Article II, Section 4, a president can be impeached only for "Treason, Bribery, or other high Crimes and Misdemeanors." Once the House votes to impeach, the Senate tries the president on the charges in the articles (by the authority of a clause in Article I, Section 3). The Senate actually conducts a trial, with the senators sitting as judges and swearing a special oath for that purpose. The chief justice of the Supreme Court presides at the trial, and the representatives who sponsored the impeachment resolution act as prosecutors. A two-thirds vote of the Senate is necessary for conviction.

A pro-Union Democrat from Tennessee, Johnson was named as Lincoln's running mate in the 1864 election to balance the National Union ticket. Unlike Lincoln, Johnson seemed to favor harsh treatment for the seceded Southern states when the war was over. But once he became president, Johnson drew back abruptly from his views, angering Republican congressmen who favored crushing all possible resistance on the part of Southern whites to the victory of the Union armies, the destruction of slavery, and the extension of citizenship and constitutional rights to the freed slaves.

The House voted to impeach Johnson for a long list of allegations. At the heart of the impeachment was the Tenure of Office Act, which had been enacted by Congress over Johnson's veto in 1867. The act provided that the president could not remove cabinet members or other executive officeholders without congressional consent—thus resurrecting an issue that had been settled in the First Congress in 1789. Republicans in both the House and the Senate passed this law to prevent Johnson from dismissing their allies in the cabinet, specifically Secretary of War Edwin M. Stanton. But Johnson dismissed Stanton anyway, saying the act was unconstitutional. Seizing on this obvious violation of the statute, so-called Radical Republicans in the House pushed through impeachment charges against him.

In the trial of the president before the Senate, Johnson's counsel, William M. Evarts, argued that the Constitution provided that the president and other officers of the government could be impeached only for specific, indictable offenses, rather than for major disagreements over constitutional interpretation or public policy or for actions designed to frustrate the workings of the government.

Under the Constitution, a two-thirds vote of the Senate is required to remove the president or any other officeholder. While a majority of the Senate voted to remove Johnson from office, he escaped removal by one vote. The seven Republican Senators who voted—with twelve Democrats—against removing Johnson saw their political careers destroyed by their decision. But Johnson himself completed his term of office and returned to public life after he left the presidency, representing Tennessee in the Senate in 1875, the same year in which he died.

Although on occasion other movements to impeach the president have surfaced—as when Harry S Truman removed General Douglas MacArthur from his command during the Korean War in 1951—nearly all these have evaporated quickly. The only sustained effort to impeach a president since 1868 was prompted by the Watergate break-in during the presidential campaign of 1972. In the summer of 1974, the House referred to its Judiciary Committee proposals to impeach Richard M. Nixon on several grounds—for obstruction of justice for refusing to turn over to the House documents pertaining to the Watergate scandal, and on various charges arising from Nixon's exercise of war powers in the Vietnam War and the impoundment of appropriated funds.

The Judiciary Committee rejected the argument of Nixon's counsel—harking back to Evarts's argument in the Johnson impeachment—that a president could only be impeached for indictable criminal offenses. Instead, the committee argued for what has been since called the "abuse of power" theory of impeachment—that is, that serious and substantial breaches of the public trust warrant impeachment as a way to maintain the integrity of the presidency. In late July, the committee voted to recommend three articles of impeachment to the full House. Article I charged Nixon with obstruction of justice. Article II advanced the "abuse of power" theory, and Nixon was accused of "violating the constitutional rights of citizens, impairing the due and proper administration of justice in the conduct of lawful inquiries [and] of contravening the law governing agencies of the executive branch and the purposes of the agencies." Article III focused on Nixon's assertion of executive privilege in refusing to comply with the committee's subpoenas for certain documents. Two other proposed articles, dealing with the bombing of Cambodia and Nixon's alleged manipulation of his personal finances and income-tax filings, failed to win a majority of support in the committee.

In his struggle to assert his executive rights against a federal grand jury presided over by U.S. District Judge John Sirica and convened by a special prosecutor who was investigating the Watergate affair, Nixon took his case to the Supreme Court. However, the Court unanimously rejected his arguments against complying with a grand-jury subpoena for documents and the tapes of conversations held by Nixon and his aides in the Oval Office. Subsequently, Nixon released transcripts of three key tape recordings that provided a basis for indicting him for obstruction of justice. It then became clear that the full House would follow the lead of the Judiciary Committee, which voted to impeach him on that ground, and that the Senate would vote to convict Nixon and remove him from office. Faced with that outcome—but before the full House voted or a trial ever took place in the Senate—Nixon resigned from office on August 9, 1974.

The impeachment controversies surrounding Johnson and Nixon have left unsettled the question of what constitutes an impeachable offense. Some scholars now incline toward the broader definitions advanced by the House Judiciary Committee in 1974.

◆◆◆ Does the President Have to Commit a Crime to Be Impeached?

Probably not. Most scholars agree that any federal official who can be impeached can be impeached for serious misconduct that is not a crime. It is true, however, that historically almost all the officials that have been impeached have committed crimes.

A number of the Americans who worked on drafting the Constitution believed that impeachment should be used only against criminals. Indeed, they felt that there was no reason to impeach a president because, if he committed a crime, he could be indicted by the courts, and if he merely were a bad president, voters would remove him from office in the next election. Furthermore, as Rufus King of Massachusetts said, the concept of separation of powers would be weakened if one branch of government could remove the head of another branch: "The three great departments of Government should be separate and independent. . . . [This would not] be the case if the Executive should be impeachable."

Despite these objections, the Constitution was written to give the House of Representatives the power to impeach, and it has used it on several occasions against persons who had not committed a crime. John Pickering, a district judge in New Hampshire, was impeached and removed by the Jeffersonian Republicans in 1804 because he was insane, alcoholic, and perhaps most of all, an ardent Federalist. He was charged only with malfeasance and general unfitness for office. Then the Jeffersonian Republicans tried—unsuccessfully—to use the impeachment power to remove from the Supreme Court Samuel Chase, a Federalist, although Chase had committed no crime. Indeed, as Alexander Hamilton said at the start of Chase's trial in the Senate, the impeachment was "of a nature which may with peculiar propriety be denominated *political.*"

In 1868—again unsuccessfully—the House of Representatives tried to remove President Andrew Johnson, on the grounds that he had dismissed the secretary of war, Edwin M. Stanton, in violation of the Tenure of Office Act of 1867 and that he had criticized, insulted, and ignored the actions of Congress. In defense of Johnson, former Supreme Court Justice Benjamin R. Curtis argued that the Tenure of Office Act was unconstitutional because it denied the president the right to decide who was to remain in his cabinet—an argument finally confirmed by the Supreme Court in 1926—and that a president could not be impeached for the "political act" of criticizing Congress. Johnson was impeached by the House but later acquitted by the Senate.

The articles drawn up against President Richard M. Nixon in 1974 were chiefly allegations of violations of the law. However, one of them did not allege an indictable offense but, instead, cited Nixon for refusing to honor subpoenas issued by the House Judiciary Committee for tapes and other material needed for its investigation of the Watergate scandal.

Most federal officials who have been impeached and convicted have been found guilty of crimes. Of the twelve persons, including Johnson, who have been impeached by the House, nine were federal judges. The Senate has voted to convict four, all of them federal judges. Of the four, John Pickering, the Federalist judge mentioned earlier, did not commit a crime. Another judge may have committed crimes but was not removed specifically on those grounds. That man, Halsted L. Ritter, a United States district judge in Florida, was acquitted in 1936 of six specific criminal charges, including tax fraud and bribery, but was removed from office on a seventh catchall charge that the criminal charges in the six other counts brought the judiciary into disrepute. West H. Humphreys, a United States district judge in Tennessee, was removed from office in 1862 for advocating secession and accepting office as a Confederate judge (arguably the crime of treason). And, Robert W. Archbald, of the United States Commerce Court, was removed by the Senate in 1913 for bribery and corruption.

It is as yet unclear if the courts have the power to review congressional impeachment actions. The issue has never been raised.

◆◆◆ Can the President Send Congress Home?

Yes, if Congress cannot agree on its own when to adjourn. But no president has ever exercised this authority.

Under Article II, Section 3, of the Constitution—which deals with the president's powers regarding both houses—he may "in Case of Disagreement between them, with Respect to the Time of Adjournment . . . adjourn them to such Time as he shall think proper."

Ordinarily, Congress adjourns itself when one house proposes a resolution to adjourn that the other house adopts. However, if the other house prefers a different date, the difference between the two is ironed out in a joint session of Congress. Each house may also adjourn for three days or less without the consent of the other (Article I, Section 5). Occasionally, one of them will adjourn for multiple three-day periods, with pro forma, one-minute sessions every three days—a work device that has never been constitutionally tested.

The first dispute under the constitutional provision arose in 1835, during the presidency of Andrew Jackson. Congress that year passed a bill fixing its own date of adjournment for the 1836 session. President Andrew Jackson vetoed the bill, claiming that setting an absolute date so far in advance invaded his authority to set dates of adjournment if Congress could not agree on one. His veto was not overridden. There was also considerable speculation that President Woodrow Wilson would have had to use this power to end the 1914 session of Congress when its members seemingly could not agree on a date. However, they ultimately settled the matter on their own.

The president—under the same section of the Constitution—also enjoys the authority to summon Congress into a special session. That has happened a number of times, though presidents are wary of doing so because once Congress meets it may consider any issues it wishes, not just what the president intended. William Howard Taft discovered that when he called both houses into extra session to consider a trade-reciprocity bill in 1909. Along with that bill, Congress considered many other bills, some in direct conflict with what Taft wanted.

On many occasions, the Senate alone has been called into an extra session to ratify a treaty with a foreign nation. This poses no threat because the Senate, without the House, has little other power on its own. The House has never been called into an extra session by itself.

◆◆◆ Who Else Besides the President Takes an Oath to "Preserve, Protect and Defend the Constitution"?

Nobody. Only the president's oath of office, provided in Article II, Section 1, of the Constitution, contains those exact words. Article VI does require that every other elected or appointed federal and state officeholder take an oath swearing "support" of the Constitution—but it's not necessarily the exact same oath that the president takes.

The first oath proposed for the president appears in the records of the Constitutional Convention for August 6, 1787, in a report of the Committee of Detail. The committee suggested that the president swear or affirm that he would "faithfully execute the office of President of the United States of America." (The alternative of affirming instead of swearing was designed to accommodate members of religious groups such as the Quakers whose convictions forbid swearing oaths.)

Several weeks later, George Mason and James Madison proposed an amendment to the oath, adding the following language: "and will to the best of my judgment and power preserve, protect and defend the Constitution of the United States." The delegates adopted this addition despite James Wilson's remark that it was unnecessary. Then, in a further refinement several weeks later, the phrase "judgment and power" was replaced by the word "abilities," which itself was changed to "Ability" in the final text:

> I do solemnly swear (or affirm) that I will faithfully execute the Office of President of the United States, and will to the best of my Ability, preserve, protect and defend the Constitution of the United States.

Article VI dealing with the oath taken by all other federal as well as state officeholders derives from the Virginia Plan, a set of resolutions that served as the basis for the work of the Convention. It originally required "that the Legislative, Executive and Judiciary powers within the several States ought to be bound by oath to support the articles of Union." The resolution was approved on June 11, but the next month Elbridge Gerry of Massachusetts successfully moved to extend the requirement to "the officers of the National Government." And late in August, the delegates, almost without discussion, adopted the motion of Charles Pinckney of South Carolina to add that no religious test would ever be required. So Article VI provides:

> The Senators and Representatives . . . and the Members of the several State Legislatures, and all executive and judicial Officers, both of the United States and of the several States, shall be bound by Oath or Affirmation, to support this Constitution; but no religious Test shall ever be required as a Qualification to any Office or public Trust under the United States.

Under the authority of Article VI, Congress has promulgated the official oaths for various government officers. The language of these oaths has been modified from time to time. The oath for most federal officeholders took its present form in 1884, that of the special oath taken by all federal judges in 1893. The oath for state officers, adopted in its present form in 1947, serves as a companion oath of the one each takes to uphold his or her state office.

The Supreme Court ══════════════

♦♦♦ Why Is There a Supreme Court?

Primarily because the men who framed the Constitution were suspicious of governments and wanted to diffuse the power of the national one that they were formulating for the thirteen original states. Their distrust was based on experiences with the eighteenth-century monarchies of Great Britain and the European continent. So the Framers set up a system of checks and balances, and the judicial branch of the government they created was given the power to curb the actions of the other two branches, the executive and the legislative.

The Supreme Court they created has been called "the most distinctive feature" of our system of government because it is empowered to interpret the Constitution and to nullify the actions of the other branches. To put it another way, our Supreme Court is, as one scholar has observed, the "supremest supreme court in the world." Its uniqueness prompted the noted nineteenth-century French politician, traveler, and writer Alexis de Tocqueville to say that "a more imposing judicial power was never constituted by any people."

Actually, the idea for such a court was not entirely new. The American patriots had recognized that there would be a need to settle disputes between the states. Under the Articles of Confederation ratified during the Revolutionary War in 1781, the Confederation Congress could establish a court to hear disputes between states. In fact, it did so once in a dispute between Pennsylvania and Connecticut—and its decision was considered final and binding. Seven of the men who served on that court participated in the Constitutional Convention of 1787 in Philadelphia— and so helped to set up the Supreme Court. In fact, one of them, James Wilson of Pennsylvania, not only played a major role at the Convention, but also became a justice of the Supreme Court when it was established.

The Supreme Court was the only court created under the Constitution, but the details of its makeup were not mentioned. The Court did not become a reality until the first Congress passed the Judiciary Act of 1789 on September 24 of that year. The act authorized the president to appoint a court consisting of a chief justice and five associate justices.

The Judiciary Act spelled out a number of other matters, too. For one thing, it created lower federal courts to serve under the Supreme Court. In addition, the act defined the appellate jurisdiction of the Court. The Constitution provides that the Supreme Court has original jurisdiction—the power to hear a case at its inception—over "Cases affecting Ambassadors, other public Ministers and Consuls, and those in which a State shall be Party" (Article III, Section 2). But the Constitution left to Congress the power to define the scope of the Court's appellate jurisdiction—its authority to review the determinations of lower federal courts and of state courts. The 1789 Judiciary Act did just that.

The Constitution does not expressly confer upon the Supreme Court, or other federal courts, the power to declare federal or state laws unconstitutional. However, before the Constitution was adopted, the power of judicial review had been exercised by several state courts in cases involving state law—and these cases were well known to the Framers. It is not surprising, therefore, that, beginning with the cases of *Marbury* v. *Madison* in 1803 and *Fletcher* v. *Peck* in 1810, Chief Justice John Marshall firmly established the authority of federal courts to review the constitutionality of both federal and state laws, and while some scholars have challenged this authority, the Supreme Court and other federal courts have routinely exercised it. In Marshall's view, "all those who have framed written constitutions contemplate them as forming the fundamental and paramount law of the nation" and it is "the province and duty of the judicial department to say what the law is."

Marshall's logic led to the power of judicial review—the power to interpret the Constitution that is shared by all courts, state and federal, not only by the Supreme Court. Although the Supreme Court is the ultimate arbiter of the meaning of the Constitution, lower federal courts as well as state courts interpret it daily. This means that any federal or state court may declare a federal law or a state statute unconstitutional.

This awesome judicial power, which the Supreme Court wields so mightily, has provoked many attempts in the past two hundred years to curb the Court—by increasing the number of justices, by suspending its sessions, by reducing its appellate jurisdiction. But there has never been an attempt to abolish it. And it's clear that any such attempt would contravene the explicit mandate of the Constitution: "The judicial Power of the United States, shall be vested in one supreme Court" (Article III, Section 1). Under the Constitution, we must have a Supreme Court.

◆◆◆ Were There Always Nine Justices?

No. In fact, at one time ten justices sat on the Supreme Court.

Article III of the Constitution, which creates the judicial branch of the federal government, does not specify how many justices the Court should have; it simply creates the Court and allows Congress broad power to decide its structure, size, and jurisdiction—a power that Congress did not hesitate to use for the Court's first one hundred years.

Under the Judiciary Act of 1789, Congress created a six-justice Supreme Court, with five associate justices presided over by a chief justice. When the Supreme Court first convened in New York City on February 2, 1790, only four justices—Chief Justice John Jay of New York and Associate Justices William Cushing of Massachusetts, James Wilson of Pennsylvania, and John Blair of Virginia—were present. Associate Justice John Rutledge of South Carolina never attended a session of the Court from the date of his appointment until he resigned in 1791, although he did carry out his duties of serving on the circuit courts in South Carolina and Georgia. Because of his ill health and his desire to accept an appointment to serve as chancellor of Maryland, Robert Hanson Harrison of that state declined his appointment as an associate justice of the Supreme Court; James Iredell of North Carolina, appointed to the seat Harrison had chosen not to accept, did not take office until August 1790, at the Court's second session.

In addition to the Supreme Court described above, the Judiciary Act of 1789 established circuit courts and district courts as trial courts below the Supreme Court, with technical matters determining which kinds of cases each court heard. A district judge was appointed to hear cases in the district court in each state. But no circuit judges were appointed. Instead, the act required the justices of the Supreme Court to "ride circuit"—that is, to sit with the district judge in each state to hear cases in the federal circuit courts. Originally, there were three circuits, and the act required two justices to sit on each circuit court—which is probably why the Supreme Court first had six justices. A later amendment to the Judiciary Act of 1789 relaxed the circuit-riding requirement, providing that only one justice sit in each circuit. Congress also reorganized the judicial system by creating six circuits, one for each justice.

As the country and the pressure of judicial business grew, Congress created new circuits and added seats to the Supreme Court. A new Seventh Circuit was set up in 1807, and the court was expanded to seven justices. In 1837, two more circuits and two more justices were added, bringing the Court to its present size for the first time. Then, in 1863,

Congress, with the enthusiastic support of President Abraham Lincoln, created the Tenth Circuit and a tenth seat on the Court—the largest the Court has ever been. This was done ostensibly to cover the far western states of California and Oregon (and later Nevada), but a tenth justice appointed by Lincoln also ensured a majority of the justices in Lincoln's favor should any constitutional challenge to his actions in the Civil War reach the Court.

The ten-justice Court lasted a brief three years as a result of bitter disputes between Congress and Lincoln's successor, Andrew Johnson. In order to deprive Johnson of the chance to nominate any justices on his own, Congress enacted over his veto in 1866 a bill to reduce the number of justices to seven by attrition: As each Justice over that number died or retired, his seat was eliminated. The Court actually shrank to eight members by the time Johnson left office three years later. That year, 1869, as a "gift" to incoming President Ulysses S. Grant, Congress restored the ninth seat, and the Court has remained at that number ever since.

In 1891, Congress created the circuit courts of appeals as appellate courts sitting above the district courts and the old circuit courts (which continued to exist). (In 1948, a revision of the Judicial Code renamed these courts as the United States Courts of Appeals.) The same act also relieved the justices of their circuit-riding responsibilities. When, in 1911, the old circuit courts were abolished, the basic structure of the present federal judiciary system—the district courts as trial courts, the courts of appeals as the first level of appellate courts, and the Supreme Court as the pinnacle—was finally in place.

Only once since 1869 has there been a serious, concerted effort to change the size of the Court. In 1937, frustrated by its repeated rejection of New Deal legislation, President Franklin D. Roosevelt proposed the reorganization of the Court. Arguing that the justices were old and overworked, Roosevelt urged that an arbitrary retirement age of seventy should be established. At the time, six of the justices, including the conservative bloc known as the Four Horsemen, were already over seventy years old. According to Roosevelt's plan, each of them could choose to retire or to remain on the Court; if he chose to remain, however, the president could appoint another justice, ostensibly to assist the elderly justice in the demanding work of the Court. Opponents of the proposal, who came from all political parties and shades of belief, contended that the plan was merely a device to "pack" the Court with Roosevelt supporters. The reorganization bill failed ignominiously. Soon afterward, however, the older justices did begin to retire, eventually permitting Roosevelt to appoint virtually an entirely new Court before his death in 1945.

◆◆◆ Does the Constitution Provide for a Chief Justice?

Yes, but it mentions the office only once—when, in Article I, Section 3, it says that "the Chief Justice shall preside" over impeachment trials in the Senate if charges are brought against a president. (This has happened only once, when Chief Justice Salmon P. Chase presided over the impeachment trial of Andrew Johnson in 1868.) The powers and duties of the chief justice as the presiding justice on the Supreme Court come from statute, custom, and tradition.

The chief justice presides not only over the open sessions of the Court but also over the private meetings and deliberations of the justices in what is called the conference. In discussion, voting, and writing opinions, he is a "first among equals" who enjoys special, though limited, privileges as the result of long-standing practice. Thus, by tradition, the chief justice speaks first at the conference in discussing the cases that have come before the Court, with each associate justice following in decreasing order of seniority. In voting at the conference, the junior justice votes first, with each justice voting in increasing order of seniority, the chief justice last— though, like each one of them, he has only one vote. If the chief justice is one of the majority, he can decide to write the opinion for the Court himself or assign the task to another justice. (If he is in the minority, the senior associate justice in the majority assigns the writing of the opinion.)

The chief justice also traditionally swears in the president and vice president, although any qualified official has the right to do so. (Calvin Coolidge was sworn in by his father, a notary public, on the death of Warren G. Harding in 1923, though the usually cautious Coolidge also had himself sworn in again by a federal judge a week later. And Lyndon B. Johnson was sworn in aboard the presidential jet, Air Force One, by U.S. District Judge Sarah Hughes following the assassination of John F. Kennedy in 1963.)

In addition to his duties on the Court, the chief justice is the titular head of the federal judicial system. Beginning with Chief Justice William Howard Taft in 1921, this has become an increasingly important aspect of the office. The current chief justice, Warren E. Burger, is especially interested in judicial administration. He has fostered the establishment of judicial centers to recommend reforms in the way federal and state courts conduct their business. Burger has also repeatedly urged that Congress set up a fourth level of federal courts between the courts of appeals and the Supreme Court—an "Intercircuit Tribunal" to resolve legal conflicts among federal courts of appeals.

The office of chief justice has evolved gradually ever since George Washington appointed John Jay of New York the first chief justice in 1789. Of the fourteen chief justices in the past, by far the most important have been Jay, John Marshall of Virginia, Taft of Ohio, Charles Evans Hughes of New York, and Earl Warren of California.

Jay, who served until 1795, led the Court in firmly establishing that it would not provide "advisory opinions" to other branches of government. He expressly rejected Washington's request that the Court do so. Jay's stand, which kept the Court from being drawn prematurely into political controversies, also served to establish the Court as an equal, independent branch of government. (Some state supreme courts—such as those of Massachusetts and New Hampshire—do render such opinions—that is, they answer hypothetical or "What if?" questions about how to draft a statute, how to enforce a law or treaty, or whether a certain action is constitutional.)

With Jay's retirement, the Court entered a period of decline in its influence and status. The Eleventh Amendment, which was ratified in 1795, overturned the Court's first major constitutional decision—*Chisholm v. Georgia*. Then, too, the Court's prestige was damaged when many of the first justices refused to serve longer than a few years because of the difficulties in serving on circuit courts.

The Courts of the late 1790s, when John Rutledge of South Carolina and then Oliver Ellsworth of Connecticut presided, were unfortunately weak ones. But after them came perhaps the greatest chief justice of all, John Marshall, who is considered the symbol of American constitutional law. Marshall, who served from 1801 to 1835, raised the Court to the level of arbiter of all constitutional disputes, both between branches of the federal government and between the federal government and the states. His opinions are considered classics of jurisprudence. Marshall also instituted the "opinion for the Court"—the written ruling that reflects the majority's opinion—at a time when it was traditional for each justice to present his own view of the issues posed by a case.

William Howard Taft, appointed in 1921, had dreamed all his life of becoming chief justice. His major interest was in overhauling the federal judiciary; he was the first chief justice to see the office as including the responsibility of leading and overseeing the entire federal court system. Taft was a prime mover in the passage of the so-called Judges' Bill, the Judiciary Act of 1925. It gave the Court the power to pick and choose which cases it would hear. Taft was also the principal force behind the construction of the Supreme Court Building. Previously, the Court had met in a small chamber in the Capitol that had been the Old Senate Chamber.

Appointed by President Herbert Hoover in 1930 to succeed Taft, Charles Evans Hughes was one of only two justices who left the Court (as Hughes did in 1916 to run for president) only to return later as chief justice. (The other was John Rutledge, who was appointed in 1789, resigned in 1791 to become chief justice of the Supreme Court of South Carolina, and was reappointed to the United States Supreme Court as chief justice in 1795, only to be rejected by the Senate after having served a few months as an appointee of the president made while the Senate was in recess.) Hughes continued Taft's work of systematizing the Court's internal business and led it discreetly yet effectively in opposing President Franklin D. Roosevelt's "Court-packing plan." Hughes never spoke publicly against the measure, although he made veiled attacks on it in speeches to legal organizations and bar associations, pointing out that there was a difference between tyranny and reform. Hughes's most important blow against the bill was his devastating letter to the Senate Judiciary Committee refuting Roosevelt's claim that the "nine old men" needed help. Hughes pointed out that an expanded Court would actually make more work for itself because there were would be more justices to consult, argue, and disagree with.

Earl Warren was governor of California when President Dwight D. Eisenhower appointed him chief justice in 1953. Liberals were appalled at the nomination; as attorney general and later governor of that state, Warren was known as a tough official who had little patience for civil liberties issues and who had been the most enthusiastic supporter of the government's internment of thousands of Japanese and Japanese Americans in detention camps during World War II. Warren surprised everyone, however, by directing the most significant constitutional revolution of modern times. The Warren Court, as it came to be known, advanced individual rights and liberties in dozens of areas, almost always with Warren in the lead. Warren himself was proudest of his authorship of the opinions in *Brown v. Board of Education*, which outlawed segregation, and *Reynolds v. Sims*, which established the constitutional principle of "one person, one vote." Warren's most controversial activity was his chairmanship of the special commission appointed in 1963 by President Lyndon B. Johnson to investigate the assassination of President John F. Kennedy and the subsequent shooting of the principal suspect in the case, Lee Harvey Oswald, by Jack Ruby. Although right-wing critics of the Court repeatedly called for Warren's impeachment, he was widely respected as a symbol of the Constitution and the Bill of Rights by the time he retired from the Court in 1969.

◆◆◆ **How Are Supreme Court Justices and Other Federal Judges Selected?**

The process is a relatively simple one: They are appointed by the president, subject to confirmation by a majority vote of the Senate. But presidents—eager to nominate justices and judges who will uphold their legislative programs and executive actions—have often been disappointed in their own choices.

The Constitution says nothing whatsoever about the qualifications necessary to be named a justice. In fact, you don't have to be a lawyer to be one, though there never has been a justice who wasn't. On the other hand, no justice before the twentieth century had a law-school degree. Oliver Wendell Holmes, Jr., appointed in 1902, was the first justice to have one. Until then, all the justices had "read law" rather than attended law school—that is, they learned the law by serving an apprenticeship in an attorney's office, a practice that was prevalent well into the first half of the twentieth century, when going to law school became an established custom. The last justice never to attend law school was James F. Byrnes, who read law in South Carolina and was appointed to the Supreme Court in 1941. The last justice who attended law school without obtaining a law-school degree was Stanley F. Reed, who was solicitor general when he was appointed in 1938. Reed had attended both Columbia and Vanderbilt law schools but did not complete either school's course.

Before filling a vacancy on the Court, a president often consults with his attorney general, the solicitor general, and the chairperson of the Senate Judiciary Committee, to which all judicial nominations are first referred. Figured into his decision are such variables as the nominee's judicial philosophy, home state, political affiliation, ethnic and religious background, and since 1981 when Sandra Day O'Connor became the first woman to serve on the bench, the nominee's sex. In addition, the president also takes into account the probable reaction of the American Bar Association, which rates candidates for the Court on a scale ranging from "extremely well qualified" to "unqualified." The ratings have proved extremely influential. The association's criticism of President Richard M. Nixon's nomination of G. Harrold Carswell of Florida to the Court in 1970 helped to lead to its defeat in the Senate.

With regard to the naming of federal circuit and district judges, a custom with no constitutional basis called senatorial courtesy obliges the president to consult also with the senators from the states where the judge will sit. In some instances, when the senators are from different political parties, they agree to allow the minority senator to name some of the nominees proposed to the president. These candidates also face evaluation by the American Bar Association, which has screening panels for each of the nation's twelve geographical circuits. Failure to take either senatorial courtesy or the association's views into account can doom a nomination, as President Jimmy Carter discovered when he disregarded the recommendation of Senator Edward M. Kennedy of Massachusetts, who was then chairman of the Senate Judiciary Committee. Kennedy wanted Professor Archibald Cox of the Harvard Law School appointed to a vacancy on the United States Court of Appeals for the First Circuit, which includes Massachusetts. Cox also had the endorsement of the association and Massachusetts's other Senator, Paul Tsongas. The president's own choices for the appointment were not favored by the senators. Finally, he, they, and the association agreed on Professor Stephen Breyer, also of Harvard, who was eventually named to the court and confirmed by the Senate in late 1980.

Ever since the passage of the Judiciary Act of 1789, the process of selecting judges has been plagued by controversy. When Chief Justice John Jay resigned his office in 1795 to accept election as governor of New York, John Rutledge of South Carolina applied to President George Washington to succeed Jay. Rutledge, a delegate to the Constitutional Convention from South Carolina, had been appointed an associate justice in 1789 but had resigned in 1791 without ever sitting on the Court (though he apparently did "ride circuit"). Washington appointed Rutledge as a "recess appointment" under Article II, Section 2, of the Constitution because Congress was not in session when Jay resigned. When the Senate returned, it rejected Rutledge, chiefly because he had bitterly and publicly denounced the Jay Treaty, the agreement with Great Britain that Jay had negotiated in 1794, while chief justice, on special assignment from Washington. Rutledge's opponents also spread rumors that Rutledge was deranged, including one that he had attempted suicide when he learned that the Senate had rejected his nomination.

Perhaps the most controversial appointment to the Court was President Woodrow Wilson's appointment of Louis D. Brandeis in 1916. Brandeis withstood furious attacks focusing on his political views and his religion (he was the first Jewish appointee to the Court). He survived the controversy with grace and dignity and won confirmation by a comfortable margin.

Occasionally, either the president or the Senate will play politics with a nomination. In 1937, President Franklin D. Roosevelt, smarting from the defeat of his Court reorganization bill (the so-called Court-packing plan), determined to appoint Senator Hugo L. Black of Alabama to succeed retiring Justice Willis Van Devanter. Black had been an ardent supporter of the bill and Roosevelt wanted to ruffle his Senate opponents but leave them powerless to object because Black himself was a senator. On the other hand, in 1954, when President Dwight D. Eisenhower nominated John Marshall Harlan, grandson of the like-named justice who had served from 1877 to 1911, irate southern senators filibustered to delay the nomination for a year in protest over the Court's decision, in *Brown* v. *Board of Education*, that overturned public-school segregation.

Frequently, a president will try to shape constitutional doctrine by appointing like-minded justices and judges. For example, in spite of the fact that his Court-packing plan did not succeed, Franklin D. Roosevelt eventually reshaped the Court in his image. After stewing for his entire first term in office because he didn't have a single chance to appoint a justice (and after watching the Court strike down dozens of his New Deal laws), he was able to appoint virtually the entire Court as the result of either retirements or deaths.

Sometimes, however, a president's effort to shape the Court's philosophy backfires. Dwight D. Eisenhower suffered perhaps the greatest disappointment of any president, because the genial and seemingly bland Earl Warren turned out to be the leader of what has been called the Warren revolution in American constitutional law.

Ronald W. Reagan has appointed many federal district and appellate judges who share his judicial and political philosophy, leading many scholars to predict a major shift to the right in the development of American law.

◆◆◆ Can a Justice Be Impeached?

Yes. In this century and as recently as the 1970s there have been attempts to impeach a Supreme Court justice, but only one justice has ever come to trial in the past two hundred years.

A Supreme Court justice, as well as every other federal court judge, is subject—under Article II, Section 4, of the Constitution—to impeachment by the House of Representatives and trial by the Senate for "Treason, Bribery, or other high Crimes and Misdemeanors." In fact, with three exceptions—the impeachment of Senator William Blount of North Carolina in 1797 (charges dismissed but expelled from the Senate), that of Secretary of War William W. Belknap in 1876 (acquitted but resigned), and that of President Andrew Johnson in 1868 (acquitted)—all the impeachments under the Constitution have been of federal judges.

The only justice to go to trial was Samuel Chase, a Marylander who had signed the Declaration of Independence but had opposed ratification of the Constitution. Chase had become a militant Federalist by the time George Washington appointed him to the Court in 1796, and Chase frequently displayed his partisan views while presiding over a circuit court. Jeffersonian Republicans bitterly resented his hostility toward them, especially his obvious delight in presiding over trials of members of their party for violations of the Sedition Act of 1798, which had been passed by a Federalist-dominated Congress to suppress dissent during the United States' undeclared naval war with France.

Aside from Chase's undeniable faults, the Jeffersonians who dominated Congress viewed his impeachment as a step in their strategy to wrest control of the federal courts from Federalists. Although they lost the election of 1800, the lame-duck Federalists quickly drew up and passed the Judiciary Act of 1801. It created numerous federal judgeships, including a new set of judges to preside in the circuit courts in order to spare the Supreme Court justices the burden of circuit riding and to establish vacancies for Federalists. The outgoing president, John Adams, signed the bill into law and spent his last night in office signing commissions to be delivered to the new judges.

However, the Jeffersonians quickly enacted the Judiciary Act of 1802, which repealed the 1801 Act. And worried that the Supreme Court would rule their new act unconstitutional, Congress exercised its power to cancel the Court's 1802 term. The Jeffersonians need not have worried; the Court subsequently upheld their action. However, in the case of *Marbury* v. *Madison* in 1803, Chief Justice John Marshall firmly established the Court's power to review and rule on acts of Congress—in a case, in fact, resulting from Marshall's own failure, while Adams's secretary of state, to deliver one of the "midnight commissions."

The Jeffersonians were aghast at the implications of the decision. They decided to use impeachment as a way to get rid of opposition officeholders. In 1804, Congress used its impeachment power to remove from office John Pickering, a mentally unstable and alcoholic Federalist who was the district judge for New Hampshire. Federalists protested in vain that a judge could only be removed from office for actual wrongdoing.

Chase came next, in 1805. The prosecution was led by John Randolph of Roanoke, an eccentric Virginia Republican who despised both Jefferson and Marshall, both of whom were distant cousins. Randolph's erratic conduct crippled the impeachment effort, as did the fairness displayed by Vice President Aaron Burr. As president of the Senate, Burr presided over the impeachment trial, although he was under indictment for the murder of Alexander Hamilton in their famous duel at Weehawken, New Jersey, in July 1804. Burr was hated by Jeffersonians and Federalists alike. However, he presided with such dignity and impartiality that he won grudging praise from both sides. It was, by the way, his last act as vice president, or as a public official of any kind.

Chase survived the impeachment attempt—and that persuaded the Jeffersonians to abandon their plans to move next against Marshall himself. The failure also ensured the gradual acceptance of the narrow view that an impeachable offense had to be an indictable criminal offense. Every impeachment charge brought against a federal judge since then—except for the 1862 impeachment of West H. Humphreys of the U.S. District Court for Tennessee for accepting a judicial post under the Confederacy—has been for bribery of some form.

While no Supreme Court justice since Chase has been impeached, talk of impeachment cropped up in 1937 against Justice Hugo L. Black and in the late 1960s and early 1970s against Justices Abe Fortas and William O. Douglas. Black was accused of deliberately suppressing the fact that he had briefly been a member of the Ku Klux Klan in the late 1920s. In a national radio broadcast, Black eventually conceded that he had been a member, but he pointed out that he had resigned almost immediately after joining. His radio talk effectively silenced calls for his impeachment.

Fortas was an associate justice when President Lyndon B. Johnson nominated him to succeed retiring Chief Justice Earl Warren. But questions about his financial dealings, especially his acceptance of money from a foundation headed by a financier under investigation for fraud, led Fortas to withdraw his name from consideration and, in 1969, to resign from the Court.

Douglas faced an attack from then-Representative Gerald R. Ford, who filed charges focusing on Douglas's views on the First Amendment, his "scandalous" private life (four marriages, three divorces), and alleged financial improprieties, including taking fees for giving lectures. The House Judiciary Committee held hearings in 1970–1971 but no bill of impeachment emerged because in the committee's view an impeachable offense had to involve conduct that could result in criminal conviction.

In recent years, federal grand juries have investigated and occasionally indicted for bribery various federal judges sitting on lower courts. In one such case in 1974, the U.S. Court of Appeals for the Seventh Circuit ruled that a federal judge could be tried in federal court on a federal grand-jury indictment even without being impeached.

◆◆◆ Can a Supreme Court Justice Be Forced to Retire?

No, but he or she can be persuaded to do so. Justices—and most other federal judges, for that matter—serve for life, or as Article III, Section 1, of the Constitution puts it, they "shall hold their Offices during good Behaviour." This means that, unless he or she is impeached, nobody can *force* a justice to leave the bench. But a justice can be persuaded to resign by the threat of impeachment, as Abe Fortas was in 1969 over the acceptance of a fee from a private foundation. Or he or she can be convinced to resign for reasons of health, as Stephen J. Field was in 1897 and William O. Douglas was in 1975.

Constitutional amendments have been offered to change the lifetime terms of the justices, but none has ever won approval by both houses of Congress. One amendment was suggested following the effort in 1805 to impeach Samuel Chase, who was charged with bias while presiding over trials involving political repression under the Sedition Act. The amendment, proposed by Representative John Randolph, the chief prosecutor at the impeachment, would have permitted the president to remove a justice at the request of a majority of both houses. In 1957, a constitutional amendment was introduced in Congress that would have limited the terms of justices to four years, but nothing came of it either.

Although Congress cannot force a justice to retire, it can create incentives. By statute, any justice—or any federal judge for that matter—who is over seventy years old and has served more than ten years continuously, or is over sixty-five and served fifteen years continuously, can retire at full salary. To sweeten the option, Congress has provided that a justice who retires may continue to serve as a judge in lower federal courts. Several justices have availed themselves of this opportunity and played an active role in lower-court cases after retirement. For example, both Tom C. Clark, who retired in 1967, and Potter Stewart, who retired in 1981, subsequently served as trial and appellate judges throughout the country.

Sometimes, efforts to get a justice to retire come from the justice's colleagues. In 1896, John M. Harlan was deputized by the other justices to suggest to eighty-year-old Stephen J. Field, who had become senile, that he retire. Although Field refused at first to do so, he finally submitted his resignation the next year. Several justices urged William O. Douglas to retire after he suffered a stroke that left him partly paralyzed. But even after he officially retired, Douglas tried to participate in several key Court cases. Like some other retired justices who had not returned to private practice, Douglas was allowed to keep an office in the Supreme Court Building, had a skeleton staff, and had access to papers related to cases before the Court. And even though he was legally not a member of the Court, Douglas claimed that he had a right to take part in the deliberations of the Court, and he even drafted opinions in several cases. Chief Justice Warren E. Burger finally persuaded him to stop interfering in the Court's work.

Burger himself and Justice Lewis F. Powell, Jr., will both turn seventy-nine in the fall of 1986. In fact, Burger will celebrate his eightieth birthday on September 17, 1987, the very day that will mark the 200th anniversary of the Constitution.

The most mundane influence Congress has over the Court concerns salaries. The chief justice now earns $104,700 annually, the associate justices $100,600. These salaries cannot be reduced—the Constitution is clear about that. Article III, Section 1, says that the "Compensation . . . shall not be diminished during their Continuance in Office." But Congress can deny any increases. Or it can give the justices a smaller increase than it gives others. It did just that in 1964—without giving any reason—when the salaries of high-ranking federal employees were raised $7,500 but those of the justices only $4,500.

Despite all this, the opportunity to serve for life leaves the justices reasonably immune from, and above, politics—as the Framers of the Constitution intended.

◆◆◆ How Often Is the Supreme Court in Session?

The time varies slightly, but usually three days a week for two weeks each month during an annual term that lasts roughly nine months.

Congress plays a role in determining when the Court is in session. In one instance, Congress actually prevented the Court from handling a sensitive issue by canceling two consecutive Court terms. It could do so under its constitutional power to regulate the timing and length of the Court's sessions (Article III, Section 2). This is just what a newly elected Republican Congress did in 1802 because it feared the Court might declare its repeal of the Judiciary Act of 1801 unconstitutional. The Court did not resume its sessions until February 1803—and has sat regularly since then.

When it was first established in 1790, the Supreme Court sat for two terms each year—the first in February and the second in August. During the first year of its existence, the Court, which was not yet the influential branch of government that it is today, sat for a total of twelve days and decided no cases.

Since those early years the terms of the Court have decreased in number and increased in length. Today's Court has only one term each year, which is designated by the year in which it begins. The term officially opens on the first Monday in October and lasts for about thirty-six weeks. Although each term formally extends until the beginning of the next, the business of the term is actually conducted between October and a date in late June or early July when the Court has reached and announced decisions on all the cases it has heard.

Before the formal opening of a term, the justices meet to consider the petitions for hearing that have accumulated during the summer. Once the term begins, such petitions are disposed of as they are received. When the Court decides to review a case early in the term, the case usually is argued and decided in the same term; cases accepted later in the term may not be heard until the following term. Beginning in October, the Court alternates between *sittings* and *recesses* of about two weeks each. The Court may also meet for special sessions, as it did during the height of the school-desegregation crisis in the late 1950s.

During the weeks it is in session, the Court holds public sessions on Mondays, Tuesdays, and Wednesdays. The public sessions usually last from 10:00 A.M. to 3:00 P.M. with an hour-long break for lunch at noon. The Court hears oral arguments at the sessions, during which each side has only a half hour to present its case—a time limit that includes the time required to answer any questions the justices might ask from the bench (such questions are usually many and pointed). The time limit is not, however, inflexible; the Court sometimes allows each side an hour. In the landmark *Brown* v. *Board of Education* school-desegregation case in 1954, the Court allocated fourteen hours for oral argument, and in a water-rights suit between two western states in 1963 it set aside sixteen hours.

The first thing that happens at some of the public sessions of the Court is the announcement of the results in cases that have been decided. This task, which occupies only a few minutes of the Court's public time, may be the only reason for convening public sessions of the Court late in the term, after the Court has stopped hearing oral arguments in cases. At that point in the term (May and June), the justices devote their time almost exclusively to writing the opinions in the cases they have heard—and the Court's public sessions usually last less than half an hour. The Court usually does not hear oral arguments after April, although some cases have been argued and decided as late in the term as June.

The most sensitive work of the Court is conducted at a periodic private meeting called the *conference*. In weeks when the Court is hearing oral arguments at public sessions, there are two such weekly conferences. On Wednesday afternoon, the Court discusses the cases argued on the previous Monday. On Friday, the justices hold a day-long conference to discuss the cases argued on Tuesday and Wednesday and to consider pending motions and the most recently received petitions for hearing. The Friday agenda may include as many as seventy-five items. When the Court is not hearing oral arguments, there is usually one conference—on Friday—to discuss motions and petitions for hearing.

The secrecy of the conferences is scrupulously guarded. No pages or clerks are present, and no formal record is kept of the discussions. Notwithstanding this general rule of secrecy, serious leaks have sometimes occurred. The single most serious one happened after the Court decided, in the controversial *Dred Scott* case in 1857, to strike down the Missouri Compromise. The Court held that blacks were not—and could not be—American citizens with rights that the white majority was bound to respect. The decision, masterminded by Chief Justice Roger B. Taney, was the Court's attempt to settle the constitutional, and political, issue of slavery once and for all. Two proslavery justices, John Catron and Robert C. Grier, informed President-elect James Buchanan of the vote one month before it was officially announced, and Buchanan then endorsed the impending decision in his inaugural address two days before the Court handed it down. Then, too, antislavery Northern newspapers published extracts from the dissent of Justice Benjamin R. Curtis in advance of the official announcement. These breaches of confidence stunned other members of the Court as well as the public.

The only recent leak occurred in 1979 when ABC News reported two days before the scheduled announcement in a libel case that Justice Byron R. White had written an opinion for the Court that was critical of the media. As a result, Chief Justice Warren E. Burger fired a typesetter from the Court's print shop.

Otherwise, it is generally accepted that the "Purple Curtain"—the drapes that hang behind the justices in the courtroom and hide the doors that lead to their deliberating room—is essential to the Court's functioning.

◆◆◆ Can Anyone Argue a Case before the Court?

Ordinarily not. Occasionally, the Supreme Court has allowed a person involved in a suit who is not a lawyer to argue his case. And sometimes a lawyer who has not been admitted to practice before the Court will be allowed to argue a particular case. But such exceptions are few and far between.

The Court's rules require that anyone appearing before it be a member of the Supreme Court Bar. That sounds restrictive, but since the Court was established, more than 100,000 lawyers have been admitted. To become a member, an attorney must be admitted to the practice of law in the highest court of a state for three years, be of good moral and professional character, and pay a fee of $100.

The criteria for admission to the Supreme Court Bar are not strict, and most applicants receive rubber-stamp approval. Recently, however, Chief Justice Warren E. Burger has argued for a tighter review of applicants. His concern was underscored in 1982 when a lawyer who had earlier misrepresented himself as having been admitted to practice in Colorado applied for admission to the Supreme Court Bar.

Despite the large number of lawyers who have been admitted, few actually argue a case before the Court. Many lawyers seek admission only to enhance their status in the eyes of clients. Of those who do appear, the ones who appear most frequently are the solicitor general and his assistants, who represent the federal government before the Court.

The modern record holder of those who have argued cases is Erwin N. Griswold, a former dean of the Harvard Law School and former solicitor general, who argued 117 times. Other lawyers who have appeared before the Court a great number of times include Daniel Webster, John W. Davis, and Walter Jones. Historians have been unable to establish the exact number of cases that Webster argued but estimate that it was in the neighborhood of 185 to 200. Perhaps the most famous case argued by the longtime Massachusetts senator involved his alma mater, Dartmouth College. In 1819, he persuaded the Court that New Hampshire could not tamper with the charter given to the college in 1769 by King George III and the old colonial government of New Hampshire.

Davis, who argued 140 cases between 1913 and 1954, was a Wall Street lawyer who had been solicitor general and had unsuccessfully run for president in 1924. In 1952, he convinced the Supreme Court to invalidate President Harry S Truman's seizure of steel mills during the Korean War. In 1954, he made his last appearance before the Court, representing South

Carolina in school-desegregation cases. (He was opposed by Thurgood Marshall, who was then counsel for the NAACP Legal Defense Fund; in 1967 Marshall was appointed to the Supreme Court.)

Jones—the all-time record holder with 317 cases between 1801 and 1850—was a Virginian who had studied law with George Washington's nephew (and future justice) Bushrod Washington. Jones was known for his "silver voice and infinite analytical ingenuity and resources." He served as the U.S. attorney for the District of Columbia for nineteen years and at the same time maintained a thriving private practice. Jones took part in the most important constitutional argument of his career in 1819 when he was counsel for Maryland in *McCulloch* v. *Maryland,* the case in which Chief Justice John Marshall rejected Maryland's attempt to tax the Bank of the United States.

Attorneys are admitted to the Supreme Court Bar for life, unless they resign or are disbarred for misconduct. That happened in the 1970s when Robert C. Mardian, a former assistant attorney general implicated in the Watergate scandal, was suspended from practice in California. When Mardian's right to practice in California was later restored, the justices also allowed Mardian to resume his membership in the Supreme Court Bar.

Occasionally a person involved in a case may want to be represented by an attorney who is not a member of the Supreme Court Bar. Such an attorney may be allowed to argue an individual case.

The Court also may allow a person to argue a case *pro se*—for himself—even if he or she is not an attorney. That has happened only a few times in the Court's history.

Some Court observers believe the Court may have to allow defendants in criminal cases to represent themselves before it because the Court ruled in 1975 that the Sixth Amendment grants a defendant in a criminal case the right to proceed to trial *pro se* if he or she voluntarily and intelligently chooses to do so rather than accept a court-appointed lawyer. That right, in any case, would *not* extend to civil cases. In 1984 the Court denied the motion of Larry Flynt, publisher of *Hustler* magazine, to represent himself before the Court in a civil case. Flynt did appear so that he could hear the argument of his case and began screaming obscenities at the Court—prompting Chief Justice Warren E. Burger to order that he be held in contempt, the first time that has ever happened in the Court chamber.

◆◆◆ What Was the First Federal Law That the Court Declared Unconstitutional?

Section 13 of the Judiciary Act of 1789. It was invalidated in 1803 in the case of *Marbury* v. *Madison*, a landmark case that both established the Supreme Court's power to review federal laws and represented a major battle in the political war between Federalists and Jeffersonian Republicans during and after the election of 1800.

The Federalists had lost that election but were determined to control some branch of the federal government. Both for that reason and to do something to alleviate the complaints of the justices and lower-court judges that they were overworked, the lame-duck Federalist Congress quickly enacted, and the outgoing president, John Adams, signed, the Judiciary Act of 1801, which created more district judgeships, provided for judges on the circuit courts, and added some justiceships of the peace for the District of Columbia. Adams appointed Federalists to these positions, the Senate confirmed the nominations, and Adams signed the commissions for the new judges—some as late as the evening of his last day in office. The outgoing secretary of state, John Marshall, had just been appointed chief justice of the Supreme Court. In the confusion attending the nation's first peaceful transfer of power from one party to another (the nation's first president, George Washington, had not represented any political faction as such), Marshall failed to deliver some of the "midnight commissions." Among them was one destined for William Marbury, a newly appointed justice of the peace for the District of Columbia.

James Madison, the new secretary of state, discovered the commissions in his desk. After consulting with the new president, Thomas Jefferson, Madison refused to deliver them. Believing that he was entitled to his, Marbury filed suit in the Supreme Court against Madison, seeking a writ of *mandamus*—that is, an injunction ordering Madison to perform his official duty and deliver the commission to him.

The new chief justice found himself in a dilemma of his own making. If he did not issue the writ, he would be conceding powerlessness in the face of Madison's refusal to deliver the commission. If he issued the writ, he had no way to enforce the order—and, of course, he could not count on the help of the Jefferson administration.

The delight of Jeffersonians at Marshall's predicament turned to outrage when the chief justice handed down his opinion, representing a unanimous Court, in February 1803. Neatly, Marshall turned the order of issues presented by the case upside down. First, he asked, was Marbury entitled to his commission? Of course, Marshall replied, delivering an extensive analysis of the difference between an official's "ministerial" responsibilities—duties he is to perform mechanically, without exercising judgment—and his responsibilities for framing public policy. The delivery of the commission was a ministerial act, and Marshall denounced the administration's refusal to perform it.

Next, Marshall asked, did the laws of the United States give Marbury a remedy for his injury? Again, Marshall answered that they did, asserting that the Court could order an executive official to perform a purely ministerial act. And a writ of *mandamus* would ordinarily be in order.

Finally, Marshall asked, could the Court grant the writ Marbury was seeking? That sprang the trap. The section of the Judiciary Act of 1789 under which Marbury brought suit, Section 13, gave the Court the power to consider an application for a writ of *mandamus* as part of its original jurisdiction—which is why Marbury went directly to the justices in the first place rather than beginning in a lower federal court. But the Constitution strictly limits the Court's original jurisdiction, and the power to consider as an original matter applications for a writ of *mandamus* is not included in it. Thus the Judiciary Act of 1789 extended the Court's original jurisdiction beyond the limits set forth in the Constitution. If a statute says one thing and the Constitution says another, Marshall continued, they must be laid side by side to see whether the statute fits within the Constitution. If it does not fit, it is unconstitutional, null and void. Marshall concluded that Section 13 was void, and he regretfully refused to issue the writ. Marbury never got the job.

Marshall's opinion riled the Jeffersonians. He had used the opportunity to read the administration a long and eloquent lecture on its obligation to perform its duties. And Jefferson and his allies were furious at Marshall's bold assertion of the power to review federal laws and to strike them down if—in the eyes of the justices—they violated the Constitution. The Jeffersonians resented Marshall's assertion that "[i]t is emphatically the province and duty of the judicial department to say what the law is." That was a restatement of Alexander Hamilton's assertion of judicial review in *Federalist* essay No. 78. Whether they liked it or not, Marshall's words permanently settled the question of the Supreme Court's authority over federal law.

The brilliance of Marshall's opinion was that the Court did not have to rely on anyone else to enforce its decision. The body that had to refrain from unconstitutional conduct was the Court itself—and it did just that by refusing to issue the writ of *mandamus* that Marbury sought.

After *Marbury v. Madison*, the Court did not hold another major federal law unconstitutional until its controversial decision in the infamous *Dred Scott* case in 1857, which invalidated part of the Missouri Compromise of 1820 and held that blacks "were beings of an inferior order, and altogether unfit to associate with the white race, either in social or political relations; and so far inferior that they had no rights which the white man was bound to respect."

◆◆◆ What Was the First State Law That the Court Declared Unconstitutional?

A Georgia statute of 1796, in a case—*Fletcher* v. *Peck*—that was the climax of a notorious and gigantic land-fraud scandal.

In 1795, the Georgia legislature granted huge tracts of land—which it had refused in the 1780s to turn over to the Confederation Congress—to four New England land-speculation companies for the sum of $500,000. The territory included nearly all of present-day Alabama and Mississippi. All the members of the legislature had been bribed to approve the grants. Almost immediately, the people of Georgia rose up in fury; at the next election, they elected a new legislature that quickly passed a law in early 1796 revoking the land grants and offering refunds to the speculators who had bought the land from the original grantees. The so-called Yazoo land controversy boiled on for decades because the speculators refused to take refunds. They argued that they had bought their land in good faith from companies that had bought the land from the state government in good faith—and thus they were entitled to keep their purchases. The alleged bribery of the legislators, they claimed, was irrelevant to the validity of the grants of land.

Eventually, in 1803, John Peck sold Robert Fletcher 15,000 acres of the Yazoo lands, and Fletcher sued Peck. He argued that Peck had had no claim to the land that he had sold Fletcher because (1) Georgia had no valid claim to the land it granted to the land companies; (2) the land grants of 1795 were procured by corruption and therefore illegal; and (3) the 1796 repeal statute had voided the grants. Therefore, Fletcher claimed, Peck had defrauded him and was liable for the purchase price and for damages for fraud. Modern scholars have concluded that Fletcher's suit was collusive, a put-up job designed to get an advisory opinion from the Supreme Court upholding the land grants and the later land sales that relied on them.

Fletcher v. *Peck* was brought in the U.S. Circuit Court for Massachusetts, and in 1806, after an extensive jury trial, Peck won on all counts. Fletcher then appealed to the Supreme Court. He was represented by Luther Martin, an old Maryland Anti-Federalist leader who had successfully defended both Justice Samuel Chase in his impeachment trial in 1805 and Aaron Burr in his treason trial in 1807. Peck was represented by John Quincy Adams. The first appeal was thrown out for technical grounds in 1809, but Fletcher and Peck tried again later that year. Their attorneys signed an agreement waiving all technical defenses that would prevent the Court from hearing the case on its merits. Because President James Madison had appointed Adams ambassador to Russia, Joseph Story, a noted Massachusetts lawyer, took over Peck's defense. Story had been counsel for one of the four Yazoo land companies, but he was unembarrassed by his apparent connection with the frauds and presented a slashing and brilliant defense of the transactions to the Court. Martin's argument was curiously lifeless and vulnerable to attack, and historians of the case have viewed his behavior as an additional indication that the case was a put-up job.

In early 1810, Chief Justice John Marshall announced the Court's decision. In his opinion, Marshall accepted the entire line of reasoning laid out by Story. Georgia, he agreed, indeed owned the land transferred by the 1795 grants and had the authority to grant that land. And if the legislature had the authority to act, any attack on the motives of the legislators in approving the grants was not relevant to whether the grants were valid or not. Moreover, he continued, the 1796 repeal act was an improper exercise of judicial rather than legislative power because only a court can declare a grant invalid, not a legislature. And finally, Marshall said, the 1796 repeal act was unconstitutional because it violated the Constitution's ban (in Article I, Section 10) on any state statute or other action that would impair the obligations of contract—and a land grant is a contract just like any other contract.

As a result of *Fletcher v. Peck,* until the late 1890s, those who challenged state laws regulating employment and public health and safety consistently cited this so-called Contract Clause, and about half of the Court's decisions striking down such state laws relied on that clause as interpreted in *Fletcher v. Peck.* The case's greatest legacy, however, was the example it set for those who seek to vindicate their political goals and agendas by litigation in federal courts. Later suits, brought for better causes and begun legitimately, have confirmed the critical role of the Supreme Court in constitutional decision making with regard to rights such as free speech, racial equality, and the right to worship.

◆◆◆ Does the Supreme Court Strike Down Federal or State Laws Often?

Not really, at least as far as federal laws are concerned.

The Supreme Court has explicitly overturned on constitutional grounds only about 110 acts of Congress in its nearly two hundred years of existence. In the same period, it has struck down nearly nine times as many state laws.

A law is generally presumed to be constitutional, an expression of the will of the majority of the people in the nation or state that passed it. When the Court invalidates a statute, it is acting in the face of popular sentiment to ensure that the rights and principles set forth in the Constitution remain intact.

The Constitution does not expressly confer upon any federal court the power to overturn federal legislation. However, the Supreme Court assumed the power—long hinted at by state courts in the 1780s and lower federal courts in the 1790s—in the first case that presented the justices with a clear chance to assert it, *Marbury v. Madison* in 1803.

The Court's power to review the constitutionality of state laws derives largely from the Supremacy Clause of the Constitution, Article VI, which states:

> This Constitution, and the Laws of the United States which shall be made in Pursuance thereof; . . . shall be the supreme Law of the Land; . . . any Thing in the Constitution or Laws of any State to the Contrary notwithstanding.

Actually, the pace at which our courts have been declaring laws unconstitutional has accelerated over the years as the nation has grown and, particularly in recent years, as the interest in civil rights has spread. Between 1803 and 1868 the Supreme Court held only three federal acts and fifty-three state laws unconstitutional. By contrast, in one recent four-year period, the Court invalidated nine federal laws and seventy-six state laws. And, in a 1983 opinion invalidating a provision authorizing either house of Congress to override the decision of an executive agency by voting its disapproval, the Court drew into question the constitutionality of similar "legislative veto" provisions in nearly two hundred federal statutes. It is possible, therefore, that in that one case, *INS v. Chadha*, the Court struck down more federal statutes than it had invalidated in the entire previous history of the republic.

◆◆◆ Why Doesn't the Court Decide Every Case That Is Brought to Its Attention?

Even though most people who say, "I'm taking my case all the way up to the Supreme Court" really don't do it, the Court is swamped with people who do. So Congress has, for the most part, given the Court the right to pick the most important and urgent cases.

In 1891, Congress created a new kind of writ, borrowed from old common-law practice: the writ of *certiorari* (from the Latin phrase meaning, roughly, "Let's see the record from the court below"). It was adopted to give the justices the power to pick and choose which cases they might want to hear. Created for only a few, select kinds of cases in 1891, the writ of *certiorari* grew in importance because of the Judiciary Act of 1925. That statute, for which the justices had lobbied Congress, divided the Court's jurisdiction into two classes—mandatory appellate jurisdiction and *certiorari* (or discretionary) jurisdiction. The relatively small number of those falling within the mandatory appellate jurisdiction includes cases in federal and state courts declaring acts of Congress unconstitutional and decisions of federal courts declaring state laws unconstitutional. The Court's discretionary jurisdiction represents most kinds of cases that the Court is asked to hear.

Rule 17 of the Supreme Court Rules describes the decision to grant a writ of *certiorari* as "a matter of sound judicial discretion" to be made only for "special and important reasons." The list of examples set forth in Rule 17 includes: cases in which a state court has decided an important federal question for the first time or in a way that conflicts with decisions of federal courts; cases in which a federal court of appeals has decided an issue in a way that conflicts with another court of appeals on the same point; cases in which a decision of a federal court of appeals conflicts with applicable state or territorial law; cases in which a federal court of appeals has decided an important question of federal law that has not been, but should be, decided by the Supreme Court; cases in which a federal court of appeals has decided a federal question in a way that conflicts with applicable decisions of the Court, and cases in which a federal court of appeals has "so far departed from the accepted and usual course of judicial proceedings or has so far sanctioned such departure by a lower court as to call for an exercise of [the Supreme Court's] power of supervision."

A party seeking review by the justices—the appellant or petitioner— files papers arguing that the case merits review. The appellee or respondent (the party opposing review) files papers in opposition. This first set of papers focuses on whether the case deserves the attention of the justices. If the Court chooses to deny review, it doesn't have to give any reasons why, though sometimes one or more justices will file a dissent.

The "Rule of Four" is an informal but long-standing Court custom that provides that the vote of four justices is required before the Court will schedule a case for argument on the merits. If the justices vote to grant review, the parties submit formal briefs and appear before the Court to argue the merits of the case. Sometimes, in a case before the Court on *certiorari*, the justices change their minds after a case has been accepted for review, and even after the parties have filed briefs and argued their positions before the Court. They may dismiss a writ of *certiorari* as improvidently granted—that is, the justices concede that they made a mistake in accepting the case for review, though that doesn't mean that they won't consider a later case posing the same issue.

◆◆◆ Does the Court Ever Change Its Mind about Constitutional Issues?

Yes. Although by and large the Court adheres closely to its precedents—that is, its earlier decisions—it occasionally changes its mind. When it does, sometimes the justices expressly overrule decisions made by an earlier Court. Sometimes they interpret a precedent in a way that modifies or narrows it. And sometimes they simply ignore earlier pronouncements and announce a new legal rule—thereby burying the old one without even referring to it.

Why the justices change their minds varies from case to case. The Constitution is a "living document" that evolves as our nation grows and changes. It is always necessary to clarify the meaning of an earlier case. And, the identity of the justices—and hence the political and philosophical makeup of the Court—constantly change.

The most dramatic changes of mind are the instances when the Court expressly overrules an earlier decision. For example, in 1963, the justices in *Gideon* v. *Wainwright* overruled the Court's 1942 decision in *Betts* v. *Brady* and held that every person accused of a serious crime has a Sixth Amendment right to counsel and, if the accused cannot pay for it himself or herself, a right to state-appointed counsel. In the nearly two decades between the two decisions, changes in the Court's personnel and in society as a whole prompted a major shift in the justices' thinking about the rights of indigent defendants in criminal cases. As a result, the justices in 1963 were ready to endorse the view that Justice Hugo L. Black had expressed in a dissent in the *Betts* case. (Black was still on the Court and, as might be expected, voted with the majority in the *Gideon* decision.)

That Black's dissent in *Betts* v. *Brady* became the basis of the majority opinion in the *Gideon* case illustrates the special importance that a justice's dissent can have: Sometimes it becomes the seed of a later ruling. Such dissents represent what Chief Justice Charles Evans Hughes called the "conscience of the law." Justices who dissent are freer to express their views because they do not have to hone them—as the author of a majority opinion does—to accommodate the views of other members of the Court. This often allows dissenting justices to write as creatively as they may wish—and to suggest innovative approaches to problems. Some of the greatest opinions ever delivered in the Court were dissents, and many dissents have been remembered long after the majority opinions have faded into oblivion.

The last decade has witnessed another dramatic change in the Court's mind—this time on an important issue of federal-state relations. In *National League of Cities* v. *Usery*, the Court, by a vote of five to four, invalidated a 1974 federal law that extended the minimum-wage and maximum-hour requirements to cover state and local government workers. The Court in that 1976 decision held that, with respect to their own employees, state and local governments were immune from federal regulation of labor relations under the Tenth Amendment, which provides that "powers not delegated to the United States by the Constitution, nor prohibited by it to the States, are reserved to the States respectively, or to the people." However, in 1985, in *Garcia* v. *San Antonio Metropolitan Transit Authority*, the Court "revisited" the question it had faced in the *Usery* case. In another five-to-four decision, it found that its earlier ruling had been based on a view of the law that was "not only unworkable but [also] inconsistent with established principles of federalism," and announced: "That case, accordingly, is overruled."

Several factors contributed to the Court's change of heart. For one thing, the Court in the *Usery* decision was split. Four justices, led by Justice William H. Rehnquist, voted to uphold the states' immunity. Four others, led by Justice William J. Brennan, Jr., voted to reject it. The remaining one, Justice Harry A. Blackmun, agreed with the *result* reached by the Rehnquist group but expressed reservations about its argument. Over the years, Blackmun's reservations grew stronger and stronger, until they finally overcame his agreement in the case. He wrote the opinion in the *Garcia* decision for the five-to-four majority he created by changing his vote. For another thing, from the time the *Usery* case was decided, the legal and scholarly community scathingly criticized it, agreeing with Justice Brennan, a dissenter in *Usery*, that the case hinted at a revival of wholesale limits on the exercise of federal authority.

The fact that the vote in the *Garcia* case was also five to four may mean that another reversal is likely in the future. Justice Rehnquist—the author of the *Usery* decision—alluded to that possibility in writing an unusually acerbic dissent in the *Garcia* case. He announced that in his view—which was perhaps framed by his confidence that President Ronald W. Reagan will get to replace one of the justices who were in the majority—the battle is not over. Referring to the legal argument on which he had based his decision in the *Usery* case, Rehnquist said: "I do not think it incumbent on those of us in dissent to spell out further the fine points of a principle that will, I am confident, in time again command the support of a majority of this Court."

Sometimes the Court will reject the reasoning of an earlier case—and thus an entire body of doctrine—without explicitly overruling the earlier case itself. The best example of this is the fate of *Plessy* v. *Ferguson*, the 1896 case upholding a Louisiana state statute requiring segregated railway coaches. Justice Henry B. Brown wrote for the Court that all a state had to do to satisfy the Fourteenth Amendment's Equal Protection Clause was to provide (or to require that railroads and other "common carriers" provide) separate-but-equal facilities for blacks and whites. In 1954, in his landmark opinion announcing the unanimous Supreme Court decision in *Brown* v. *Board of Education*, Chief Justice Earl Warren wrote that segregation is inherently unequal. In so doing, he had to cope with the *Plessy* decision. He did, declaring that "the doctrine of 'separate but equal' has no place" in American life.

Despite all these examples, it is nevertheless exceptional for the Court to ignore or overrule an earlier Court's decision. Justices are reluctant to overturn past decisions because they realize that what they do has far-reaching implications and influence and that this influence depends on the stability and authority of their decisions. For the Court to overturn past decisions on a regular or even frequent basis would compromise its stature and integrity. The justices think long and hard before they vote to throw out an earlier ruling. As Justice Robert H. Jackson once quipped: "We are not final because we are infallible, but we are infallible only because we are final."

◆◆◆ How Does the Supreme Court Enforce Its Decisions?

Practically speaking, it can't. Alexander Hamilton, for one, recognized (in the *Federalist* essay No. 78) that "the judiciary is beyond comparison the weakest of the three departments" of our system of government—"the least dangerous branch." The Supreme Court can issue certain writs and injunctions and, like other courts, cite people for contempt, but it has no police power or enforcement agency of its own, and it must rely on the executive branch of the federal and state governments—and the public's respect for our legal system—to carry out its orders.

The Court has the power to issue writs or injunctions that require a person to do something or to stop an activity. If the person ignores the Court, it is empowered by the Judiciary Act of 1789 to hold that person in contempt and "to punish by fine or imprisonment, at the [Court's] discretion." Although these powers seem to give the Court broad authority to enforce its judgments, the powers are sometimes more apparent than real.

The most striking example of failure to comply with a decision of the Court involved President Andrew Jackson. In 1829 Georgia, anxious to open its land for settlement, extended its authority over large portions of Cherokee Indian territory. The Cherokee were peaceful farmers who had developed a written alphabet for their language and had written a constitution for their tribal government—accomplishments unique among the Indian tribes of that period. (Under Article I, Section 8, of the Constitution, Indian tribes are treated as separate and sovereign nations.) Eager to assert its sovereignty over the Cherokees' land (so that the state could confiscate the land and sell it to white purchasers), Georgia convicted a Cherokee named Corn Tassel of murder. The Supreme Court agreed to hear his claim that the Georgia courts did not have jurisdiction over him, but the state ignored the fact that the case was pending in the Court and executed Corn Tassel on December 24, 1830—before the Court could hear his case. Then, in an 1832 case involving the same Cherokee territory, the Court ruled that Georgia was unconstitutionally interfering in Indian affairs. The state announced that it would resist the Court's ruling, and Jackson, who agreed with Georgia's position, refused to interfere. Tradition has it that Jackson said, "Well, [Chief Justice] John Marshall has made his decision, now let him enforce it." In general, however, the other branches of the federal government have been quick to comply with the Court's decisions.

Today, the Court as an institution enjoys broad public support, based upon the prestige it has accumulated over the years. This gives its mandates almost unquestioned force. For example, in 1974, despite President Richard M. Nixon's claim of executive privilege, the Court ordered him to turn over to the Watergate grand jury tapes of his conversations with advisers. The president complied in large part because of the public support the justices had for their decision.

Public opinion does not always favor specific decisions of the Court, of course; indeed, a principal function of the Court is to resist such pressure. In the face of widespread defiance of particular decisions, however, the Court can draw on the public's deep respect for the Court as an institution to insist that its decision be enforced. This is usually sufficient to carry the day. For example, the Court has not backed off from its decisions striking down mandated school prayers and Bible reading in public schools, even though many towns and school districts still maintain such practices.

On rare occasions, in fact, the justices not only reaffirm their commitment to a previous decision but will even go out of their way to declare that they will not change their minds. The best example is the Court's reaction to the political and public resistance throughout the South to the justices' unanimous 1954 school-desegregation decision, *Brown* v. *Board of Education*. In Arkansas, Governor Orval Faubus and the state legislature led a campaign of "massive resistance" that included passing a state law in 1957 suspending the state's requirement of compulsory school attendance for any student attending a racially mixed school, and that same year, adopting a state constitutional amendment directing the legislature to use any constitutional means to oppose the Court's decision. When a federal district court ordered desegregation of the public schools of Little Rock, politicians opposed the order and riots broke out around Central High School. Faubus called out the National Guard to resist enforcement of the desegregation order. Federal authorities obtained an injunction against the governor, and President Dwight D. Eisenhower first sent in federal soldiers, then replaced them with detachments of the Arkansas National Guard under federal orders, to ensure that the desegregation order was enforced.

The school board then successfully petitioned the district court for a postponement of the desegregation plan, arguing that the violence and unrest in Little Rock would make it impossible to put the plan into effect or otherwise to run the schools. Black parents who had originally brought the suit to compel desegregation appealed the postponement, and the U.S. Court of Appeals for the Eighth Circuit agreed with them. The Supreme Court took the rare step of meeting in a special term in August (usually the justices are in a long recess from the end of June to the beginning of October) and issued a unanimous decision upholding the

Eighth Circuit and rejecting the plea for a postponement. The Court moved swiftly to allow the school board time to make plans for the 1958–1959 school year. In an opinion signed by all the justices, the Court denounced the obstructionist efforts of Faubus and the state legislature, blaming them for the violence and unrest that plagued Little Rock. The justices also reminded the state officials of their oath to uphold the federal Constitution and repeated basic constitutional doctrine that the Supreme Court is the authoritative interpreter of the Constitution and that its decisions must be obeyed.

◆◆◆ Is the Supreme Court the Only Court That Can Declare a Law Unconstitutional?

No. Both state courts and the lower federal courts can and often do declare laws unconstitutional. And, in those cases where the Supreme Court has reviewed such decisions, it has frequently upheld the lower courts.

The power of judicial review—that is, the right of courts to pass on the constitutionality of statutes established by Chief Justice John Marshall's opinion in the case of *Marbury v. Madison*—is not a power reposing only in the Supreme Court; it is shared by all the courts in the nation. State courts and lower federal courts share the right and responsibility to test the constitutionality of laws that come before them. And they have not been reluctant to do so. One of the most famous cases in which a lower federal court declared a statute unconstitutional was *Roe v. Wade*, a 1972 case involving a Texas law that prohibited abortions unless the mother's life was in danger. A federal district court in Texas found the law unconstitutional. In 1973, the Supreme Court, which took the case on direct appeal from the district court, agreed, though for a different reason.

Similarly, in 1983, the Connecticut Supreme Court declared unconstitutional a state law barring an employer from firing or refusing to hire a worker who would not work on his sabbath, because the statute violated the First Amendment's ban on any law "respecting an establishment of religion." The U.S. Supreme Court upheld the Connecticut court's decision in 1985.

An important function of the U.S. Supreme Court is to police the use of the power of judicial review by state courts and lower federal courts. Sometimes, these courts interpret the federal Constitution in ways that the justices find unacceptable. In recent years, for example, state courts have tended to read the rights guaranteed by the Fourth, Fifth, and Sixth

Amendments in a way that is more protective of criminal defendants than the Supreme Court believes is appropriate. In such cases, the Court frequently has reversed the ruling of the state court. Thus, in a 1985 case in which the California Supreme Court had ruled that the Fourth Amendment required the police to obtain a warrant before searching a mobile home, the U.S. Supreme Court reversed the state court's decision. In doing so, it invoked an exception to the warrant requirement that the Court had developed to permit searches of automobiles without a warrant. In the California court's view, a mobile home was more like a home than a car. The Supreme Court disagreed—and its view prevailed.

Sometimes, when a state court wants to be more protective of individual liberties than it perceives the U.S. Supreme Court is willing to be, the state court will base its decision on the state, rather than the federal, constitution. This insulates the state court's decision from review by the Supreme Court. State courts are the final arbiters of the meaning of state constitutions, and as long as their interpretations of those constitutions do not violate the U.S. Constitution, they cannot be set aside by the Supreme Court. For example, some state courts have used their state constitutions to provide greater protection for criminal defendants than the Supreme Court's interpretation of the U.S. Constitution would require. Thus, although the Court has interpreted the Fourth Amendment as barring only evidence obtained directly in unreasonable searches by government agents, the Montana Supreme Court has interpreted that state's constitution to permit defendants to insist on the exclusion at trials of evidence obtained in similar searches by private persons, such as neighbors, employers, or private investigators. Ordinarily, state criminal decisions providing defendants with protections going beyond those in the federal Constitution are the exception rather than the rule, but there are more such decisions now than in the past.

◆◆◆ What Other Courts Does the Constitution Authorize?

Whatever other courts—in addition to the Supreme Court—that Congress chooses to establish under the authority given it in either Article III, Section 1, of the Constitution or in Article I, Section 8.

The very first Congress, which met in 1789, exercised its option under Article III, Section 1, to establish a system of federal trial and appellate courts below the Supreme Court. Ever since, there have been lower federal courts, although Congress has periodically reorganized the system as the nation grew. The essential shape of the federal judiciary as we know it today was fixed by Congress in the Judiciary Acts of 1891 and 1911. It is essentially a three-tier system—the federal district courts as trial courts, the courts of appeals as appellate courts above them, and the Supreme Court at the top of the pyramid. There are a few "specialized" courts that deal with special types of cases (for example, tax or customs matters), but by and large they operate parallel to the main system.

The district courts are the basic trial courts of the federal judiciary. The nation (including the District of Columbia and Puerto Rico) is divided into ninety-one federal judicial districts. There is at least one district court in each state, and several populous states are divided into as many as four districts. Congress has authorized the appointment of 563 district judges. Although some judicial districts—such as the Western District of Arkansas, the Northern District of Iowa, and the Eastern District of Oklahoma—have only one district judge, most districts have two or more judges, with the largest, the Southern District of New York, having twenty-seven.

The business of the federal district courts has changed dramatically over the last forty years, reflecting the more active role played by the federal government since the New Deal—increasing regulation of business activity, the emergence of the welfare state and a fundamental rethinking of the role of the federal government in assuring justice and individual rights. For example, the Civil Rights Act of 1964 and the Voting Rights Act of 1965 have spawned a multitude of cases challenging racial and sexual discrimination. Similarly, the Truth-in-Lending and Fair Credit Reporting acts are examples of federal regulation of the economy that have stimulated the growth of consumer-protection litigation. Other sources of the rising tide of litigation include federal securities and antitrust statutes.

The work of the courts of appeals is primarily appellate—reviewing cases from the district courts. There are now thirteen courts of appeals: one for the District of Columbia, one for each of eleven numbered circuits that include anywhere from three to ten states and territories, and a Court of Appeals for the Federal Circuit, created in 1982 to hear appeals in cases from certain specialized courts. There are now 168 judgeships authorized for the thirteen courts of appeals. The number appointed for each court ranges from six judges for the First Circuit (Maine, New Hampshire, Massachusetts, Rhode Island and Puerto Rico) to twenty-eight for the Ninth Circuit (Alaska, Arizona, California, Hawaii, Idaho, Montana, Nevada, Oregon, Washington, and Guam). Normally, cases are heard by panels of three judges. However, because of heavy caseloads, frequently a district judge within a circuit is designated to sit temporarily as a member of a panel of the court of appeals. To cope with the enormous number of appeals filed each year, courts of appeals have also had to restrict or do away with oral arguments in many cases and to cut back on the number of opinions they publish. In 1960, for example, 3,899 cases were filed in all the courts of appeals; by 1978, filings were five times the 1960 level (or 18,918) and by 1983 they had jumped another 56 percent (to 29,630 cases).

Some judges and commentators, including Chief Justice Warren E. Burger, now argue that the work load of the Supreme Court is so large and unmanageable that a fourth level of federal courts should be created. They propose a new court—called variously a National Court of Appeals, a National Court of the United States, or an Intercircuit Tribunal—to relieve the Supreme Court's burden and to contribute to greater coherence in federal law by eliminating conflicts between decisions of the various courts of appeals. However, opponents of the proposed new court contend that it would actually generate more work for the justices, who would have to choose between three options—hearing a case, refusing to hear it, or referring it to the new court. At present, they have only two options—to hear a case or to refuse it. Moreover, opponents of the proposed new court argue that it would encourage more cases and add yet another layer to the judicial process, increasing delays in the final resolution of cases and adding costs for litigants and the system as a whole.

The basic federal judicial system just described was established by Congress under the authority given to it in Article III, Section 1, of the Constitution. Article I, Section 8, of the Constitution also gives Congress the authority "To constitute Tribunals inferior to the supreme Court"— and Congress has created some courts (such as the federal bankruptcy courts) under the authority given to it in Article I. The distinction is not an academic one. Courts established under Article I are very different from courts created under Article III. For example, whereas Article III judges are appointed for life (the Constitution says they "shall hold their Offices during good Behaviour"), Article I judges may be appointed for limited terms only. So, given "good Behaviour," a federal district judge may not be removed from office; but a bankruptcy judge has no such security.

The States ══════════════════════

◆◆◆ Which Came First, the States or the Federal Government?

That's a chicken-versus-egg riddle that still perplexes some historians. And it's a question with political ramifications as well; many proponents of federal decentralization, including President Ronald W. Reagan, use the argument that the states created the federal government to buttress their support for states' rights.

The original thirteen states began as colonies of England, founded between 1607 and 1733; the first was Virginia, the last Georgia. Several, such as Virginia, were founded by the Crown as economic ventures initially run by private companies under royal charters; these later became Crown colonies run by England itself. Others, such as Pennsylvania and North Carolina, were proprietary colonies, founded by an individual person with a royal grant of land and the power to administer it; these colonies were almost the personal property of their proprietors, who later had to yield to British pressure and give up their proprietorships, so that these colonies later became Crown colonies as well. Still others were founded by other countries and conquered by England; for example, New York was originally founded by the Dutch as Nieuw Amsterdam, but was conquered by England in 1664 and renamed New York.

The colonists were separated from the mother country by a vast ocean and thus were left virtually alone for most of their history. Their many quarrels with the royal governors sent to rule them and with the proprietors ruling under royal grants developed their taste for political action and for self-government. Institutions and doctrines such as representative assemblies, judicial review, and the separation of powers were born and developed quickly on American soil. By 1776, when the colonists declared their independence, Americans had extensive experience with political systems and with self-government to draw on in framing their own constitutions and legal systems.

In May 1776, though, the colonies had not yet declared their independence. Although a few colonies—South Carolina, New Hampshire, and Rhode Island—had recast their colonial charters to remove all references to King George III and England, none had actually reorganized themselves as independent states. That month the Second Continental Congress passed a resolution calling on the colonies to frame new forms of government in case it should become necessary to separate from England. Nearly every colony answered this call. Thus, it is an interesting question, though ultimately an unanswerable one, whether the states came first or whether they were called into being by the Second Continental Congress, which is the direct ancestor of the federal government. James Wilson, one of the most important of the delegates to the Constitutional Convention of 1787, argued that Congress, and therefore the nation, came first, because Congress had issued the call to create new charters of government. But this argument does not account for the three colonies that had reworked their charters before Congress passed that resolution.

◆◆◆ How Does a New State Join the Union?

By the only kind of bill that Congress can pass but that it cannot repeal: a bill of statehood. Article IV, Section 3, of the Constitution says, "New States may be admitted by the Congress into this Union"—but once admitted, a state cannot be merged with another state or be split into two states without its consent.

Actually, five states have been formed from other states, chiefly because the citizens in the area felt either geographically or socially separated, or both, from the other residents of the state.

Vermont was the first state admitted to the Union that had been part of another state. The territory now known as Vermont had long been the subject of conflicting claims by New Hampshire, Massachusetts, and especially New York. At the height of the Revolution, Vermont declared its independence and constituted itself an independent republic in 1777. New York's attempts to reclaim Vermont surfaced repeatedly in the Confederation Congress in the 1780s, but Congress chose to let the matter rest until after the ratification of the Constitution. Finally, because of the persuasive efforts of John Jay and other moderate New Yorkers, the state abandoned its attempt to reclaim Vermont, and Vermont joined the Union in 1791.

The territory comprising Kentucky and Tennessee was part of the western lands ceded by Great Britain to the American states in the Treaty of Paris of 1783 ending the Revolutionary War. Virginia had claimed what is now Kentucky but transferred its claims to the United States, and Kentucky was admitted as a state in 1792. Tennessee at first was claimed by both Virginia and North Carolina. From 1784 to 1787 its residents tried to form the state of Franklin, but North Carolina was able to quash the movement because it still claimed the territory. Once North Carolina ratified the Constitution in late 1789, it gave up its claim, and in 1790 Congress stepped in to govern the area as a federal territory. In 1796 Tennessee joined the Union as the sixteenth state.

Maine, which had been visited by the English explorer John Cabot in 1498, was once part of Massachusetts. It was admitted to the Union in 1820 as part of the Missouri Compromise—as a free state to balance Missouri's admission as a state where slavery was allowed.

West Virginia was formed in 1863 after Virginia seceded. Residents in the western part of the state did not want to join the Confederacy and were allowed to form their own state. The Virginia legislature never approved West Virginia's admission, but the federal government did. In fact, during the remainder of the Civil War, the federal government recognized the West Virginia legislature as reflecting the legitimate will of Virginia also.

The most recent states to join the Union were, first, Alaska, then Hawaii, both in 1959. In doing so, they followed a historical five-step procedure. First, the citizens of each territory held a referendum on whether they wanted statehood. After the people in the territory approved the idea, Congress passed an enabling act, which authorized the election of a territorial legislature to draft a state constitution. Once that document was drafted, Congress had to approve it. Then, Congress had to pass a statehood bill. Finally, as soon as that bill was signed by the president (for Alaska and Hawaii, Dwight D. Eisenhower), the new state was admitted into the United States. And, once admitted, it was on equal footing with every other state. As the Supreme Court put it in a case involving Oklahoma's right to decide the location of its capital:

> [W]hen a new state is admitted into the Union, it is so admitted with all of the powers of sovereignty and jurisdiction which pertain to the original States, and . . . such powers may not be constitutionally diminished, impaired or shorn away by any conditions, compacts or stipulations embraced in the act under which the new State came into the Union.

Historically, Congress has imposed conditions upon territories wishing to become states. For example, it would not let Utah become a state for decades until Utah banned polygamy; it did so and was admitted in 1896.

And New Mexico was granted statehood in 1912 only after it agreed to spend certain revenues for education. The impact of such conditions, however, is usually not as significant as it was in the case of Utah because, as the Court's language in the Oklahoma case makes clear, once a new state is admitted, no conditions can be enforced against it—not even those to which it agreed. Thus, in 1907, the year that Oklahoma was admitted, Congress made the prospective state promise that it would keep its capital in Guthrie for seven years. But, once admitted, Oklahoma refused to do so—and the Supreme Court backed it up.

Sometimes the question of statehood can be controversial, as it is in Puerto Rico. There are numerous Puerto Ricans who would like to see the island become the fifty-first state; others would prefer that it become a sovereign nation; still others believe it should remain a free commonwealth associated with the United States—a status it achieved in 1952—because otherwise special tax and trade benefits it enjoys would be lost.

◆◆◆ Has a Proposed State Ever Had Trouble Joining the Union?

Yes, a number of states have. One, the state of Franklin, was actually denied admission, but that was before the Constitution was ratified, when the Articles of Confederation were still in effect.

Congress—according to the Supreme Court's interpretation of Article IV, Section 3, of the Constitution—has the right to impose conditions before it grants statehood, and at times it has imposed some that states have had a hard time meeting. Also, on occasion, an established state has objected to the creation of a new one because of the economic and political competition it poses.

The state of Franklin was proposed in 1784 by residents of what was then the frontier of the nation (in what is now eastern Tennessee), who felt that they were not properly represented by the state legislatures of Virginia, North Carolina, and Georgia. The frontiersmen decided to form their own state and named it in honor of Benjamin Franklin. They then petitioned the Confederation Congress for admission. Virginia and Georgia were willing to cede land to the proposed state, but North Carolina strongly objected. Unlike other states, it had not ceded to the Confederation government its claims to western lands acquired under the Treaty of Paris, which ended the Revolutionary War. North Carolina also claimed that the frontiersmen were in open rebellion. Its opposition persuaded the Confederation Congress to refuse Franklin's admission. (Ten years later, after North Carolina had ceded its claims under the new Constitution, the area in question was admitted with its approval as the state of Tennessee.)

Both Maine and Missouri experienced difficulty being admitted into the Union. Before the Civil War, Southern slave states did not want more free—that is, nonslave—states admitted because they feared that if an overwhelming number were free states, slave states would be forced to abandon slavery. The Southern states insisted that the admission of nonslave states into the Union be paired with the admission of slave states to ensure the sectional balance of power. This plan was called the Missouri Compromise because it resulted in the admission of Missouri and Maine as paired free and slave states. Maine's admission, in fact, was held up for more than a year to work out this compromise in 1820.

The readmission of rebellious Southern states after the Civil War caused a considerable amount of dispute. Although these states were never technically excluded from the Union, they were denied their role in the federal government, and Congress at the time considered them to be legally excluded under the Fourteenth Amendment. Many people did not want the Southern states readmitted until they had totally eliminated all vestiges of slavery. Gradually, however, despite short-lived experiments intended to compel enforcement of the freed blacks' civil rights, the states were in fact readmitted without any mandatory elimination of discrimination, though slavery itself had been abolished.

The most famous controversy concerning a new state surrounded the admission of Utah in 1896. The citizens there were mostly Mormon and practiced polygamy. Congress would not permit it to become a state until it explicitly forbade polygamy in its state constitution—which it eventually did.

◆◆◆ Can a State Secede?

No. If there was any doubt about that, it was settled by the Civil War, in which the federal government defeated the attempt by eleven Southern states to quit the Union and form the Confederate States of America.

The issue of secession raises a fundamental question about the nature of the Constitution and the Union. The Federalists argued that the Constitution was created by the people of the United States and that the states were subordinate to the Union. The emerging Republican party of Thomas Jefferson argued that the states were the constituent parts of the Union and that they had created the Constitution. Though it was never expressed as such, lurking beneath the surface of the Jeffersonian argument was the possibility that a state could choose to leave the Union. As early as 1798, Virginia and Kentucky passed resolutions denouncing the Alien and Sedition Acts, passed by Federalists during the undeclared war with France. Both the Kentucky Resolutions and the Virginia Resolutions, as they were called, said that the laws were unconstitutional and that any state could interpret the Constitution just as well as the federal government could. The Kentucky Resolutions, drafted by Jefferson himself, said that a state could nullify federal laws within its borders. The Virginia Resolutions, drafted by James Madison, said a state could "interpose" itself between its citizens and an unconstitutional law, thereby forcing the federal government to reexamine the law.

Ironically, when the first actual move to secede came—during Madison's administration and the War of 1812—die-hard New England Federalists mockingly cited the Kentucky and Virginia Resolutions as sound precedent for their action. Bitterly opposed to the war effort, they sought to take the New England states out of the Union, hoping either to form their own independent nation or to ally themselves with Canada or England. The Federalists met in late 1814 in Hartford, Connecticut, but the conclusion of the war that same year put an end to their movement. Then, in 1830, in reaction to unfavorable federal tariff laws, South Carolina passed various statutes nullifying the laws. Drawing extensively on the doctrines enunciated by Kentucky and Virginia in 1798, John C. Calhoun insisted that states could secede from the Union. Madison, in retirement, was horrified and indignantly denied that either he or Jefferson had intended to condone secession. President Andrew Jackson convinced South Carolina to back off from its threat of secession through a combination of threatening to take swift military action against South Carolina and at the same time reducing the burden put on the state by the tariff.

However, the possibility of secession still existed and was not put to rest until the Civil War, which established through military force that no state can leave the Union. This was confirmed in 1869 by the Supreme Court in a case involving bonds issued to Texas ten years before it seceded to join the Confederacy. During the war, the state had sold them. The Court upheld the state's reconstructed government's effort to recover the bonds or compensation for them, saying that all attempts to secede are null and void. The Court was, nevertheless, careful to limit the scope of its decision to strike down only laws that seceding states had passed that actually aided the rebellion itself. Thus, Jackson's defiant toast at an 1830 Jefferson Day banquet remains valid: "Our Federal Union: It must be preserved."

◆◆◆ What Are States' Rights?

In the words of the Tenth Amendment, the powers "reserved to the States respectively." But the exact nature of those powers has been a matter of debate and controversy almost since the Constitution was adopted. Who decides, a state or the federal government, whether slavery is legal? Who decides who can vote in state or national elections? Who decides who can serve on juries? Each of these questions—and numerous others—raises issues concerning states' rights.

Over the years, the division of authority between the federal government and the states has been hotly debated. States have tried to stave off what they saw as federal encroachments on their authority by invoking the doctrine of states' rights. The ultimate right, at least to supporters of the doctrine in the nineteenth century, was that of secession; invoking it led to the Civil War.

The doctrine has been raised increasingly in the 1980s by proponents of the so-called New Right, such as President Ronald W. Reagan, to support their argument for cutting the federal budget and reducing the federal government's involvement in social programs for education, welfare, and medical care.

The origins of the doctrine date from colonial times. Each of the original thirteen states was founded independently of the others and retained exclusive sovereignty over its territory. As early as the 1640s, in the New England Confederation, an attempt was made to form a defense network against the Indians. The same motive led to the Albany Congress of 1754. The colonies came together for the Stamp Act Congress of 1765; it, as well as the First and Second Continental Congresses, in 1774 and 1775 respectively, came into being as a response to England's oppressive tax and commerce policies. American political leaders agreed that concerted action by all the colonies was necessary to oppose the actions of Parliament and the Crown successfully.

John Adams recalled in 1813 that the task of securing the unanimous adoption of the Declaration of Independence by the Second Continental Congress was as difficult as getting thirteen clocks to strike as one. Although many leading Americans such as Patrick Henry and Tom Paine spoke of all Americans as being members of one nation, in reality the people themselves came to think of themselves that way only gradually. That slowness was reflected by the four years of negotiations it took to secure unanimous adoption by the states of the Articles of Confederation in 1781. Americans in those days distrusted strong central government. To

Americans then, government was best that remained closest to the people. And they preferred local government to state government, and state government to a general government.

As the defects of the Articles became apparent in the mid-1780s, some political leaders seriously considered breaking up into thirteen separate states or several regional confederacies. But supporters of a stronger general government insisted that union must be preserved. The Constitutional Convention of 1787 saw as its main objective the continued existence of the Union, either by revising the Articles or—as the delegates actually did—by replacing them with a new charter of government. Though their action indicated a shift in political thinking in favor of a powerful, energetic, centralized government, the older view persisted at the Convention. The Constitution that was written was designed "to form a more perfect Union"—a union not only of individuals but also of states. Some delegates, such as Alexander Hamilton of New York, favored reducing the states to mere administrative districts. Others—Luther Martin of Maryland, for example, and both Robert Yates and John Lansing, of New York—left the Convention rather than continue to participate in the creation of what they feared would be an omnipotent national government. The Convention's solution to this dilemma, as James Madison of Virginia described it in the *Federalist* essay No. 39, was to draft a constitution that was "in strictness, neither a national nor a federal constitution, but a composition of both." In this context, a federal government operates on and is responsible to the political entities constituting it—that is, the states. A national government operates on and is responsible to the people. Madison noted that the new Constitution combined both federal and national elements in its structure and function; he believed this mix, rather than a pure constitution of either type, was best designed to preserve a republican form of government—that is, a government run by a legislature and an executive, both of which are elected directly or indirectly by the people and are responsible to them.

The question of states' rights, then, is where to draw the line between the powers retained by the states and those granted to the central government under the Constitution. The Tenth Amendment, which reserves all powers not expressly granted to the federal government to the states or the people, ostensibly provides constitutional justification for states' rights arguments. However, Anti-Federalists who opposed the Bill of Rights regarded this amendment as mere window dressing, claiming that it would have no effect against federal usurpations under the "implied powers" argument developed by Hamilton. They proved prophetic, because states' rights disputes persisted.

Of all the disputes over states' rights in the nineteenth century, the most critical was posed by the "peculiar institution" of slavery. In the *Dred Scott* case in 1857—a victory for states' rightists—the Supreme Court ruled that a state could allow slavery within its borders and withhold individual constitutional rights from blacks. The Civil War that followed settled the question of a state's right to secede. It also settled similar issues. One was nullification, or a state's alleged right to nullify a federal law; another was interposition, by which a state could theoretically interpose itself between a federal law and its citizens to prevent the law's operation. The North's victory in the war solidified the nationalist view of the Constitution: that it was framed and adopted by the people of the United States, in their national capacity, and not by states as political units.

Over the last five decades, the Supreme Court has come to play an important role in the centralization of our society, primarily through its interpretation of two constitutional provisions—the Commerce Clause (Article I, Section 8) and the Tenth Amendment. Beginning with the New Deal, the Court has interpreted the Commerce Clause, which gives Congress the power to regulate interstate commerce, in the broadest possible way. Today, Congress and the federal government can regulate just about anything as "interstate commerce" and this has facilitated the growth of government regulation. At the same time, the Court has given a very narrow interpretation to the Tenth Amendment, which reserves to the states powers not delegated to the federal government by the Constitution. Today, that amendment does little to check the encroachment of the federal government on state concerns.

The states do enjoy some independence, however. They have the right to be free from federal taxation. They also enjoy a limited immunity from suits in federal courts, though they can be sued by another state or by the United States. They cannot be deprived of their equal representation in the Senate or otherwise be discriminated against by the federal government. Nor can the federal government create a new state with powers greater than those of the existing states.

Perhaps the most significant power that states have is their power to amend the Constitution. However, the procedure provided by the Constitution is so cumbersome that it is rarely invoked. Two-thirds of the states' legislatures must agree on calling a convention to propose an amendment, and three-fourths of the states' legislatures or three-fourths of state ratifying conventions must then approve it (Article V).

◆◆◆ Did Any State Ever Have Its Boundaries Changed?

Yes. Many have had their boundaries changed, chiefly as the result of a dispute with another state or with the federal government. Most of the disputes have been petty, but once in a while—as in the case of water rights in the West or the ownership of the mineral-rich outer continental shelf—billions of dollars can be involved. Disputes sometimes find their way to the Supreme Court, but most are settled beforehand.

Of course, boundaries have been changed when new states were formed from old states, which has happened five times: Vermont, which was admitted in 1791, from land claimed by New York, New Hampshire, and Massachusetts; Kentucky, in 1792, from land claimed by Virginia; Tennessee, in 1796, from land claimed by North Carolina and Virginia; Maine, in 1820, from part of Massachusetts (pursuant to the Missouri Compromise, as a free state, to balance the admission of Missouri, a slave state, that same year); and West Virginia, in 1863, from Virginia. All but West Virginia were admitted to the Union with the consent of the original states, as required by Article IV, Section 3, of the Constitution. West Virginia, formed from the pro-Union counties of Virginia that opposed secession in 1861, was admitted into the Union without Virginia's consent during the Civil War.

Since 1790, more than a hundred boundary disputes have been settled by the Supreme Court and hundreds more have been settled without any judicial intervention. A notable one, originally between California, Arizona, and several Indian tribes over water rights to the Colorado River, took thirty-one years to settle from the time the litigation began in 1952; by the time the settlement was reached, three other states had joined the case.

A fairly typical dispute might involve the exact location of the boundary or ownership of uninhabited islands located between the two states. For example, the interstate compact establishing the Port Authority of New York and New Jersey in 1923 also settled some border disagreements involving uninhabited islands between the two states.

In 1985, a dispute arose over which of those two states owns the island on which the Statue of Liberty stands (a matter not covered by the 1923 agreement). Advocates on each side appealed to different documents dating from the nineteenth century. The case is still pending.

◆◆◆ Can One State Sue Another State?

Yes, but only before the Supreme Court. Boundary disputes—the most common type of conflict between states—have often been decided by the Court. It has also heard cases in which one state has sued another for violation of a contract and cases in which one state has tried to stop another from interfering with or diverting its water supply.

Though it was rarely used, the Articles of Confederation provided a method for settling disputes between states: the Confederation Congress would appoint a committee from its own members to arbitrate the matter. The Framers of the Constitution decided that a permanent mechanism for settling such disputes was needed. They realized that surrendering the power to conduct diplomatic relations or to make war to the federal government should not leave the states without a way to settle grievances against each other. So they gave the Supreme Court what is called original jurisdiction in all suits "in which a State shall be a Party" (Article III, Section 2).

The original jurisdiction of the Supreme Court is very special, because in such cases the Court acts as a trial court (usually it acts as an appellate court). In such cases, it actually receives evidence and determines the facts of the case, applying the law to the facts as it finds them. (Usually, the Court applies the law to facts that were determined by a lower trial court.) The justices do not hear the evidence themselves in original jurisdiction cases; instead, they appoint a "special master" (a judge or an expert appointed just for the case) who hears the testimony and prepares "findings of fact" for the justices. Technically, in at least some of the lawsuits that come within the Court's original jurisdiction, the litigants have a right to a jury trial. But since the 1790s, when three jury trials were held before the Supreme Court, the Court apparently has not conducted a jury trial in an original jurisdiction case. In 1950, Tennessee requested a jury in a case that was before the Court as a matter of original jurisdiction, but the Court denied the request, ruling that the state had no right to a jury in that case.

Today, not all cases "in which a State shall be a Party" come within the Court's original jurisdiction. For example, the Eleventh Amendment, ratified in 1798, bars all federal courts—including the Supreme Court—from hearing suits brought against a state by a citizen of another state or of a foreign country. Such suits must be brought in a state court (though, interestingly enough, under a 1979 Supreme Court ruling, not necessarily in a court of the state being sued).

Moreover, even if a case comes within the Court's original jurisdiction, the Court won't necessarily decide to hear the suit. The Constitution lists the cases that come within the original jurisdiction of the Court—those "affecting Ambassadors, other public Ministers and Consuls" as well as "those in which a State shall be a Party"—but it does not say that the Supreme Court is the *only* court that can hear those cases as an original matter, nor does it say that the Supreme Court *must* hear those cases. And, although there is a hint to the contrary in the 1803 case *Marbury v. Madison,* Congress has—ever since the Judiciary Act of 1789—assumed the power to make the Supreme Court's original jurisdiction in part concurrent, or shared, with that of lower federal courts or state courts. For example, today, by act of Congress, suits involving ambassadors, other public ministers, and consuls can be tried either in the Supreme Court or in other courts. As a practical matter, this means that the Court does not hear such cases.

Similarly, the same act of Congress provides that many cases in which a state is a party may be instituted in courts other than the Supreme Court—specifically, suits between the United States and a state, or actions by a state against the citizens of another state or against aliens may be brought in courts other than the Supreme Court. But Congress has mandated that, where one state sues another state, *only* the Supreme Court can hear the case.

Just because a state is interested in the outcome of a case does not mean that the Court can or will hear it. And what determines whether the Court will take the case has nothing to do with the subject of the dispute or the amount of money at stake. The key is the identity of the parties involved. For example, the Court does not have jurisdiction to hear, as an original matter, a suit brought by a state against a city located in another state. Such a suit would have to be brought in a state or lower federal court that has jurisdiction.

The Court will hear disputes between states if the state bringing the suit establishes that it is acting to protect or to advance the interests of the entire state, not just some of its citizens or companies. Similarly, the Court will require the state seeking to bring the suit directly in the Supreme Court to show that the other party is actually another state, rather than some other entity or person. Thus, when Alabama in 1934 challenged the validity of an Arizona law that prohibited the sale in the open market of goods made by convicts, the Court refused to hear the case. And, in 1954, the Court refused to hear the claim of both Alabama and Rhode Island that a federal statute, under which Congress had ceded land to Texas, was unconstitutional.

◆◆◆ Can the State Take Away My House and Land If I Don't Want to Sell Them?

Yes. Under a power known as eminent domain, any government—city, state, or federal—can take away your house and land. But it must comply with the requirements of the Fifth and Fourteenth amendments—that is, it must be able to demonstrate that it is taking the property for a public purpose and that you are being paid a fair price in return.

The government frequently must "take" private property through condemnation when it wants to build a new school building, a park, an airport, or an urban development. Nobody questions that government could hardly go on if it could not take property in this way. But there are limits: The government cannot just take anything it wants in any way it wants. The so-called Takings Clause of the Fifth Amendment—which has been applied to the states by the Fourteenth Amendment—commands that government may not take private property except for "public use" and that, when it does take property, it must pay the owner "just compensation."

Because of the Takings Clause, two constitutional issues arise every time the government takes private property: whether the government is taking the property for a public use and whether it has given the owner a fair market price for it. Courts sometimes find it easy to determine whether the government has paid "just compensation," because they can refer to the prices being paid for similar property on the open market. On the other hand, where the property taken is unique (such as a railroad) or where only a small piece of a larger plot is taken, the determination of "just compensation" can be difficult. Similarly, it is usually easy for the courts to decide whether the government is taking the property for a public use, though even this can sometimes be a problem if the public use is not an obvious one. The general rule is clear: A government cannot confiscate your property just to turn it over to a private person or company—no matter how much it pays you. But the application of this principle is not always simple.

Consider the case of the Hawaii Land Reform Act of 1967—a law passed by the Hawaiian legislature that radically redistributed the ownership of land in that state. Before Hawaii was part of the United States, it was an independent monarchy, and the kings of Hawaii had granted huge tracts of land to private persons, including American citizens who had settled there. By 1967, 72 private landowners owned 47 percent of Hawaii. Because the state and federal governments owned 49 percent of the state's land, only 4 percent of Hawaii was available for anyone else. The legislature decided that this "concentrated land ownership was responsible for skewing the state's [real estate] market, inflating land prices, and injuring the public tranquility and welfare." It passed a law designed to break up the large estates, condemning the properties under the state's right of eminent domain and transferring the property to tenants. The landowners were compensated but sued to overturn the law because, they claimed, the state was taking private property for a private use. The Supreme Court disagreed and upheld the Hawaii statute. It ruled that it was well within the state's powers to "reduce the perceived social and economic evils of a land oligarchy" created in the previous century under the old monarchy. Writing for the Court, Justice Sandra Day O'Connor declared:

> [Just because] property taken outright by eminent domain is transferred in the first instance to private beneficiaries does not condemn that taking as having only a private purpose. Government does not itself have to use property to legitimate the takings; it is only the taking's purpose, and not its mechanics, that must pass scrutiny under the Public Use Clause [of the Fifth Amendment].

The *Hawaii* case illustrates something that Justice William O. Douglas said thirty years earlier: "The role of the judiciary in determining whether [the eminent domain power] is being exercised for a public purpose is an extremely narrow one." The Court usually defers to a legislature's determination that it is doing something for a "public" purpose—and the Court rarely will second-guess the legislature on that point.

One additional question about the Takings Clause has developed. Suppose that, rather than condemning property and taking ownership of it, the government merely "regulates" its use—perhaps in a way that substantially reduces its value. When is such a government regulation of the way you use your own property so burdensome that it amounts to a taking under the Takings Clause? If the property owner's loss is just an incidental result of an otherwise valid regulation, the government does not have to compensate the property owner. Justice Oliver Wendell Holmes, Jr., established this rule in a 1922 case, *Pennsylvania Coal Co. v. Mahon*, when he said: "While property may be regulated to a certain extent, if regulation goes too far it will be recognized as a taking."

In that case, the coal company had deeded to a man named Mahon surface rights to some land, but it retained the right to exploit mineral deposits below the surface. Later, the state passed a law barring the mining of anthracite coal where the mining might cause the surface land to subside or sink. When the coal company announced that it was going to mine the coal below Mahon's land, he sued for an injunction, citing the new state law. The coal company argued that the statute was unconstitutional because it took away the company's mineral rights without compensating it—in other words, the regulation amounted to a taking. The Supreme Court agreed and struck down the statute.

Since the *Mahon* case, the issue of distinguishing between a regulation and a taking has arisen with regard to zoning and landmark-preservation ordinances. In general, the Court has rejected efforts to overturn such local and state rules. In one instance in 1980, it upheld a zoning ordinance against a challenge brought by a real-estate developer. The developer had acquired five acres of unimproved land in Tiburon, California, a scenic suburb of San Francisco. After he purchased the land, the city adopted zoning changes placing the land in a zone where the developer could build only one single-family residence on each acre. The developer sued, claiming that the ordinance was unconstitutional because it "took" his property without compensating him. The Supreme Court disagreed. Writing for the Court, Justice Lewis F. Powell, Jr., said that the law was not a taking, but only a regulation that was designed to protect residents "from the ill effects of urbanization." In Powell's view, the regulation benefited the developer as well as his neighbors "by serving the city's interest in assuring careful and orderly development of residential property."

Similarly, in 1978, the Court upheld a decision of the New York City Landmarks Preservation Commission declaring Grand Central Terminal a landmark and forbidding any changes to its exterior without commission approval. The Penn Central Railroad had sought to build a high-rise office tower above it and, when its request for a permit to do so was denied, sued, claiming the application of the law was a taking. The Supreme Court rejected the railroad's claim, however, pointing out that Penn Central could sell the "air rights" above the terminal—that is, its right to build a taller office building on the site—to the developer of a neighboring site who could then erect a building nearby using the terminal's "sun-and-shadow" limits. The landmark designation, the Court said, therefore did not totally deprive Penn Central of property and thus was not a taking.

Some recent decisions indicate that the present Supreme Court is prepared to take the Takings Clause seriously. In 1982, for example, it invalidated a New York law that compelled landlords to permit a cable television company to install its cable and some other small equipment on landlords' rental property and that gave the landlord only a one-time payment of one dollar for the intrusion. New York argued that the law was merely a regulation of the use of the property. The Court agreed with the

landlord that the ordinance was a taking, saying, "[W]hether the installa-
tion is a taking does not depend on whether the volume of space that it
occupies is bigger than a bread box." The key was that the law authorized a
"permanent physical occupation of [the landlord's] property." Since there
had been no real compensation for the taking, the Supreme Court held
the law unconstitutional.

In a 1984 case, the Supreme Court extended the Takings Clause to
intangible property. Under the Federal Insecticide, Fungicide, and Roden-
ticide Act, the Environmental Protection Agency refused to permit the
Monsanto Company to market certain pesticides unless it would first
disclose its formulas and methods to the agency. But disclosure to the
agency would have made that information generally available. Monsanto
argued that this procedure was a taking because the trade secrets involved
were its property. The Supreme Court said that trade secrets were sufficiently similar to more tangible forms of property to qualify as property for
purposes of the Taking Clause. Of course, that didn't end the matter.
Before Monsanto could win, the Court had to determine that a taking had
occurred and that compensation was in order. It did, and the case was sent
back to the lower court to determine what the compensation should be.

◆◆◆ Is It Possible for My City to Prevent My Favorite Sports Team from Moving?

Yes, but don't bet on it. The power of eminent domain—the right of the
government to take property against the will of its owner—has always been
around. But only recently have cities attempted to apply it to sports teams.

The Fifth Amendment does limit the city's power of eminent domain by
providing that private property may not be taken unless it is for a "public
use" and "just compensation" is paid. Other than that, the power of
eminent domain is nearly unlimited. For example, just about any property
can be taken—and that includes a football team and the players' contracts
with the team that make its existence possible.

Your city would be on pretty strong ground in arguing that it was taking
the team for a "public use." Courts have been very liberal in interpreting
this term. For example, courts frequently have approved the condemnation
of land so that stadiums and sports complexes could be built. And, in
1982, in a celebrated case involving the Oakland Raiders, the California
Supreme Court ruled that Oakland could force the owners to sell the

football team to the city in order to keep the team there. The court even said that the city could resell the team to local buyers who pledged to keep the Raiders in Oakland.

If your city did take possession of your favorite team by eminent domain, it would have to pay its former owners "just compensation" for it. That might be a problem, because the market value of a professional baseball or football team can exceed $50 million. If the city wants to "condemn" the team, it would have to pay that market price.

One word of caution: If you want your city to use its power of eminent domain to keep your favorite team around, be sure the city acts before the team physically moves—because once the team shifts to an out-of-state location, the city will find it difficult to use its power of eminent domain. That happened to Baltimore when the owners of its football team, the Colts, moved the team, bag and baggage, to Indianapolis literally in the middle of the night in March 1984. By the time Baltimore got around to trying to do something about the move, it was too late.

Even if your city does start its lawsuit on time, there still may be a problem. Unless the city can persuade the court to issue an injunction forbidding the team to move, the owners of the team might move it while the lawsuit works its way through the court system. That's why the Oakland Raiders are now the Los Angeles Raiders. After the California Supreme Court decided that Oakland could use its power of eminent domain to keep the team in town, it had to send the case back to the trial court so that the court could decide issues such as whether the particular condemnation was for a "public use" and, if it was, what the amount of compensation should be. While all the legal maneuvering has been going on, the Raiders have been playing in Los Angeles. If at the conclusion of the lawsuit Oakland wins, it may move the team back as the new owner. But, for now, the team continues to play in Los Angeles.

Part Two

OUR RIGHTS AND LIBERTIES

The Right to Vote ========

Eighteen. The Twenty-sixth Amendment, ratified in 1971, establishes that. The amendment was adopted in large part because of the Vietnam War, when many Americans who were not old enough to vote were drafted into the armed forces. This paradox gave birth to the slogan, "Old enough to fight, old enough to vote."

The Twenty-sixth Amendment does not grant the right to vote to *all* eighteen-year-old American citizens, however. Many over eighteen are not permitted to vote because they are disqualified for reasons having nothing to do with their age. For example, they are mentally incompetent or guilty of certain crimes. The amendment merely guarantees that citizens who are eighteen years of age or older shall not be discriminated against on account of age when it comes to setting qualifications to vote.

Moreover, the amendment does not mandate an absolute minimum voting age. It requires only that anyone eighteen or older be allowed to vote. Thus, theoretically, a state could pass a law giving sixteen-year-olds the right to vote in elections—even in presidential elections—though that's unlikely.

And, finally, the amendment does not require the states to permit seventeen-year-olds to vote in a primary election, even if they will be eighteen by the time of the general election. This, too, gives the states latitude—but in this case latitude to restrict rather than to expand the vote. Some states, such as Ohio, have chosen to bar all persons under eighteen from primary elections.

The Constitution originally said nothing about age as a qualification for voting. The Framers left virtually all questions about voting qualifications to the states, which had varying age requirements tied to whatever "age of majority" was recognized by a particular state. In fact, the first mention of age did not come until the adoption of the Fourteenth Amendment in 1868 following the end of the Civil War. Its second section, which was written to ensure voting rights for blacks, effectively set a minimum age of twenty-one years for all elections—an age probably chosen because most states considered twenty-one to be the age of majority.

Congress tried to lower the voting age to eighteen in all federal *and* state elections in the Voting Rights Act of 1970, but the state-election provisions were struck down by a deeply divided Supreme Court later the same year in a case involving Oregon's requirement that citizens be twenty-one to vote in *state* elections. Four justices believed that Congress had the power to grant eighteen-year-olds the right to vote in both federal and state elections. Four others, however, maintained that only states could control voter qualifications. The ninth justice, Hugo L. Black, maintained that Congress could pass laws regarding federal elections but not state elections. Black provided the fifth vote upholding Oregon's twenty-one-year-old minimum for state elections.

That decision, in effect, left those states who wanted to set a higher age requirement than eighteen with the expensive task of maintaining separate records for federal and state elections. Accordingly, they were receptive to ratifying the Twenty-sixth Amendment, which Congress proposed on March 23, 1971, three months after the Court's ruling. It was officially ratified on June 30, 1971—a record three months later.

◆◆◆ Did Any Women Have the Right to Vote before the Nineteenth Amendment Was Ratified?

Most did, although the very first state to grant women the right to vote—back in the 1790s—did so by mistake and then reversed itself.

In 1919, the year before the Nineteenth Amendment was adopted, women had the right to vote in all elections, both state and federal, in thirty of the nation's forty-eight states. And those thirty states contained more than two-thirds of the population of the United States.

Up until the amendment, the decision whether to grant women the franchise in either federal or state elections was left to the states. The Supreme Court had made that clear in 1875. In fact, it wasn't until 1970, a half-century after the amendment went into effect, that the Court, in a five-to-four decision in a case dealing with the vote of eighteen-year-olds, ruled that Congress could regulate federal elections in any way it wished.

The women's suffrage movement spanned 130 years, but its beginnings were not auspicious. During the Revolution, Abigail Adams urged her husband, John Adams, to "remember the ladies" and admit women to a full role in American political life, but Adams treated her plea as a joke;

and when President Thomas Jefferson was asked whether he would consider appointing women to federal office during his administration, he rejected the idea out of hand. New Jersey unwittingly started the ball rolling when drafting its state constitution in 1790; its provision on suffrage did not restrict the vote to men, and women thus voted in New Jersey's elections until 1807, when the state legislature remedied the "mistake" and stripped them of the vote.

The first state to grant women the franchise on a permanent basis was Wyoming. Because the number of voters (rather than the number of citizens) was a critical factor in determining whether a territory could become a state, Wyoming shrewdly allowed women to vote in territorial elections as early as 1869, and when Wyoming became a state in 1890, it continued that right, a move that proved vital to the suffrage movement throughout the nation.

Wyoming's example was so successful that it encouraged other states to follow suit. Colorado adopted a state constitutional amendment granting its women the suffrage in 1893. Idaho followed in 1896. Utah ran into a problem after it granted women the right to vote in 1870 while still a territory. Exercising its right to control the laws in territories, Congress took away the suffrage from Utah's women in 1887. However, once Utah became a state in 1896, it restored their right to vote.

The next state to allow women to vote, Washington, didn't do so until 1910, when the suffrage movement began to develop momentum and effectiveness. From 1912 to 1920, twenty-six other states adopted similar measures. During this time, Jeannette Rankin, a Republican from Montana, became the first woman to sit in the House of Representatives. Elected in 1916, she was the only representative to vote against President Woodrow Wilson's call for a declaration of war in 1917 and was defeated for reelection the next year. Returning to the House in 1940, she was the only representative to oppose President Franklin D. Roosevelt's call for a declaration of war in 1941 and was defeated in the 1942 election. Rankin, in fact, was the only member of either house of Congress to oppose American involvement in either war.

In 1920, the right of all women to vote in all elections was made applicable throughout the nation by the Nineteenth Amendment, which says:

> The right of citizens of the United States to vote shall not be denied or abridged by the United States or by any State on account of sex.

◆◆◆ Do I Have to Speak English to Vote?

No. Congress has expressly forbidden tests, including one for competency in English, as a prerequisite for voting.

The right to vote has changed dramatically in the last two centuries. The Constitution says nothing about language or literacy requirements for voting. Article IV, Section 4, does guarantee that "every State in this Union" will have "a Republican Form of Government." But the Supreme Court has consistently refused to interpret this provision in any broad fashion that would mean that the provision, by itself, guarantees certain voting rights for everyone. Consequently, the Fourteenth, Fifteenth, Nineteenth, Twenty-fourth, and Twenty-sixth amendments have all been adopted to add such rights to the Constitution. They are the source of much of Congress's authority to enact voting-rights laws.

Despite these amendments, though—the first of which were ratified soon after the Civil War to protect blacks—securing voting rights for everyone without any restrictions whatever was slow in developing. Many states required complex literacy tests as a prerequisite. Some even required a voter to "understand and explain" an article of the Constitution.

Interestingly, the huge influx of immigrants—most of whom were from Europe—to America during the nineteenth century and into the twentieth failed to spur any movement to relax English-language requirements, probably because the dominant impulse was to assimilate the new Americans into the American mainstream—an impulse that coincided with the newcomers' desires to be assimilated.

From about the late 1920s on, Congress and the Supreme Court began to tear down the barriers to voting that the states had erected. And, although the Court refused to declare literacy tests uniformly unconstitutional in 1959, six years later it did say that they were unconstitutional unless a state could show that the test did not serve a discriminatory purpose.

In the last generation, language requirements became the focus of national attention because of the rise of Hispanic Americans as the nation's single largest ethnic group. Spanish-speaking citizens—primarily Mexican Americans in the Southwest and Puerto Ricans in the Northeast—insisted that bilingualism be adopted in education and in the voting process.

As part of the Voting Rights Act of 1965, Congress suspended all literacy tests and similar devices for restricting the right to vote. The Court, citing the Fifteenth Amendment, upheld Congress's power to do so in 1970, and by 1975, Congress had permanently banned all literacy tests.

Later amendments to the act forbade the requirement that a voter had to speak English. The most recent ones even require a state to print bilingual ballots if 5 percent of a district's population speaks a primary language other than English. And, in fact, if the minority language in question is only spoken and not written—as is true for certain languages spoken by Native Americans—then the state must provide someone to explain orally what a ballot says.

◆◆◆ Did Americans Ever Have to Pay to Vote?

Yes. The poll tax was legal and still in use in five southern states until 1964. And until 1969 it was also legal to limit voting to persons who had a certain minimum income or owned a certain minimum amount of property.

When the Constitution went into effect in 1789, every one of the original thirteen states had either a poll tax or some other financial requirement for voting, such as a minimum yearly income level or amount of assets or a minimum amount of property. Some states had both the tax and a financial requirement. The idea behind both was to limit voting to "responsible" adults—that is, to men (women couldn't vote then) who had a stake in the welfare of the political community.

In the 1820s and 1830s state constitutional conventions eliminated many of the minimum-income or property requirements. But the poll tax was another matter. Southern states used such taxes to keep blacks from voting following the Reconstruction Era in the late nineteenth century.

In 1937, the Supreme Court upheld the constitutionality of a Georgia poll tax in both state and federal elections on the ground that the regulation of elections was an area of law reserved to the states. When, in 1964, the Twenty-fourth Amendment outlawing the poll tax was ratified, only Alabama, Arkansas, Mississippi, Texas, and Virginia still had poll-tax statutes.

The Twenty-fourth Amendment banned the poll tax only in federal elections, however. It was not until 1966—at the height of the civil rights movement—that the Court ruled that a poll tax in state elections was also unconstitutional. The Court held that granting the vote to some and denying it to others violated the Equal Protection Clause of the Fourteenth Amendment. It said that because "Wealth, like race, creed, or color, is not germane to one's ability to participate intelligently in the electoral process," the poll tax introduced "a capricious or irrelevant factor." Later, in a 1969 case dealing with a general wealth requirement for voting in Louisiana state elections, the Court also outlawed minimum-wealth requirements.

This right, however, is not all-inclusive. On a very few local financial issues, the Court has allowed voting to be restricted to those affected. The most significant example was a 1973 case involving a California waterbond referendum. The justices ruled that because only landowners were affected by the local law, the voting could be limited to them. That case is a narrowly limited exception to a powerful general principle that restrictions on voting are usually not allowed.

◆◆◆ Can I Be Prevented from Voting If I Move to Another State?

Only for a limited number of reasons. You have to be a bona fide resident of the state, and you may have to meet the state's minimum-residency requirement. And, very often, you have to declare your party affiliation to be eligible to vote in a primary. But otherwise, your right to vote is secure because, even though the Supreme Court ruled in 1959 that states have "broad powers to determine the conditions under which the right of suffrage may be exercised," later Court rulings and laws enacted by Congress have limited a state's ability to exercise these powers.

All states have state constitutional provisions and statutes defining the qualifications for voting. The rule that you must be a resident of a state or city before you vote in its election is based on the principle that, although nonresidents may be affected by what the city or state does, drawing geographical boundaries is the best way to set up rules about who can vote. The Supreme Court has sanctioned establishing the right to vote on residency, but it has struck down efforts by states to set artificial limits based on it. Thus, the Court has invalidated both a Maryland law that denied the vote to persons living on the grounds of the National Institutes of Health, a federal enclave carved out of Maryland property, and a Texas law that denied the vote to military personnel who moved to Texas during the course of their military service.

A requirement that you have to be a resident of the state for some specified period of time is permissible, but only within very strict limits. In 1972, the Court struck down a Tennessee statute that required one-year residence in the state and three months of residence in the county before a citizen became eligible to vote. The Court conceded that residency requirements might help the state prevent voter fraud, but said that such fraud could be prevented by a much shorter period. The Court suggested that thirty days would be enough. Requiring one year of residence to be eligible to vote, it said, violated two constitutional rights—the right to vote and the right to travel from state to state—therefore the Tennessee law was held to be unconstitutional. The following year, the Court allowed Arizona and Georgia to cut off voter registration fifty days before an election to permit the state to prepare accurate voting lists, but the justices indicated that fifty days was near the limit that the Constitution allowed. In presidential elections, Congress requires the states to continue to register voters until thirty days before the election.

Often states require voters who wish to vote in a party primary to establish their affiliation with the political party either at the time of the primary or by a specified time before the date of the primary. Such rules are designed to guard against voters' switching over to a rival party in order to influence it in ways inconsistent with the beliefs of its real members. The Court has been much more willing to tolerate residency requirements for primary elections than for general elections. Although it invalidated an Illinois statute prohibiting a person from voting in the primary election of a political party if he or she had voted in the primary of any other party within the preceding twenty-three months, the justices allowed New York to insist that a voter be an enrolled party member for eleven months before voting in that party's primary. Not all states have followed New York's approach, however. Many do not require a voter to be a registered member of a party to vote in its primary. For example, Wisconsin freely permits what is called *crossover voting*.

One related matter: States sometimes require candidates for elective state office to have lived in the state for a given period before the election—no doubt by analogy to the constitutional requirement that representatives be United States citizens for seven years (Article I, Section 2), senators be United States citizens for nine years (Article I, Section 3), and the president be a natural-born citizen (Article II, Section 1). (Presidents must also have resided "within the United States" for fourteen years before their election.) The Supreme Court has never dealt in detail with these state residency requirements, but lower courts have upheld them.

◆◆◆ Does the Constitution Provide for Political Parties?

No, but it doesn't prohibit them, either. In fact, it protects them. And parties have become an integral part of our political system.

At the time of the Constitutional Convention in 1787, there were no formal political parties, though there had been ill-defined factions in colonial politics and pro-Crown Tories and anti-Crown Whigs in the Revolutionary Era. The Framers of the Constitution made no formal provision for parties in the new charter because they distrusted them. To most of the Framers, parties were the same as factions, which they defined as groups—whether minorities or majorities—bent on selfish, short-term goals that would injure society as a whole. Thus, they designed the structure of the Constitution to guard against such groups.

The best explanation of what the Framers sought to guard against is found in James Madison's now-classic *Federalist* essay No. 10. Because factions were inevitably harmful to the public good, Madison argued, anyone seeking to put together a republic had to face the problems they caused. Because liberty, the major cause of faction, was at the same time the great good that all Americans wanted to preserve, Madison acknowledged that you could not get rid of the causes of faction. But you could control their effects, both through making the nation large enough that no majority could seize control of the government and injure the rights of minorities, and through splitting up the powers of government among three separate and equal branches so that no one branch could dominate the government and nation.

In fact, although the structure of government established in the Constitution was designed in part to restrict the political power of factions, the First Amendment helped to nurture the growth of what became political parties as we know them. Because they are vehicles of political expression—the core of what the First Amendment is meant to safeguard—political parties have benefited greatly from the protections of that key constitutional provision.

Almost by accident, and certainly against the expectations of the Framers of the Constitution, political parties developed from the beginning of government under the Constitution. In fact, some historians have argued that the division between supporters and opponents of the Constitution during the ratification controversy in the months immediately following the Constitutional Convention did not go away after the Constitution was adopted; rather the protagonists merely shifted and transformed themselves into the parties of the 1790s.

The first organized political parties, the Federalists and Jeffersonian Republicans, evolved because of the polarization of public opinion resulting from the fiscal policies of Alexander Hamilton, a leading Federalist and secretary of the treasury in the administration of President George Washington. Hamilton's centralized economic policy—which set those favoring a strong national government and one allied with the rich and well-born against states' rights advocates and those opposed to creating a wealthy aristocracy—sparked fervent political controversy. In the 1790s divisions intensified because of the French Revolution, which set those who favored a relatively stable aristocratic system and opposed the excesses of the Revolution against those who favored a broad-based democracy and opposed the efforts of European powers to restore the French monarchy.

By March 4, 1801, when Thomas Jefferson assumed the presidency in the first peaceful transition of power from one political party to another, the idea of political parties of differing views coexisting side by side had finally taken hold, and we have had political parties ever since. Although some have declined or disappeared—such as the Federalists in the 1810s and the Whigs in the 1850s—America's national political life has always been dominated by two major, broad-based political parties, with occasional splinter or third parties contributing new ideas to American political debate—such as the Populists of the 1890s, who proposed regulation of large businesses, the income tax, and direct election of senators. Also, political parties have become the basis for the organization of the Senate and the House, with each house having a fully developed party structure of majority and minority leaders and whips (that is, assistant leaders), and a combination of party membership and seniority to determine which senators and representatives chair or serve on which key legislative committees.

Political parties have been and are such an important part of the American electoral process that we have permitted, and in some cases insisted upon, government regulation of them. Every state has enacted laws that limit, to some extent, the freedom of political parties. In particular, most states regulate the processes by which parties nominate candidates for national, state, and local office and select delegates to national political conventions. The Constitution permits the states great latitude in shaping them.

Occasionally, however, some state or party practices have been found to violate the Constitution. For example, Supreme Court decisions in the so-called white primary cases of the 1920s into the 1950s struck down successive attempts to prevent blacks from participating in Democratic party politics in Texas, which at that time was a one-party state. The

Court said that excluding blacks from the Democratic primary—at first by explicit statutory language, later by more subtle means—effectively took away their right to vote. Thus it invalidated the white primary system as a violation of the Fifteenth Amendment, which had been ratified in 1870 expressly to give blacks equal voting rights with whites.

◆◆◆ How Was a National Election Day Established?

By statutes enacted by Congress in 1845 (for Presidential elections), in 1872 (for elections for the House of Representatives), and in 1914 (for senators, following the ratification in 1913 of the Seventeenth Amendment, which provides that senators be elected directly by the people).

Nothing in the Constitution requires a single national election day. Nothing in the Constitution requires that the presidential and vice presidential electors be elected on the same day as members of the Senate and the House of Representatives. In fact, nothing in the Constitution requires that members of the Senate and of the House of Representatives be chosen on the same day. And nothing in the Constitution requires that the presidential and vice presidential electors be chosen on the same day in every state. The only national election day mandated by the Constitution is the day on which the electors in each state, once elected, vote for president and vice president—for Article II, Section 1, of the Constitution provides that *that* day "shall be the same throughout the United States."

Essentially, the Constitution grants to Congress the power to choose when elections for federal office occur. Article I, Section 4, which deals with congressional elections, provides:

> The Times, Places and Manner of holding Elections for Senators and Representatives, shall be prescribed in each State by the Legislature thereof; but the Congress may at any time by Law make or alter such Regulations, except as to the Place of Chusing Senators.

And Article II, Section 1, which deals with the election of presidential and vice presidential electors, says:

> The Congress may determine the Time of chusing the Electors, and the Day on which they shall give their Votes; which Day shall be the same throughout the United States.

Because of Anti-Federalist charges during the ratification controversy that followed the Constitutional Convention of 1787—charges that Congress could use the authority granted by Article I, Section 4, to interfere with state election laws and procedures—the first Congress chose to leave elections for senators and representatives completely in the hands of the states. In 1792, Congress exercised its authority under Article II, Section 1, by enacting a law providing that presidential electors should be chosen in each state *within* thirty-four days preceding the first Wednesday in December 1792, and every fourth year thereafter. Thus, Congress did not require that the states choose the electors on the same day. It did provide, however, that the electors would vote for president and vice president on the first Wednesday in December.

In 1845, Congress changed the 1792 statute to provide that presidential and vice presidential electors be *chosen* on the first Tuesday after the first Monday in November. This was the first true national election day—but only the presidential election was involved.

By 1872, Congress had become fed up with the delays, haggling, and uncertainties in the ways states handled elections to the Senate and the House. In a case under the federal voting rights statutes in 1884, Justice Samuel F. Miller described and explained how Congress began to straighten out the mess:

> [T]o remedy more than one evil arising from the election of members of Congress occurring at different times in the different States, Congress . . . required all the elections for such members to be held on the Tuesday after the first Monday in November in 1876, and on the same day of every second year thereafter. . . .
>
> In like manner Congress has fixed a day, which is to be the same in all the States, when the electors for President and Vice-President shall be appointed.
>
> Now the day fixed for electing members of Congress has been established by Congress without regard to the time set for election of state officers in each State, and but for the fact that the State Legislatures have, for their own accommodation, required state elections to be held at the same time, these elections would be held for Congressmen alone at the time fixed by the Act of Congress.

These statutes fixed the elections for presidential and vice presidential electors and for members of the House on the same day—and, as Justice Miller pointed out, the states tended to fix their own elections on that day for convenience.

At that time, however, senators were still selected by the legislatures of the states. State legislatures had no fixed day on which they would select senators—and often it took days, weeks, or even months for a legislature to agree on a candidate, during which all other business was suspended. Public frustration with these delays and with charges that senators were frequently "bought" by large corporations that bribed state legislators eventually secured the ratification of the Seventeenth Amendment in 1913, which did away with the old system and gave the people the power to choose their senators by direct popular vote. In 1914, Congress enacted a law fixing the election day for senators as the same day used to elect representatives and presidential and vice presidential electors.

Thus, it appears that originally there was no set and definite plan to create a national election day on which all federal, state, and local elections were to be held. Rather, because of what might be called a case study in historical accident, our national election day (the first Tuesday after the first Monday in November) has evolved.

There has been talk in Congress in recent years about prohibiting national radio and television broadcast networks from airing results on election day until the polls are closed throughout the nation. Many politicians are concerned that voters in the West who find out how those in eastern states have voted may then decide not to bother voting at all. There have also been a number of proposals to expand the time of voting from one day to two or more in order to increase voter turnout.

◆◆◆ Can I Give as Much Money as I Want to a Political Candidate?

Not if the candidate is running for president, vice president, the Senate, or the House. Federal legislation restricts the amount of money that an individual can contribute to a federal election campaign. State, county, and city elections are another matter. Many, but not all, states have enacted similar provisions limiting contributions in local elections.

For most of the twentieth century, reformers have tried to abolish or restrict the influence of money in federal elections. Charges that ambassadorships and other government posts were "sold" to the highest bidder compounded public fears that elections could be determined by the size of a campaign war chest rather than by the vote of the people. Early federal statutes—such as the Corrupt Practices Act of 1925, passed in the wake of the Teapot Dome scandal during President Warren G. Harding's administration—proved ineffective. Many contributors and candidates simply ignored the limits on contributions and any requirements that they had to disclose their contributions. The issue reached a high point as the cost of mounting a successful campaign via television commercials rose to astronomical levels. Amid speculation that the 1972 election would be the most expensive in American history, Congress enacted the Federal Election Campaign Act of 1971. It amended the law two years later in light of the Watergate scandal's revelations that the Committee for the Re-Election of the President (Richard M. Nixon) had "laundered" campaign contributions to hide who gave the money and what it was being used for.

The Federal Election Campaign Act limits to $1,000 the amount that any individual can give to any candidate for federal office. It also limits the total amount of an individual's contributions to all candidates for federal office to no more than $25,000 in any given calendar year.

Reviewing the law in a 1976 case challenging it as a violation of First Amendment rights, the Supreme Court agreed that the law did curtail the ability of contributors to "speak" their political views through gifts of their money. But, it declared, "a limitation upon the amount that any one person or group may contribute to a candidate . . . entails only a marginal restriction upon the contributor's ability to engage in free communication." The Court said that the intent of the law—to prevent corruption in political campaigns—outweighed any "marginal restriction." On that basis, the Court upheld as constitutional the provisions of the law restricting contributions to candidates, and a similar rationale has been used to uphold state statutes.

As originally passed, the Federal Election Campaign Act placed limitations not only on *contributions* to candidates but also on *expenditures* on behalf of candidates. For example, the act limited even expenditures by a candidate from his or her own personal funds. The Court struck down that feature of the law because it cut too deeply into the rights of expression protected by the First Amendment. A candidate, the Court said, has a right to advocate his or her candidacy "vigorously and tirelessly." And, clearly, an individual's expenditure of his or her own money in his or her own campaign could not have a corrupting influence on the candidate. Indeed, the Court concluded that the use of personal funds tends to reduce a candidate's dependence on outside contributions and thereby counteracts the coercive pressures that attend contributions by others. So there's no limit on what candidates can spend on their own campaigns.

Separate federal laws prohibit federal employees from contributing to the reelection campaign of a federal officer. These laws are meant to eliminate any pressure that a federal worker might feel about giving to a superior's campaign.

In addition, Congress has enacted restrictions on how and how much corporations, labor unions, and other associations can give to those running for office. They can establish separate funds "to receive and make contributions on behalf of federal candidates," but the law limits their solicitations to stockholders, executive and administrative personnel, employees, or members of the organization. Direct corporate involvement in a federal campaign is prohibited—a ban that many states have also imposed on local elections.

◆◆◆ Can a Candidate Spend as Much as He or She Wants to in a Political Campaign?

Yes and no. A candidate for public office can generally raise and spend unlimited sums of money for a campaign. However, in a presidential campaign, a candidate who accepts federal campaign financing is restricted from spending over a certain limit.

The Federal Election Campaign Act of 1971 and companion legislation limited the amount that may be spent on a campaign for federal office by the candidate and by individuals or groups on the candidate's behalf. It even limited the candidate's expenditures from his or her personal or family resources to $25,000. The bill also strictly limited contributions to a candidate's campaign.

The federal law was soon challenged by a host of political leaders and groups, representing the full breadth of the political system, who saw it as an infringement on their First Amendment right to freedom of speech.

Generally, the Supreme Court upheld as constitutional the limitations on *contributions* to candidates and struck down as unconstitutional limitations on independent *expenditures*. In particular, the Court invalidated the law's provisions limiting what a candidate can spend out of his or her own personal or family funds and the ceiling on overall campaign spending. The Court declared:

> A restriction on the amount of money a person or group can spend on political communication during a campaign necessarily reduces the quantity of expression by restricting the number of issues discussed, the depth of their exploration, and the size of the audience reached. This is because virtually every means of communicating ideas in today's mass society requires the expenditure of money. The distribution of the humblest handbill or leaflet entails printing, paper, and circulation costs. Speeches and rallies generally necessitate hiring a hall and publicizing the event. The electorate's increasing dependence on television, radio, and other mass media for news and information has made these expensive modes of communication indispensable instruments of effective political speech.

Although Congress cannot force candidates to limit their expenditures, it can try to persuade them to do so voluntarily by offering them public funds. Currently, public financing is available only for presidential elections. The Federal Election Campaign Fund, established in 1971, offers major-party candidates large amounts of money if the candidate limits his or her total nomination expenditures to $10 million and general-election spending to $20 million. In 1980—the last presidential campaign for which final figures are available—the fund gave $29.4 million to both President Jimmy Carter and Ronald W. Reagan to cover expenses from the end of their parties' nominating conventions to election day.

A candidate is free, however, to refuse public financing and to raise and spend as much as he or she wants, which is what former Governor John B. Connally of Texas—a state with many wealthy political contributors—did in his 1980 bid for the Republican presidential nomination. But Connally's resulting image as a "fat cat" fatally injured his campaign in the eyes of many voters; his efforts secured him only one "multi-million-dollar delegate," and he dropped out of the campaign months before the nominating convention.

A relatively new phenomenon—a product of the heavy federal regulation of elections that began with the Federal Election Campaign Act—is the political action committee, or PAC. PACs are organizations set up to receive and spend funds to influence directly or indirectly the election of, or defeat of, candidates for office. Typically, most contributors have no role in deciding which specific candidates the PAC will support or oppose, what strategies and methods the PAC will employ, and the amounts of money the PAC will spend. PACs frequently raise money by direct-mail solicitations.

Sometimes PACs make direct contributions to the war chest of a candidate. The Federal Election Campaign Act limits such contributions—and any other expenditures in cooperation with a candidate or his or her agents—to a maximum of $5,000 for each candidate for federal office.

At other times, PACs make expenditures completely independently of the candidate—but in support of his or her candidacy. For example, in 1980 and again in 1984, two self-styled conservative PACs—the National Conservative Political Action Committee and the Fund for a Conservative Majority—spent millions of dollars, collected from over 200,000 donors, on radio and television ads to encourage Americans to vote for Ronald W. Reagan. The expenditures were "independent" in that they were not made in coordination with the official Reagan election campaign committee or any of its officials. Indeed, the efforts of both groups were at times viewed with disfavor by the official campaign committee as potential sources of harm or embarrassment.

Until 1985, federal law severely limited such independent expenditures by PACs on behalf of candidates such as President Reagan. But that year, as a result of a suit brought by those two groups (after they had been cited for violating the law) challenging the limits on First Amendment grounds, the Supreme Court struck down the statutory restrictions on such spending. In the justices' view, limits on truly independent spending on behalf of a candidate were more like family expenditures on behalf of a candidate—which cannot be limited—than contributions to a candidate's war chest—which can be limited.

Religion ===================================

◆◆◆ By What Right Can Congress Have a Paid Chaplain?

Although to many the practice of having a minister pray at the start of a legislative session seems to violate the principle of separation of church and state, the Supreme Court held in 1983 that it is constitutional.

The Court's decision came in a case involving the Nebraska legislature, which had hired a chaplain to recite a prayer at the beginning of each of its meetings. The Court upheld the practice, rejecting the contention of one legislator that it was a violation of the First Amendment. The majority of the justices based their reasoning primarily on history. Writing for the Court, Chief Justice Warren E. Burger pointed out that the First Congress, which proposed the Bill of Rights to the states, had itself authorized the appointment and payment of chaplains. "Clearly," the chief justice said, "the men who wrote the First Amendment Religion Clause did not view paid legislative chaplains and opening prayers as a violation of that Amendment."

Moreover, the chief justice pointed out that legislators are adults who are "presumably not readily susceptible to 'religious indoctrination,'" and that therefore there would be no "pressure" on them simply because a prayer drawn from a religion other than their own was being said by their colleagues. He thus distinguished the Nebraska case from practices that directly affect young children, such as opening a school day with a prayer—a practice that the Court has repeatedly struck down.

The chief justice was not troubled by the fact that the same chaplain, a Protestant, had served for sixteen consecutive years or that all his prayers were "in the Judeo-Christian tradition." The legislature had appointed him, Burger observed, because "his performance and personal qualities were acceptable." There simply was "no indication that the prayer opportunity has been exploited to proselytize or advance any one, or to disparage any other, faith or belief."

In a dissenting opinion, Justice William J. Brennan, Jr.—who was joined by Justice Thurgood Marshall—severely criticized the majority's use of historical evidence instead of the traditional test for determining a violation of the First Amendment's mandate that church and state be separate. In just about every case involving separation of church and state over the last two decades, the Court has used the so-called tripartite test, which strikes down any challenged government action unless it has (1) a clearly secular purpose, (2) a primary effect that neither advanced nor inhibited religion, and (3) a capacity to operate without entangling the government and religion. By using this test, Brennan argued that in the Nebraska case "any group of law students . . . would nearly unanimously find the practice to be unconstitutional."

Brennan also questioned the significance of the historical evidence relied on by the majority: "Legislators, influenced by the passions and exigencies of the moment, the pressure of constituents and colleagues, and the press of business, do not always pass sober constitutional judgment on every piece of legislation they enact." Moreover, he said, historical evidence drawn from two centuries ago could not properly be applied to a very different world today.

◆◆◆ Can a Nativity Scene Be Displayed on Public Property?

Yes. Although the crèche is one of the world's most inspiring religious symbols, the Supreme Court in 1984 said that Pawtucket, Rhode Island, could erect at taxpayers' expense a Christmas display, including a crèche, as part of the observance of the holiday season.

The Pawtucket crèche, on property owned by a group of local citizens, was erected by the city in cooperation with the local merchants' association. Writing for a five-to-four majority, Chief Justice Warren E. Burger said that the Constitution does not "require complete separation of church and state." Indeed, he went on, "it affirmatively mandates accommodation, not merely tolerance, of all religions, and forbids hostility toward any." Burger said that there was "an unbroken history of official acknowledgement by all three branches of government of the role of religion in American life from at least 1789"—including the establishment of Thanksgiving as a national holiday, the adoption of the motto "In God We Trust," and the annual proclamation of a National Day of Prayer. He argued that "an absolutist approach" in applying the Establishment Clause of the First Amendment, which forbids Congress from making any law "respecting an establishment of religion," is "simplistic and has been uniformly rejected by the Court."

The chief justice maintained that the display of a crèche was different from the posting of the Ten Commandments in a public classroom— which the Court had previously prohibited. That, he said, was done "purely as a religious admonition," while the crèche must be viewed "in the context of Christmas season"—that is, rather than being "a purposeful or surreptitious effort to express some kind of subtle governmental advocacy of a particular religious message," the crèche was merely a depiction of "the historical origins of this traditional event long recognized as a National Holiday." He likened it to "the exhibition of literally hundreds of religious paintings in governmentally supported museums."

Addressing the argument that "political divisiveness" would result if the crèche were displayed—with Pawtucket residents dividing along religious lines over whether the city should pay for erecting the crèche—the chief justice pointed out that the crèche had been displayed for forty years without friction.

In the Pawtucket case, it was the city that wanted to erect the crèche. That is not always the case. Sometimes a private group wants to put up a crèche in a public place. The question whether a city can be required to allow that was addressed later in 1984 by the United States Court of Appeals for the Second Circuit after Scarsdale, New York, denied the request of a group of local churches to erect a nativity scene in a village park during the Christmas season. Scarsdale had permitted the group to do so for many years, but in 1981 its board of trustees voted to deny the group's request. The board argued that it was required to deny the application in order to comply with the Establishment Clause of the First Amendment. However, the court of appeals ruled that because the park was a "traditional public forum," the village was barred by the First Amendment's Free Speech Clause from excluding from it *any* form of expression—including religious expression—just because of its content. Relying on the Supreme Court's ruling in the Pawtucket case, the court of appeals said that if Scarsdale were to "permit the display of a crèche in a traditional public forum at virtually no expense to it," its action could not be viewed as a violation of the Establishment Clause. Moreover, the court noted, the sponsors of the crèche had agreed to erect a sign making it clear that the display was sponsored by a private group. "No reasonable person," it added, "will draw an inference that the Village supports any church, faith or religion associated with the display of a crèche during the Christmas season."

The Scarsdale case was heard by the Supreme Court in 1985, but the Court divided four to four over the case (one Justice was ill when it was argued and thus did not participate in the decision). When the Court divides equally, the votes of the individual justices are not announced and no opinion is issued. The effect is that the lower court ruling is affirmed—that is, left standing—and the issue remains unresolved until a similar case comes before the Supreme Court.

◆◆◆ Why Can't My Child Pray in School?

But he can. Your child is absolutely free to pray in a public school—so long as he or she does it on his or her own. Nothing in the Constitution or in any decision of the Supreme Court stops a child from individually and silently reciting any prayer at any time during the school day. A youngster can recite grace before meals or pray silently for success on an exam. In fact, in places such as lunchrooms, where students generally are permitted to talk freely, your child can even recite a prayer out loud.

The question has a different answer, however, if a prayer is recited in an organized manner as part of an official school program. The Court ruled in 1962 that a school district in New York could not require recitation of a twenty-two-word "nondenominational" prayer composed by the state's Board of Regents because the practice violated the First Amendment's Establishment Clause, which says that "Congress shall make no law respecting an establishment of religion." The Court held that "the constitutional prohibition against laws respecting an establishment of religion must at least mean that it is no part of the business of government to compose official prayers for any group of the American people to recite as a part of a religious program carried on by government." The Court explained that the framers of the Bill of Rights had added the First Amendment to the Constitution because they realized that "one of the greatest dangers to the freedom of the individual to worship in his own way lay in the Government's placing its official stamp of approval upon one particular kind of prayer." The Court emphasized that it did not matter whether the prayer was "nondenominational" or that no student would be forced to recite it. The government's official sponsorship, it said, was enough to render the prayer invalid because the Establishment Clause is based on the premise that "a union of government and religion tends to destroy government and degrade religion."

A year later, the Court used the same reasoning to strike down a Pennsylvania law that required students to recite at least ten verses from the Bible at the opening of each school day. Individual students chose the verses, and the reading was followed by the recitation of the Lord's Prayer.

The Court rejected Pennsylvania's argument that the Bible readings were established to further the "secular purposes" of "promotion of moral values . . . and the teaching of literature." They were, the Court said, "religious exercises" prohibited by "the command of the First Amendment that the Government maintain strict neutrality" in matters of religion.

In 1985, the Court declared that an Alabama statute that authorized a period of silence at the beginning of every school day "for meditation or voluntary prayer" also was unconstitutional. Its sponsor had inserted into the legislative record a statement that the statute "was an effort to return voluntary prayer to the public schools." Taking into account the fact that separate legislation had already established a period of silence for "meditation," the Court concluded that Alabama had added the words "voluntary prayer" in order to "convey a message of State endorsement and promotion of prayer."

The decision in the 1985 Alabama case was based on the specific facts and history of the Alabama statute, however. A law creating a "moment of silence" that is enacted for legitimate purposes—rather than as part of an effort to circumvent the Supreme Court's prohibition of state-sponsored prayer in the schools—would probably pass constitutional muster. As the Court explained, "The legislative intent to return prayer to the public schools is, of course, quite different from merely protecting every student's right to engage in voluntary prayer during an appropriate moment of silence during the school day."

Though state-sponsored prayers are clearly prohibited in public schools, it is not clear whether students have the right to form voluntary prayer groups and meet during school hours. In 1981, the Court ruled that *college* students have the right to do so on school premises. The Court reasoned that the right to pray is part of the right of free speech. Because the college—the University of Missouri—had allowed other, nonreligious groups to meet on its property, the Court said that it could not discriminate against religious speech by banning religious groups from meeting under similar conditions.

Different considerations are presented, however, when *elementary-* or *secondary-school* students try to hold prayer meetings in public schools. Because they are younger and more impressionable than college students, and because they are in school by virtue of a state's compulsory attendance laws, there is a greater possibility that providing classroom space for the prayer group will be viewed as state endorsement of religion. For these reasons, the five United States courts of appeals that have considered the issue have said that the Establishment Clause forbids public high schools and elementary schools from providing classroom space for such prayer groups.

The Supreme Court now has before it the case of some Williamsport, Pennsylvania, high-school students whose school board refused to allow them to meet to pray on school premises during a regularly scheduled activities period. It remains to be seen whether the justices will take the same view of this issue as that taken by the circuit courts.

◆◆◆ Can I Be Forced to Send My Child to School If It's against My Religion?

Perhaps. You do have a constitutional right to send your child to an accredited private school—the Supreme Court has said so. And, if you have religious objections, a state probably cannot force you to send your child to a secondary school, as long as you provide some suitable alternative education. But the state may be able to force you to send your children to an accredited elementary school—even if, on religious grounds, you want to send the child to a *non*accredited religiously sponsored school or to provide instruction at home.

In 1925, the Supreme Court recognized the right of parents to send their children to an accredited private school when it overturned an Oregon statute that required parents of all children between the ages of eight and sixteen to have their children attend a public school. The Society of Sisters, which operated a number of Catholic schools, had challenged the law, saying that it would deprive parents of their right to send their children to a school where they would "receive appropriate mental and religious training." The Court found the Oregon statute "unreasonably interfered with the right of parents and guardians to direct the upbringing and education of children under their control." As the Court explained, "The child is not the mere creature of the state; those who nurture him and direct his destiny have the right, coupled with the high duty, to recognize and prepare him for additional obligations."

More recently, in a 1972 case, the Supreme Court considered a claim by members of the Amish religious sect that it was against the tenets of their religion to send their children to school beyond the eighth grade. Invoking the Free Exercise Clause of the First Amendment, they sought an exemption from Wisconsin's compulsory school-attendance law, which required all children to attend school until they reached the age of sixteen. The Amish insisted that by sending their children to high school they would "endanger their own salvation and that of their children . . . because the values they teach are in marked variance with Amish values and the Amish way of life." Moreover, an Amish child who has completed the eighth grade is expected, as the Court itself noted, to "acquire Amish attitudes favoring manual work and self-reliance and the specific skills needed to perform the adult role of an Amish farmer or housewife"—skills that can be "best learned through example and 'doing' rather than in a classroom."

In ruling for the Amish, Chief Justice Warren E. Burger, who wrote the Court's opinion, said that "a State's interest in universal education, however highly we rank it, is not totally free from a balancing process when it impinges on fundamental rights and interests, such as those specifically protected by the Free Exercise Clause of the First Amendment and the traditional interest of parents with respect to the religious upbringing of their children." In fact, Burger said, in view of the importance of the values protected by the Free Exercise Clause, "only those interests of the highest order and those not otherwise served can overbalance legitimate claims to the free exercise of religion."

Burger also pointed out that the Amish are not opposed to all education beyond the eighth grade, only to the conventional schooling provided by the ordinary high school. Indeed, he found that the Amish provided "an ideal vocational education" for their adolescents, an alternative to formal education that "has enabled them to function effectively in their day-to-day life under self-imposed limitations on relations with the world, and to survive and prosper in contemporary society as a separate, sharply identifiable and highly-sufficient community for more than 200 years in this country."

A variation on the Amish issue has developed in recent years. Some parents—Fundamentalists, for example—have religious objections to sending their children to any public school because, in their view, public schools teach "the antireligion of secular humanism." Some of these parents cite the Amish case and claim a right to send their children to a nonaccredited church school or to provide them with home instruction. By and large, those few state courts that have considered this issue have held that the state has the right to impose some requirements in these circumstances, but that the state may not do more than to ensure, by the least intrusive means possible, that an adequate education is being provided. For example, states may require that students of these nonaccredited schools take standardized tests to determine whether they are being given a proper education.

◆◆◆ Why Are Religious Groups and Charities Usually Exempt from Paying Taxes?

Because the Supreme Court has said that if your city, state, or federal government wants to exempt them, it may do so—and most have. Such exemptions are as old as the nation itself. The Court reasoned that religious groups could be exempted along with other charities because they benefit the community just as other nonprofit groups do. Moreover, it said, exempting them from taxes actually tends to reduce the involvement of government with religion.

In 1970 the Supreme Court upheld a New York statute that exempted religious groups from taxes on property they owned and used for religious purposes. For one thing, the Court said, New York had not singled out only religious institutions for the exemption but, "rather, it has granted exemption to all houses of religious worship within a broad class of property owned by nonprofit, quasi-public corporations which include hospitals, libraries, playgrounds, scientific, professional, historical, and patriotic groups"—all of which are "beneficial and stabilizing influences in community life."

Moreover, instead of "attempting to establish religion," the Court declared, New York was "simply sparing the exercise of religion from the burden of property taxation levied on private profit institutions." As the Court explained, "The grant of a tax exemption is not sponsorship since the government does not transfer part of its revenue to churches but simply abstains from demanding that the church support the state."

Although the Court recognized that the grant of exemption "occasions some degree of involvement with religion," it concluded that elimination of the exemption would "tend to expand the involvement of government by giving rise to tax valuation of church property, tax liens, tax foreclosures, and the direct confrontations and conflicts that follow in the train of those legal processes."

Finally, the Court pointed out that the practice of exempting institutions from taxation was deeply rooted in history and was an example of America's tradition of "benevolent neutrality toward churches and religious exercise generally so long as none was favored over others and none suffered interference." Congress, the Court noted, has always exempted churches from federal tax laws. That alone, it was quick to say, does not mean that Congress is right: "No one acquires a vested or protected right in violation of the Constitution by long use, even when that span of time covers our entire national existence and indeed predates it." But, the

Court declared, "an unbroken practice of according the exemption to churches, openly and by affirmative state action, not covertly or by state inaction, is not something to be lightly cast aside." It added that "nothing" in "two centuries of uninterrupted freedom from taxation has given the remotest sign of leading to an established church or religion and on the contrary it has operated affirmatively to help guarantee the free exercise of all forms of religious belief."

◆◆◆ Can a State Give a Tax Break to Parents Who Send Their Child to a Private School?

Yes. The Supreme Court said in 1983 that a state could, even if the school is a parochial one.

The Court's ruling came as a result of a case involving a Minnesota statute that permitted taxpayers to claim a deduction from gross income of up to $700 for expenses incurred for the "tuition, textbooks and transportation" of children attending elementary or secondary school. Several Minnesota taxpayers who brought the suit claimed that because nearly all the children whose parents benefited by the statute attended religiously affiliated schools, the statute had the effect of providing financial assistance to *sectarian* institutions and therefore violated the Establishment Clause of the First Amendment, which compels separation of church and state.

The Court, however, held that the statute had the *secular* purpose of "ensuring that the state's citizenry is well-educated." By educating a substantial number of students, it declared, private schools relieve public schools of a correspondingly great burden—to the benefit of all taxpayers.

The Court also said that the tax deduction did not have "the primary effect of advancing the sectarian aims of the non-public schools." The Court stressed that "the deduction [was] available for educational expenses incurred by all parents, including those whose children attend public schools and those whose children attend non-sectarian private schools or sectarian private schools." The fact that public-school parents were entitled to a deduction seems to have been important to the Court—even though, because a public education ordinarily is free, the significance of the provisions for aid to public-school parents was slight, covering such incidental costs as the tuition for a driver's education course. Nonetheless, because public-school parents were technically included in the program, the Court was able to say that the Minnesota law "neutrally provide[d] state assistance to a broad spectrum of citizens."

The Court also stressed that the aid at issue was given to the parents of the school children, not to the parochial schools or the churches they represented. On that basis, the Court concluded: "No imprimatur of State approval can be deemed to have been conferred on any particular religion, or on religion generally."

◆◆◆ Can I Do Anything My Religion Tells Me to Do?

No. Although the First Amendment protects your freedom to believe what you want, it does not give you a right to do anything you want to do in the name of religion. Obviously, you cannot practice human sacrifice. But there are other, less obviously unacceptable things you can't do either—even if your religion commands you to do them. For example, you can't practice polygamy.

The polygamy example is taken from an 1878 Supreme Court case. George Reynolds, a member of the Church of Jesus Christ of Latter-Day Saints (commonly known as the Mormon Church), was convicted under a law enacted by Congress for the territory of Utah that outlawed polygamy. He had two wives. Reynolds claimed that Mormon tenets required that he have more than one wife or face "damnation in the world to come." He said that the territorial law violated his right to exercise his religion freely. The Court disagreed. It said that the First Amendment does deprive Congress "of all legislative power over mere opinion," but it was still "free to reach actions which were in violation of social duties or subversive of good order." Polygamy, the Court declared, was an "odious" practice that has "from the earliest history of England . . . been treated as an offense against society." Laws, the Court added, are made to govern actions, "and while they cannot interfere with mere religious belief and opinions, they may govern practices. Suppose that one believed that human sacrifices were a necessary part of religious worship, would it seriously be contended that the civil government under which he lived could not interfere to prevent a sacrifice?"

State courts have upheld prohibitions on snake handling—even as part of a religious ritual. In 1976, the Tennessee Supreme Court upheld an injunction barring a pastor of the Holiness Church of God in Jesus from "handling, displaying or exhibiting" dangerous and poisonous snakes during his religious service. The pastor claimed that the practice was required by his religion "to confirm the Word of God." The court agreed that the handling of snakes was "central" to the man's faith, but it said that doing so "in a crowded church sanctuary, with virtually no safeguards, with children roaming unattended," posed "a clear and present danger so grave as to endanger paramount public interests."

More recently, in 1982 the United States Supreme Court upheld the conviction of a member of the Amish religious sect for failing to pay Social Security taxes. The payment of such taxes, the man said, is forbidden by his religion, which forbids participation in *any* insurance plan on the ground that such participation displays a lack of faith in Providence. He argued that his constitutional right to exercise his religion guaranteed him an exemption. The Court disagreed. It found that "it would be difficult to accommodate the comprehensive Social Security system with myriad exceptions flowing from a wide variety of religious beliefs." Moreover, the Court could find "no principled way . . . to distinguish between general taxes and those imposed under the Social Security Act." Thus, if it granted an exemption to the taxpayer in the Social Security case, the Court felt that it would be forced to grant exemptions to those who claimed they couldn't pay any taxes at all. The Court concluded: "Because the broad public interest in maintaining a sound tax system is of such a high order, religious belief in conflict with the payment of taxes affords no basis for resisting the tax."

◆◆◆ **Can I Be Forced to Accept Medical Treatment If It Is against My Religion?**

Usually not. An adult can refuse to accept treatment that is against his religious convictions even if the treatment is necessary to save his life. However, if the welfare of others is involved, courts have ordered lifesaving medical treatment and preventive measures such as vaccination, even when it violated a patient's religious beliefs. As the Supreme Court said in 1944: "The right to practice religion freely does not include liberty to expose the community . . . to communicable disease."

The issue often arises in cases involving members of the Jehovah's Witnesses, whose religious beliefs prohibit blood transfusions. For example, in 1965, the Illinois Supreme Court ruled that a Witness who, while in a hospital, repeatedly objected to taking transfusions for the treatment of peptic ulcers should not have been given the transfusions against her will. The court said that the First Amendment "protects the absolute right of every individual to freedom in his religious belief and the exercise thereof, subject only to the qualification that the exercise thereof may properly be limited by governmental action where such exercise endangers, clearly and presently, the public health, welfare or morals." The court noted that there were no minor children involved in the case and that no other person's health was threatened when the patient refused treatment; thus, there was no "clear and present danger to society." Accordingly, it concluded, "Even though we may consider appellant's beliefs unwise, foolish or ridiculous," it was improper to make her "accept medical treatment forbidden by her religious principles."

The court probably would have reached a different conclusion had the woman had minor children who were dependent on her—a point it considered in its ruling. That was the situation a year earlier in Washington, D.C., when the U.S. court of appeals there ordered that a transfusion be administered to another member of the Jehovah's Witnesses against her will. Pointing out that the patient was the mother of a seven-month-old child, the court reasoned that she had "a responsibility to the community to care for her infant." The government, the court declared, would ordinarily "not allow a parent to abandon a child," so "it should not allow this most ultimate of voluntary abandonments." Under some circumstances, the same logic would permit a court to order a patient who is pregnant to accept a transfusion if the transfusion is necessary to save the life of her unborn child.

A New York court added another factor in 1985 when it ruled that a pregnant woman who voluntarily enters a hospital to undergo surgery cannot instruct the hospital to withhold needed blood transfusions. That, the court said, would put the hospital "in an untenable position." A hospital, the court declared, "is not the patient's servant, subject to his orders . . . and to let a patient die runs counter to the reason for the hospital's existence."

◆◆◆ Can I Be Forced to Close My Store on Sundays?

That depends on where you live. In a series of cases decided in 1961, the Supreme Court held that the Sunday closing laws of several states are constitutional. But some states have never had a Sunday closing law, others that had one have repealed it, and still others that had one have seen it struck down by their state supreme court on the basis of their own state constitution.

The U.S. Supreme Court's view was clearly spelled out in a 1961 case dealing with employees of a large discount store in Maryland who were charged with violating that state's Sunday-closing law by selling a three-ring binder, a can of floor wax, and a toy submarine. The workers claimed that the purpose of the closing law—to create an "atmosphere of tranquility"—aided the conduct of church services and religious observance of the sacred day. But the Supreme Court concluded that nowadays such laws "seem clearly to be fashioned for the purpose of providing a Sunday atmosphere of recreation, cheerfulness, repose and enjoyment." In its view, "the air of the day is one of relaxation rather than one of religion."

Moreover, the Court declared, Maryland could legitimately seek "to set one day apart from all others as a day of rest, repose, recreation and tranquility—a day which all members of the family and community have the opportunity to spend and enjoy together, a day on which there exists relative quiet and disassociation from the everyday intensity of commercial activities, a day on which people may visit friends and relatives who are not available during working days." The fact that Maryland chose Sunday as the day of rest did not, the Court continued, make a difference: "People of all religions and people of no religion regard Sunday as a time for family activity, for visiting friends and relatives, for late sleeping, for passive and active entertainment, for dining out, and the like."

A companion case was brought by Orthodox Jews who, in conformance with their sabbath, closed their stores in Philadelphia from sundown on Fridays until sundown on Saturdays. They argued that Pennsylvania's Sunday-closing law therefore forced them to close their businesses for two days, penalizing them for exercising their religion. However, the Court found that while the store owners had to make "some financial sacrifice in order to observe their religious beliefs, still the option is wholly different than when the legislation attempts to make a religious practice itself unlawful." The Court said that "it cannot be expected, much less required, that legislators enact no law regulating conduct that may in some way result in an economic disadvantage to some religious sects and not to others because of the special practices of the various religions."

The Court also rejected the argument that the state was *required* to establish an exemption for those who observe Saturday as their day of rest. However, it indicated that states *could* establish such an exemption if they wanted to. "A number of states provide such an exemption," it added, "and this may well be the wiser solution to the problem."

Despite the Supreme Court decisions, some state courts have, nevertheless, invalidated their own state's Sunday-closing laws—often on the basis of the state's constitution. For example, in 1976 the New York Court of Appeals struck down that state's Sunday-closing statute on the ground that the classifications it established were unconstitutionally arbitrary and irrational. An employee of a pharmacy had been charged with selling a ceramic bank on a Sunday. In setting aside his conviction for doing so, the court concluded that the state law encompassed such a helter-skelter collection of exceptions—allowing the sale of things ranging from thoroughbred horses to soda water—that it "no longer possesses the requisite rationality in light of its avowed purpose."

◆◆◆ Can My Boss Make Me Work on My Sabbath?

Not unless your boss can prove that he or she is unable reasonably to accommodate your request for the day off. That's clear from both the Civil Rights Act of 1964 and federal court decisions that have followed it.

Under the Civil Rights Act of 1964, an employer may not discriminate against workers because of their religion—which is defined broadly to include "all aspects of religious observance and practice, as well as belief." And, the observance of the sabbath as a day of rest is one religious practice that is protected. Under the act, therefore, if an employee asks for his or her sabbath day off, the employer must accommodate the request unless the employer "demonstrates that he is unable to reasonably accommodate to an employee's or prospective employee's religious observance or practice without undue hardship on the conduct of the employer's business."

The constitutionality of this "religious accommodation provision," as it is called, has been repeatedly upheld by federal courts of appeals. The United States Court of Appeals for the Ninth Circuit, for example, concluded in 1981 that the provision has a legitimate secular purpose—"to secure equal economic opportunity to members of minority religions"— and that it does not impermissibly advance religion or excessively entangle the government with religion.

Earlier, in 1977, the Supreme Court considered a case brought against Trans World Airlines by one of its workers in Kansas City, Missouri. Larry G. Hardison, a member of the Worldwide Church of God who worked in a TWA department that had to be staffed twenty-four hours a day, seven days a week, ran into problems when he was asked to work on his sabbath (from sundown Friday to sundown Saturday). The collective-bargaining agreement with the union representing the department's workers included a seniority provision. Hardison did not have enough seniority to bid for a shift that would give him his sabbath off, however, and the union was unwilling to violate its contract. Moreover, TWA was unwilling to permit Hardison to work a four-day week because that would have meant paying someone else overtime to fill his job on Saturday. When TWA fired Hardison, he sued it under the Civil Rights Act of 1964. When the case reached the Supreme Court, the justices ruled that TWA was not required by the act "to carve out a special exception to its seniority system to help

Hardison meet his religious obligations." Moreover, the Court said, although the act did require TWA to "reasonably accommodate" Hardison's religious needs, it did not require it to pay "premium" wages to hire his replacement—the act did not require TWA to absorb that kind of cost. Thus, the airline, it said, had not unlawfully discriminated against Hardison for refusing to work on his sabbath.

On the other hand, a company that does not make a good-faith effort to accommodate a worker's sabbath and fires or forces him or her to quit is in violation of the act. For example, in 1978 the Court of Appeals for the Seventh Circuit found that an Illinois warehouse worker whose religious obligations prevented him from working on Saturdays was unlawfully fired for failing to work overtime on a Saturday. The worker, Rodges Redmond, was a Jehovah's Witness who had been appointed by his church to lead a Bible study group on Saturdays. The ecclesiastical appointment gave him a lifetime post with no leeway as to the time and day on which he could meet with his students. The court found that the company, the GAF Corporation, had not made any effort "to accommodate plaintiff's religious needs, and failed to demonstrate that it would suffer any undue hardship in accommodating the plaintiff." The court noted that GAF had six other warehouses from which it could obtain needed workers at no additional cost.

In 1985, the Supreme Court declared unconstitutional a Connecticut statute that provided that a worker could never be required to work on his or her sabbath. The Court said that the statute "arms Sabbath observers with an absolute and unqualified right not to work on whatever day they designate as their Sabbath," thereby imposing "on employers and employees an absolute duty to conform their business practice to the particular religious practice of the employee." Under the Connecticut statute, the Court reasoned, "Sabbath religious concerns automatically control over all secular interests at the workplace," with no leeway for "special circumstances" or "substantial economic burdens" placed upon the employer. "This unyielding weighting in favor of Sabbath observers over all other interests," the Court concluded, "impermissibly advances a particular religious practice" and thereby violates the Establishment Clause of the First Amendment, which forbids that.

The Court's decision in the Connecticut case does not jeopardize the protection provided by the federal Civil Rights Act of 1964. The Connecticut case dealt with a law providing for a worker's *absolute* right to observe his sabbath. The Civil Rights Act of 1964 requires employers to accommodate the religious practices of their workers *only* when reasonably possible to do so. Thus, while workers do not have an absolute right to take off from work on their sabbath, employers must try to take their religious needs into account whenever they can readily do so.

◆◆◆ Do I Have to Be Religious to Qualify as a Conscientious Objector?

No. The Supreme Court has made it clear that anyone who holds moral or ethical beliefs opposing war in general is entitled to be classified as a conscientious objector, provided that those beliefs occupy the same importance in his life as the belief in God does in the life of those who believe in God. But you cannot qualify as a conscientious objector if you only object to a specific war. All these principles were clearly established as the result of the Vietnam War, when a number of young men objected to serving in the armed forces, some of them even fleeing abroad or to Canada to avoid prosecution for evading the draft.

As early as the Revolutionary War, religious groups such as the Society of Friends (commonly known as the Quakers) refused to participate in the war because their religious beliefs forbade them to do so. Their refusals occasionally caused difficulties with the authorities, but no case ever reached the level of consideration on constitutional grounds.

In 1789, when James Madison proposed the amendments that became the Bill of Rights, he urged that one be adopted to protect conscientious objectors, but Congress ignored him. Thereafter, legislatures and courts unswervingly accepted the argument that was set forth in greatest detail in 1918 in a Supreme Court decision upholding the draft in World War I: that, under the law of nations as well as the Constitution, citizens of a nation have an absolute obligation to serve in the armed forces when called upon to do so, and that a person can avoid military service only if the government establishes a category of exemption for conscientious objectors and the person satisfies the definition. The draft law for World War I, for example, exempted ministers and theological students as well as members of certain religious sects "whose tenets exclude the moral right to engage in war." People in the last category, however, were required to perform some kind of noncombatant service, such as being medical orderlies.

The landmark case in this area, decided in the midst of the Vietnam War in 1965, came when the Supreme Court considered the claims of three young men who, while not claiming to be atheists, did not believe in God in the traditional sense. Two identified themselves as agnostic pacifists, the third as a deist of sorts and a pacifist. One of them, Daniel

Andrew Seeger, said that he preferred "to leave the question as to his belief in a Supreme Being open" and that his "religion" was a "belief in and devotion to goodness and virtue for their own sakes, and a religious faith in a purely ethical creed."

The Court accepted his belief as "sincere" and "honest." The draft law, however, granted conscientious-objector status only to those who were opposed to war based on "religious training and belief," and the law defined that crucial term as "an individual's belief in a relation to a Supreme Being involving duties superior to those arising from any human relation, but [not including] essentially political, sociological, or philosophical views or a merely personal moral code." Therefore, the law did not seem to cover Seeger and the others.

Nevertheless, the Court ruled that each of the young men was entitled to be exempted. It said that the statutory definition should be construed "broadly," that in using the term "Supreme Being," Congress was referring not to "the orthodox God" but rather to "the broader concept of a power or being." Moreover, the Court explained, a person who holds a "sincere and meaningful belief which occupies in the life of its possessor a place parallel to that filled by the God of those admittedly qualifying for the exemption" was also entitled to conscientious-objector status.

In 1970 the Court made even more explicit its holding that a person who does not hold traditional religious beliefs may qualify as a conscientious objector. Elliott Ashton Welsh, a pacifist and essentially an agnostic, specifically denied that his beliefs were "religious." Instead, he said, they had been formed "by reading in the fields of history and sociology." Nevertheless, the Court held that he was entitled to an exemption from the draft. All the draft law requires, it said, is that a person's beliefs "play the role of a religion and function as a religion" in his life. A deeply held moral or ethical code, the Court insisted, is sufficient to provide a basis for being considered a conscientious objector.

That moral, ethical, or religious objections only to a specific war, rather than to war in general, are not grounds for being considered a conscientious objector was made clear by the Court in 1971 in a case involving Guy Porter Gillette and Louis A. Negre, who said that the draft for Vietnam was unconstitutional because the war itself was unconstitutional. They argued that limiting exemption to persons who were opposed to war in any form was a violation of the Free Exercise Clause of the First Amendment. But the Court rejected that argument, saying that "valid neutral reasons exist for limiting the exemption to objectors to all war, and . . . the section [of the draft law that granted exemption only to such objectors] therefore cannot be said to be a religious preference."

Freedom of Expression ====

◆◆◆ Can I Say Anything I Want?

No. Freedom of speech is not absolute.

The First Amendment states that "Congress shall make no law . . . abridging the freedom of speech." Although the amendment appears to speak in absolute terms, and former Justices Hugo L. Black and William O. Douglas long championed the view that "no law" means precisely that—*no law*—a majority of the Supreme Court has always insisted that the "freedom of speech" which the Constitution permits is not an unlimited license to talk. Government may regulate speech in certain circumstances to protect important public interests. Thus, as Chief Justice Charles Evans Hughes observed, the government undoubtedly can stop someone from disclosing in time of war "the sailing dates of transports or the number or location of troops." Or, as Justice Oliver Wendell Holmes, Jr., wrote in one of his most famous opinions, the "most stringent protection of free speech would not protect a man in falsely shouting fire in a theater and causing a panic." Moreover, the Court has held that local, state, and the federal governments can, among other things, outlaw the sale and distribution of pornography in order to protect public morals. They can also require newspapers to pay for negligently, as well as intentionally, publishing a lie about a private individual that injures his or her good name and reputation, and they can outlaw deceptive and misleading commercial advertisements for the benefit of consumers.

Still, over the years the Supreme Court has marked off a large area of speech that government may not restrict. Its decisions have been strongly influenced by a broad vision of the central place of free speech in our constitutional system. Perhaps the most eloquent expression of that vision came in an opinion by Justice Louis D. Brandeis in 1927:

> Those who won our independence believed that the final end of
> the State was to make men free to develop their faculties; and that in

179

its government the deliberative forces should prevail over the arbitrary. They valued liberty both as an end and as a means. They believed liberty to be the secret of happiness and courage to be the secret of liberty. They believed that freedom to think as you will and to speak as you think are means indispensable to the discovery and spread of political truth; that without free speech and assembly discussion would be futile; that with them, discussion affords ordinarily adequate protection against the dissemination of noxious doctrine; that the greatest menace to freedom is an inert people; that public discussion is a political duty; and that this should be a fundamental principle of the American government.

The Court's acceptance of this vision is perhaps best illustrated by its decision in 1971 to reverse the conviction of Paul Robert Cohen for trying to convey the depth of his feelings about the Vietnam War by parading through the corridors of the Los Angeles County Courthouse wearing a jacket bearing the words "Fuck the Draft." Cohen's conviction rested entirely upon the offensiveness of the words he used to convey his message, but the Court refused the state's claim that, as a guardian of public morality, it had the power to "remove [an] offensive word from the public vocabulary." Writing for the Court, Justice John Marshall Harlan declared:

> To many, the immediate consequence of [freedom of speech] may often appear to be only verbal tumult, discord, and even offensive utterance. These are, however, within established limits, in truth necessary side effects of the broader enduring values which the process of open debate permits us to achieve. That the air may at times seem filled with verbal cacophony is, in this sense, not a sign of weakness but of strength. We cannot lose sight of the fact that, in what otherwise might seem a trifling and annoying instance of individual distasteful abuse of a privilege, these fundamental societal values are truly implicated. . . .
>
> First, the principle contended for by the State seems inherently boundless. How is one to distinguish this from any other offensive word? Surely the State has no right to cleanse public debate to the point where it is grammatically palatable to the most squeamish among us. Yet no readily ascertainable general principle exists for stopping short of that result. . . . For, while the particular four-letter word being litigated here is perhaps more distasteful than most others of its genre, it is nevertheless often true that one man's vulgarity is another's lyric. Indeed, we think it is largely because governmental officials cannot make principled distinctions in this area that the Constitution leaves matters of taste and style so largely to the individual.

Additionally, we cannot overlook the fact, because it is well illustrated by the episode involved here, that much linguistic expression serves a dual communicative function: it conveys not only ideas capable of relatively precise, detailed expression, but otherwise inexpressible emotions as well. In fact, words are often chosen as much for their emotive as their cognitive force. We cannot sanction the view that the Constitution, while solicitous of the cognitive content of individual speech, has little or no regard for that emotive function which, practically speaking, may often be the more important element of the overall message sought to be communicated. Indeed, as Mr. Justice [Felix] Frankfurter has said, "[o]ne of the prerogatives of American citizenship is the right to criticize public men and measures—and that means not only informed and responsible criticism but the freedom to speak foolishly and without moderation."...

Finally, and in the same vein, we cannot indulge the facile assumption that one can forbid particular words without also running a substantial risk of suppressing ideas in the process. Indeed, governments might soon seize upon the censorship of particular words as a convenient guise for banning the expression of unpopular views. We have been able ... to discern little social benefit that might result from running the risk of opening the door to such grave results.

◆◆◆ Can I Say Anything I Want about the Government?

Just about, because one thing is certain: The First Amendment bars government from attempting to silence its critics. As James Madison put it, "If we advert to the nature of Republican Government, we shall find that the censorial power is in the people over the Government, and not in the Government over the people."

Less than ten years after the First Amendment was adopted, Congress enacted the Sedition Act of 1798. The young nation was then on the verge of war with France, and the ideas generated by the French Revolution were widespread. The polemics between the Federalists, who were then in power and who opposed the spread of French revolutionary ideas, and the Republicans, who admired the Revolution's overthrow of the French monarchy, were bitter and occasionally even violent. The Sedition Act, an attempt by the Federalists to silence their political opponents, provided the following:

If any person shall write print utter or publish ... any false scandalous and malicious writings against the government of the

United States or either house of the Congress of the United States or the President of the United States with intent to defame the said government, or either house of the said Congress, or the said President or to bring them or either of them into contempt, or disrepute; or to excite against them or either or any of them the hatred of the good people of the United States . . . then such person being convicted shall be punished by a fine not exceeding $2,000 and by imprisonment not exceeding two years.

The Federalists vigorously enforced the Sedition Act, the victims in all cases being members of the Republican party, including the editors of the four leading Republican newspapers and three of the more outspoken Republican officeholders. The very first prosecution under the Sedition Act was brought against Matthew Lyon, a representative from Vermont, for publishing an article and a letter critical of the administration of President John Adams. Lyon was convicted, fined $1,000, and sentenced to four months in prison. While in jail, he was reelected to Congress.

The whole episode seems to have shocked the country and was an important factor in the defeat of the Federalists in the election of 1800. The Sedition Act expired by its own terms on March 3, 1801, and was not revived. President Thomas Jefferson pardoned the violators, and eventually Congress repaid their fines.

More than 160 years later, the Supreme Court decided the landmark case of *New York Times Co. v. Sullivan*. The case arose from an allegation by L. B. Sullivan, commissioner of public safety in Montgomery, Alabama, that he had been libeled by an advertisement published in the *New York Times* by the Committee to Defend Martin Luther King and the Struggle for Freedom in the South. Although the advertisement's text, which described acts of harassment and police brutality against civil-rights demonstrators, was inaccurate in minor points only, the jury found that Sullivan had indeed been defamed and awarded him $500,000 in damages.

Sullivan's suit was only the first of a number of libel actions filed by members of Alabama's white majority and aimed at punishing northern supporters of the civil-rights movement and, ultimately, at stifling the opposition of blacks to racial segregation. Suits pending at the time in Alabama courts against the *New York Times* claimed total damages of $5 million, and suits against CBS asked for total damages of $1.2 million.

The Supreme Court unanimously set aside the jury's verdict in the *Sullivan* case. It found "the central meaning of the First Amendment" in the theory of free speech that emerged from the controversy over the Sedition Act of 1798. The Court stressed the "profound national commitment to the principle that debate on public issues should be uninhibited, robust, and wide-open, and that it may well include vehement, caustic, and sometimes unpleasantly sharp attacks on government and public officials." The Court specifically ruled that the Sedition Act of 1798 had been unconstitutional and concluded that, because critical discussion of government ordinarily involves attacks on individual officers, libel suits by public officials had to be strictly scrutinized in order to prevent any government officials from using indirect means to silence their critics. To remove that threat, the Court ruled that public officials could not recover damages unless they proved that the person making the defamatory statement about them knew that it was false or acted with reckless disregard— that is, published the statement without checking or caring whether it was true or false.

◆◆◆ Do I Have to Salute the American Flag or Recite the Pledge of Allegiance?

Not if you don't want to. No government official or agency—including a school board—can force you to do either. The government cannot tell a person what to believe and cannot force a person to say something that he or she does not believe.

The First Amendment's guarantee of freedom of belief crystallized in a controversy that arose in the 1940s. In 1940, the Supreme Court upheld the action of the Minersville, Pennsylvania, school board in expelling Lillian and William Gobitis, who were members of the Jehovah's Witnesses, because they refused for religious reasons to participate in the flag ceremony. But, three years later, with the United States in the throes of World War II, the Court reversed itself, holding that the West Virginia State Board of Education could not require Walter Barnette's children, who were also members of the Jehovah's Witnesses, to participate in a flag-saluting ceremony. Alluding to the historical and contemporary struggles against totalitarianism, the Court rejected any notion that an American citizen could be forced to profess publicly any state of belief:

> [The ultimate futility of such] attempts to compel coherence is the lesson of every such effort from the Roman drive to stamp out Christianity as a disturber of the pagan unity, the Inquisition as a means to religious and dynastic unity, the Siberian exiles as a means to Russian unity, down to the fast failing efforts of our present totalitarian enemies.

It is not just religious objectors who have the right to refuse to pledge allegiance to the flag. Justice Robert H. Jackson, who wrote the Court's opinion and who later participated in the war crimes trials of high Nazi officials at Nuremberg, relied exclusively on the free-speech provisions of the First Amendment and did not invoke at all the religion clauses. He declared:

> If there is any fixed star in our constitutional constellation, it is that no official, high or petty, can prescribe what shall be orthodox in politics, nationalism, religion, or other matters of opinion or force citizens to confess by word or act their faith therein.

Thus, in 1977, the Supreme Court ruled that George and Maxine Maynard of New Hampshire had the right to cover up with tape the motto "Live Free or Die" that the state imprinted on its license plates. The Court said that the couple could not be forced to use their automobile to help the state disseminate a message that was repugnant to their personal beliefs. Although it considered the requirement to be a less serious infringement upon personal liberty than West Virginia's law requiring children to salute the flag, the Court concluded nonetheless that New Hampshire's law invaded "the sphere of intellect and spirit" that the Constitution puts beyond government control.

◆◆◆ Can I Burn the American Flag?

No. Almost all states have enacted laws making desecration of the flag a crime, and in 1968 Congress barred anyone from knowingly casting contempt upon an American flag by publicly mutilating, defacing, defiling, burning, or trampling it. The statute was prompted by a number of flag-burning incidents during protests against the Vietnam War and was intended to apply not only within the United States but also to acts of desecration by American citizens abroad.

For some people, the flag represents values and policies that are abhorrent. For the great majority of Americans, however, it is a symbol of patriotism, of pride in our history, and of the sacrifices and valor of the millions of Americans who have fought and died defending the nation. Thus, the United States has an important interest in preserving the national flag as an unalloyed, untainted symbol of national unity.

Often in times of national stress the American flag becomes a target for those who want to make a symbolic attack on the United States or its policies. But courts have ruled that the First Amendment does not give protestors the right to burn or mutilate the flag as a means of expressing their anger at or rejection of the United States. However, at the same time, precisely because it is a national symbol, the government cannot limit its use only to those who agree with American policies. That appears to be the conclusion of a case in which the Supreme Court reversed the conviction of Harold Spence, a college student, who attached a peace symbol to an American flag and hung the flag upside down from the window of his apartment soon after the American invasion of Cambodia and the shooting and killing of protesting students at Kent State University in Ohio in 1970. Spence did not permanently disfigure or destroy the flag. He created the peace symbol with masking tape, which could be easily removed, and used the flag in just about the way that flags have always been used as a means to convey ideas. (Flying a flag upside down is a traditional custom when a nation is in grave danger; it is derived from the practice of flying a ship's flag upside down as an emergency signal and call for help.) As Spence insisted, his purpose was to associate the American flag with peace instead of war and violence. The Court accepted Spence's explanation and concluded that the First Amendment protected his right to use the flag as he had.

◆◆◆ Do I Enjoy the Same Right of Free Speech as Any Other Citizen If I Work for the Government?

No. If you are one of the more than 15 million municipal, state, and federal workers in the United States today, you can be fired for participating in partisan political campaigns and in some circumstances for publicly criticizing your employer, and you can be required to take an oath to support the Constitution as a condition of your employment.

The Hatch Act, which Congress passed in 1934 and amended in 1940, and its state and local counterparts drastically limit the participation of public employees in political campaigns. Elected officials and persons in obviously political posts are generally free from the restrictions of these laws, which apply to ordinary "nonpolitical" civil servants, whose rights are strictly limited. For example, a government worker can register and vote in any election but may not solicit votes for a candidate, speak at a political rally in favor of or in opposition to a candidate, or allow his or her name to be used in campaign literature endorsing a candidate. A government employee can belong to a political party but may not run for party office, solicit funds for the party, or be a delegate to a party convention.

The Supreme Court has ruled that these limitations are reasonable. Writing in 1973, Justice Byron R. White maintained that "partisan political activities by federal employees must be limited if the Government is to operate effectively and fairly, elections are to play their proper part in representative government, and employees themselves are to be sufficiently free from improper influences." White pointed out that the Hatch Act's restrictions are "not aimed at particular parties, groups or points of view, but apply equally to all partisan activities."

Still, there is reason for skepticism about the necessity of such severe limits, and in recent years a number of states have largely removed restrictions on their employees' exercise of rights of political participation. In Alabama, for example, government workers can engage in politics while not on the job. Indiana's employees have the same right, as long as their activities do not interfere with the performance of their duties.

The Supreme Court has also recognized that sometimes a government employee can be disciplined for saying something that a citizen who is not an employee would have a perfect right to say. Still, the First Amendment does give a significant measure of protection to the speech of government employees. We have come a long way since 1892, when Oliver Wendell Holmes, Jr., who was then chief justice of the Massachusetts Supreme Judicial Court, said that a New Bedford, Massachusetts, policeman could be fired because he "may have a constitutional right to talk politics, but he has no constitutional right to be a policeman." In a 1968 case, the U.S. Supreme Court ruled that Marvin Pickering, a schoolteacher in Will County, Illinois, was illegally fired for writing a letter to a local newspaper criticizing the school board, particularly for spending funds on athletic programs at the expense of educational programs.

Yet the Court has also made it clear that a government worker's speech is not protected if it compromises the ability of government to act. For example, a worker cannot publicly accuse his or her immediate supervisor or fellow workers of corruption if that would destroy the kind of close, harmonious relationship within an office that is often essential to getting a job done. And a worker has no right to make public individual grievances that do not involve issues of "public concern."

Individuals may also be required to take an oath before they get a government job, but the Court has demanded that the words of the oath not infringe upon individual rights of belief or association. During the so-called McCarthy Era, named for the Wisconsin senator who led an anti-Communist "witch-hunt" during the late 1940s and early 1950s, public anxiety over Communist subversion, fueled in part by the cold war with the Soviet Union, prompted all levels of government to adopt security programs to identify and remove "subversives" from government jobs. At issue was an employee's "fitness" for a job as measured by his or her political views, associations, and activities. But the Supreme Court after years of struggling with the issue came to the conclusion that such oaths could not be required. An individual cannot be forced as a condition of public employment to disclaim belief in the overthrow of our institutions of government or to disclaim membership in an organization such as the Communist party as long as the individual does not embrace its unlawful aims. What the government can require from the worker is an oath addressed to the future that swears that he or she will not use illegal force to change our constitutional system.

◆◆◆ Can the Government Stop a Newspaper from Publishing Something?

Rarely, if ever, can the government stop the presses. The First Amendment was intended to prevent the government from adopting a system of *prior restraint* similar to the old English licensing system under which nothing could be printed without the approval of the state or church authorities.

The rule that prior restraints are assumed to be invalid did not become a working rule of constitutional law until 1931 in the case of *Near v. Minnesota.* That case arose from a move by County Attorney Floyd Olson to have the *Saturday Press,* a Minneapolis weekly published by Jay Near, declared a public nuisance. The issues of the paper that provoked Olson's move contained shrill and bigoted comments about Jews and blacks and exaggerated charges that law-enforcement officials were in collusion with gangsters and racketeers. A Minnesota court perpetually enjoined Near from issuing "any publication whatsoever which is a malicious, scandalous, or defamatory newspaper." The practical effect of the injunction was that Near, in order to avoid the risk of summary punishment for contempt of the court's order, had to clear material in advance with the judge. However, the Supreme Court, in a five-to-four decision, set aside the injunction.

Writing for the majority, Chief Justice Charles Evans Hughes held the injunction invalid as a prior restraint: "The liberty of the press, historically considered and taken up by the Federal Constitution, has meant, principally although not exclusively, immunity from previous restraints or censorship." It didn't matter that the *Saturday Press* was a scandal sheet and Jay Near was a not very scrupulous editor. "The fact that the liberty of the press may be abused by miscreant purveyors of scandal does not make any less necessary the immunity of the press from previous restraints," Hughes wrote.

Forty years after that case, President Richard M. Nixon asked federal judges in New York and Washington to enjoin the *New York Times* and the *Washington Post* from the continued publication of the *Pentagon Papers*, a highly secret government history of the formulation of American policy in Vietnam, including military operations and secret diplomatic negotiations. The government claimed that its publication would prolong the war, strain relations with our allies, and hinder negotiations with our enemies. However, the Supreme Court ruled that these claims would not support an injunction against publication. A majority of the justices were not persuaded that the government had shown with sufficient certainty that publishing the *Papers* would injure the national interest. Without such a certainty, they said, the government could not justify a prior restraint.

Nevertheless, the government was able to obtain court orders to prevent *The Progressive* magazine from publishing an article entitled "The H-Bomb Secret: How We Got It, Why We're Telling It." The Atomic Energy Act of 1954 prohibits the communication to any nonauthorized person of technical data about nuclear weapons that could be "utilized to injure the United States or to secure an advantage to any foreign nation." The government claimed that *The Progressive's* article contained at least a core of information that had not previously been published, together with a comprehensive, accurate, and detailed description of how to construct and use a thermonuclear weapon, which would be extremely useful to a nation that was seeking a thermonuclear capability. Understandably, U.S. District Judge Robert Warren issued the orders restraining the publication because it is difficult to argue with the logic that First Amendment rights should be subordinated, at least temporarily, when the alternative is the possibility of a nuclear catastrophe. As Warren observed: "You can't speak freely when you're dead." Still, the episode was unsettling because no appellate court was ever given the opportunity to review the lower court's decision. Six months after it began, the government withdrew its attempt to block publication when it became apparent that more than a dozen earlier articles had contained some or all of the allegedly "secret" material and that Dr. Edward Teller, often described as "the father of the H-Bomb," probably gave away the "secret" years ago in an article for the *Encyclopaedia Americana.*

◆◆◆ Can Reporters Be Forced to Disclose Their Sources?

Yes. A judge can order a reporter to disclose the identity of a confidential informant and may have to issue such an order if the informant's name is necessary to give a criminal defendant a chance to present an effective defense.

Every person has a duty, subject to rare exceptions, to give evidence required for the administration of justice. That is what the Supreme Court told President Richard M. Nixon when it required him to produce the Watergate tapes for a federal grand jury in 1974, and that is what the Court told three journalists in 1972. The reporters were Paul Branzburg of the *Louisville* (Ky.) *Courier-Journal*, who wrote two stories about illegal drug trafficking in Louisville; Paul Pappas, a newsman and photographer for a New Bedford, Massachusetts, television station who was at the headquarters of the Black Panthers just before an expected police raid; and Earl Caldwell, a reporter for the *New York Times* who covered various activities of the Black Panthers and other radical black groups on the West Coast. All three men refused to tell grand juries the names of confidential sources they had used in preparing their stories, claiming that the First Amendment gave them the right to refuse. They argued that important sources of information would dry up if journalists could be compelled to reveal the identities of confidential informants, to the detriment of the public's right to know. Nonetheless, the Supreme Court ruled, though only by a bare majority, that the three reporters had to answer the grand juries' questions. The Court did not rule that judges must always force news reporters to disclose their sources, but held instead that judges had to decide, on a case-by-case basis, which interest was more important, society's interest in prosecuting a crime or its interest in the free flow of information.

Still, many news reporters have felt so strongly that they had to protect their sources that they have been willing to go to jail rather than comply with court orders to disclose them. In one case, William T. Farr spent five days in jail for contempt of court after he refused to disclose confidential sources for a news story he wrote for the Los Angeles *Herald Examiner* on the Charles Manson murder trial in 1975. In another case that year, four reporters for the *Fresno* (Calif.) *Bee* were jailed for indeterminate sentences for refusing to disclose how they had obtained a grand-jury transcript.

The press has strongly urged legislatures to adopt statutes establishing a reporter's privilege akin to the historic privilege that protects confidential communications between a husband and wife or between a doctor and patient. Although the press has not succeeded in persuading Congress to act, more than half the states have passed so-called shield laws, which bar judges in many circumstances from ordering journalists to reveal confidential sources. In 1978, New Jersey's shield law became the focus of a nationwide controversy after the *New York Times* published a series of articles alleging that a New Jersey physician, identified only as "Dr. X," had poisoned several hospital patients. When the doctor was later tried for murder, his lawyers subpoenaed Myron Farber, the *Times*'s reporter on the story, to testify, demanding that he disclose his source and produce his notes. Farber refused, citing the shield law, but still was imprisoned for contempt of court. The New Jersey Supreme Court ruled that Farber had to cooperate because the protection of the shield law must give way when necessary to preserve a criminal defendant's Sixth Amendment right to a fair trial. At the same time, the court established some guidelines for judges confronted with the same problem in future cases. A reporter, the New Jersey court insisted, is entitled to a preliminary determination that the information sought by the defendant is "material and relevant to the defense, that it could not be secured from any less intrusive source, and that the defendant had a legitimate need to see and otherwise use it."

As the shield laws illustrate, the news media may sometimes enjoy a special status in the law, but not as a matter of constitutional right. The Supreme Court has consistently rejected claims that the freedom "of the press" guaranteed by the First Amendment grants greater rights to the press than the freedom "of speech" clause grants to individual citizens. From the viewpoint of the First Amendment, an individual distributing pamphlets in the street or making a speech at a town meeting enjoys the same rights of free expression as the mass media in this country—no more and no less.

◆◆◆ Can Reporters Be Barred from Covering a Criminal Trial?

Yes, but only under certain circumstances. A judge cannot keep reporters, or the general public for that matter, out of the courtroom unless it is necessary to protect the defendant's right to a fair trial or unless it is important to close the courtroom for some other compelling reason. And, while a judge may close a courtroom, he or she cannot issue a *gag order* that bars the press altogether from publishing stories about the case.

The Sixth Amendment's guarantee of "the right to a speedy and public trial, by an impartial jury" was a response to the sixteenth- and seventeenth-century English practice of conducting political trials out of the public eye—for example, in the Court of Star Chamber. An open trial is intended to ensure that the prosecutor, judge, and jury act legally and that the public can see that a defendant's rights are protected and that justice is done. Occasionally, however, it is hard to have both a public and a fair trial. In notorious cases, the glare of publicity can make it difficult to impanel a jury that has not in some sense already heard of the crime and judged the defendant guilty or innocent. These situations force on the courts the difficult task of choosing between a defendant's rights under the Sixth Amendment to a fair and impartial trial and a reporter's rights under the First Amendment—a conflict often referred to as "fair trial versus free press."

Although there have been a goodly number of sensational trials in the nation's history that have attracted extensive press attention, the first case posing the dilemma of fair trial versus free press to reach the Supreme Court was the conviction of Dr. Sam Sheppard for murdering his wife. In 1966, the Court reversed his conviction on the ground that the news media's hostile and distorted coverage of the case and the trial effectively declared Sheppard guilty in the eyes of the public, made the trial a mockery, and destroyed his Sixth Amendment rights. A trial judge, the Court insisted, has not only the power but also the duty to take "strong measures to insure that the balance is never weighed against the accused."

The specter of the "Dr. Sam" trial, which the Court described as a "Roman holiday," has overshadowed all the Court's later decisions. For example, following the Court's directive about avoiding harmful prejudice, a Nebraska judge issued a gag order in a notorious mass-murder case. It barred the news media from reporting on the suspect's confessions, admissions, or any other information strongly suggesting his guilt. In 1976, the case reached the Supreme Court, which unanimously struck down the gag order as a prior restraint on speech. Writing for the Court, Chief Justice Warren E. Burger found that the order was not justified by the facts of the case. However, Justices William J. Brennan, Jr., Potter Stewart, and Thurgood Marshall went further in a concurring opinion. They urged an absolute ban on gag orders, and in effect, the decision in that case has guaranteed that information about a criminal trial may not be suppressed, that the media may publish any facts about a case that they know.

As a result, trial judges turned instead to the use of orders closing pretrial hearings and trials. When this issue reached the Supreme Court in 1979—in a case involving a murder trial in Rochester, New York—the justices upheld by a narrow vote a trial judge's order barring the public and press from a pretrial hearing into the question whether the jury at the trial would be permitted to hear evidence of a confession allegedly made by the defendant. As the justices noted, the prosecution, the defense, and the trial judge all agreed on the need for the order and on the fact that nothing short of closing the pretrial hearing could safeguard the defendant's right to a fair trial.

The following year, the Court—in a case brought by a Richmond, Virginia, newspaper—dealt with a related question: whether the right of the press and the public to attend a criminal trial itself (as opposed to a pretrial hearing held in connection with the trial) is guaranteed by the Constitution. By a vote of seven to one, the Court said that it was, declaring as follows:

> Subject to the traditional time, place, and manner restrictions, streets, sidewalks, and parks are places traditionally open, where First Amendment rights may be exercised; a trial courtroom also is a public place where the people generally—and the representatives of the media—have a right to be present, and where their presence historically has been thought to enhance the integrity and quality of what takes place.

The Court did go on to note, however, that there could be certain, rare circumstances when a trial judge could close even a trial, or a part of a trial, to the public to guarantee a defendant's right to an impartial verdict. However, the justices felt the *Richmond Newspapers* case was not one where the circumstances justified closing the trial.

Subsequent Supreme Court cases have reaffirmed the right of the press and the public to attend criminal trials. In a 1982 case brought by the *Boston Globe*, the Court struck down a Massachusetts law that required the exclusion of the press and the general public from the courtroom during the testimony of a minor who had allegedly been the victim of a sex offense. Reporters for the *Boston Globe*, seeking to cover the trial of a person charged with having raped three young girls, had been barred from witnessing the testimony of the children. The Court invalidated the Massachusetts law because the exclusion of the press was mandatory— though the justices did leave open the possibility that under appropriate circumstances and in individual cases trial courts could exclude the press and public during the testimony of minors.

Two years later, a trial judge in Riverside County, California, closed the court to the public and to reporters from the Press Enterprise Company during the examination of prospective jurors for the trial of a defendant charged with the rape and murder of a teenage girl. The judge was trying to protect the privacy of the jurors and to ensure their candid answers to questions asked as part of the examination. When the case got to the

Supreme Court the justices held that the public and the press have a right to be present when jurors are questioned and selected for a criminal trial. As in both the *Richmond Newspapers* and the *Globe* cases, however, the Court did not hold the right of public access to this part of a trial to be absolute: "Closed proceedings, although not absolutely precluded, must be rare and only for cause shown that outweighs the value of openness." Chief Justice Warren E. Burger elaborated: "The presumption of openness may be overcome only by an overriding interest based on findings that closure is essential to preserve higher values and is narrowly tailored to serve that interest. The interest is to be articulated along with findings specific enough that a reviewing court can determine whether the closure order was properly entered."

The Individual ════════════════════════

◆◆◆ Do I Have the Right to Die?

There's no clear-cut answer to this question. But while the Supreme Court has yet to rule on it, some state courts have said that terminally ill patients—whose lives are so racked by suffering that death is preferable to continuing medical care—have a right to refuse life-sustaining treatment.

The decision to let a patient "die with dignity" is a complex and troubling one and has divided society and the medical profession. The most important, and noted, case involving the right to die concerned a twenty-one-year-old New Jersey woman, Karen Anne Quinlan, who lapsed into a coma after consuming a combination of gin and tranquilizers in April 1974. All the doctors consulted by her family agreed that she had suffered irreversible brain damage and was "brain-dead"—that is, EEG readings showed no brain activity—with no chance of recovery.

Quinlan's doctors refused her parents' plea to remove their daughter from a respirator so that she could "die with dignity." So the parents sued in New Jersey Superior Court to obtain a court order directing that the respirator be disconnected. The court denied the parents' application, but the New Jersey Supreme Court reversed the decision in 1976 and granted the request.

The New Jersey Supreme Court based its decision on a new interpretation of the right to privacy. It balanced Karen Quinlan's interest in having the machine turned off against the state's interest in preserving life, deciding in her favor. The court appointed Quinlan's father as her legal guardian and gave him sole authority to decide his daughter's fate. Removing Quinlan from the respirator would not be a criminal act, even if Quinlan died as a result, the court ruled, because her death "would not be homicide, but rather expiration from existing natural causes." Quinlan was removed from the respirator, but lived for nearly ten years before dying in June 1985 without ever regaining consciousness.

The year that Karen Quinlan died, 1985, the New Jersey Supreme Court decided yet another important case involving the right to die. Claire C. Conroy, an eighty-four-year-old mentally incompetent nursing-home patient, was gravely ill and bedridden, with many serious and irreversible physical and mental impairments. She could be fed only by a tube that extended from her nose through her esophagus to her stomach. Conroy's doctors estimated that, even if treatment were to continue, she would die in at most one to two years. Her guardian filed suit for a court order to have the feeding tube removed to end her suffering. But by the time the case reached the New Jersey Supreme Court, she had died. Nonetheless, the court chose to consider the right-to-die issue on its merits, noting that the question involved was not moot because it arises repeatedly. Intent on offering guidelines for future cases, the court declared:

> We hold that life-sustaining treatment may be withheld or withdrawn from an incompetent patient when it is clear that the particular patient would have refused the treatment under the circumstances involved. The standard . . . is a subjective one, consistent with the notion that the right that we are seeking to effectuate is a very personal right to control one's own life. The question is not what a reasonable or average person would have chosen to do under the circumstances but what the particular patient would have done if able to choose for himself.

The court noted that it would be appropriate to consider any views that the patient might have expressed on the matter while competent and that the consideration of medical evidence bearing on the patient's condition, treatment, and prognosis is essential in deciding whether to discontinue treatment. If the patient's wishes are unknown, the court continued, treatment may be withheld if either of two tests is satisfied: First, is there some trustworthy evidence that the patient would have refused the treatment when competent, and do the burdens of the patient's life under treatment (specifically, unavoidable pain) clearly outweigh the benefits of that life (such as physical pleasure, emotional enjoyment, or intellectual satisfaction)? Second, if there is no evidence at all about the patient's wishes, do the burdens of the patient's life with treatment outweigh the benefits, and is the pain and suffering such that continuing the treatment would be inhumane? The court specifically rejected taking into account in any way "assessment of the personal worth or social utility of another's life, or the value of that life to others." The court also stressed that the decision maker should be extremely cautious about deciding whether one of the tests had been met before authorizing the end of medical treatment.

With differing results, courts have considered the issue of death with dignity in one other type of case—that of a convicted prisoner who chooses to starve himself to death rather than languish in jail. In 1982, the Georgia Supreme Court ruled that prison officials could not force-feed a death-row inmate who had decided to starve himself to death. The court ruled that the inmate's right of privacy, including the right not to have his medical condition monitored against his will and the right not to be force-fed, outweighed the state's interest in keeping him alive. On the other hand, in 1984, the New Hampshire Supreme Court ruled just the other way in the case of a prisoner serving a life sentence without parole. The inmate sought to justify his attempt to starve himself by asserting his rights of free speech and freedom of religion, his right to privacy, and his right under the Eighth Amendment not to be subjected to cruel and unusual punishment. The court rejected all these arguments but only considered the privacy argument in detail. The court held that the state's interests in maintaining an effective criminal-justice system, in preserving internal order and discipline in its prisons, and in carrying out its duty to protect the lives in its custody outweighed the prisoner's right to die with dignity.

◆◆◆ Can I Be Prevented from Remarrying Because I Owe My Previous Spouse Child-support Payments?

No. The Supreme Court has held that the Equal Protection Clause of the Fourteenth Amendment forbids a state from preventing you from doing so.

Marriage, the Court said in a 1967 case, is a fundamental right protected by the Constitution: "The freedom to marry has long been recognized as one of the vital personal rights." Traditionally, however, marriage has been regulated by the states, and most have laws that establish a minimum age for the couple, require some type of test for venereal disease, and prohibit a person from being married to more than one spouse.

The Wisconsin legislature went much further than these traditional regulations when, in 1973, it passed a statute that said that persons under an obligation to pay child support could not marry without first getting court approval. The court, in turn, could not give its permission unless the marriage applicants proved that they were up to date on child-support payments and that their children by previous marriages were not likely to become public charges.

In 1974, Roger Redhail was denied a marriage license by a county clerk because he had not complied with the Wisconsin law. As a high-school student in 1971, Redhail had fathered a baby girl for whom he was obligated to pay $109 a month in support. But, in September 1974, when he applied for the license, he had been unemployed for two years and was $3,700 behind on his payments. The child was receiving public benefits under a government program. The woman Redhail wanted to marry in 1974 was pregnant with his child, and he and the woman wanted to legalize their relationship before the child was born. When they were refused their license, Redhail sued, claiming the Wisconsin statute was unconstitutional.

When the case reached the Supreme Court several years later, the justices ruled that the statute violated the Equal Protection Clause because it treated people with child-support obligations differently from other people. Justice Thurgood Marshall's opinion for the Court stated that, because "the right to marry is of fundamental importance, and since the classification at issue here significantly interferes with the exercise of that right, we believe that 'critical examination' of the state interests advanced [is] required." Elaborating, he declared:

> It is not surprising that the decision to marry has been placed on the same level of importance as decisions relating to procreation, childbirth, child rearing, and family relationships. As the facts of this case illustrate, it would make little sense to recognize a right of privacy with respect to other matters of family life and not with respect to the decision to enter the relationship that is the foundation of the family in our society. The woman whom [Roger Redhail] desired to marry had a fundamental right to seek an abortion of their expected child [under the Court's decision in *Roe* v. *Wade* in 1973], or to bring the child into life to suffer the myriad social, if not economic, disabilities that the status of illegitimacy brings. Surely, a decision to marry and raise the child in a traditional family setting must receive equivalent protection.

The Court found that the interests served by the Wisconsin statute—furnishing the state with an opportunity to counsel the marriage applicant and ensuring the welfare of the children involved—were substantial, but that the statute unnecessarily restricted a person's right to marry. Wisconsin, the Court said, could employ numerous other means, including criminal penalties, to make sure that the payments were made.

◆◆◆ Can I Do Anything I Want To in My Bedroom?

You can't commit murder, of course. But as far as your sex life goes, you are free to do just about anything you want. With only a few exceptions, such as laws against incest or statutory rape, no government—local, state, or federal—can tell you what to do or what not to do.

That "right to privacy" is not spelled out as such in the Constitution. In fact, the word *privacy* is not used at all. However, the Constitution has been interpreted by the Supreme Court to spell out safeguards regarding an individual's right to privacy and independence in his or her personal life. In 1928, Justice Louis D. Brandeis, the earliest champion of such rights, spoke of "the right to be let alone—the most comprehensive of rights and the right most valued by civilized men." However, it has only been in the last two decades that the Court has defined the "right to be let alone" in any detail.

The Court's first decision defining the constitutional right to privacy came in 1965 in *Griswold* v. *Connecticut,* when the Court struck down a law prohibiting the use of contraceptives by married persons. Writing for the majority, Justice William O. Douglas declared that the "specific guarantees in the Bill of Rights have penumbras, formed by emanations from those guarantees that help give them life and substance." The "penumbras" of several of these guarantees, Douglas continued, create zones of privacy that therefore can be said to be drawn from the essence of the Bill of Rights as a whole. Douglas said that the zone of privacy has come to encompass various forms of freedom of choice, including marital decisions about having children and how they should be raised. To support the novel right to privacy that he was creating, Douglas pointed to several amendments that protect a person from unreasonable government intrusion in certain matters of personal concern. The First Amendment, for example, guarantees citizens the constitutional right to associate with whomever they like. And the Fourth Amendment protects their right "to be secure in their persons, houses, papers, and effects, against unreasonable searches and seizures."

Once established, the constitutional right to privacy became a primary basis for protecting freedom of sexual choice—especially in the privacy of the bedroom. But even in the bedroom, freedom of sexual choice is not absolute. The government has the clear right to outlaw types of sexual conduct that threaten interests important to society. This is the basis of laws against incest or statutory rape, for example. Moreover, states, invoking what they perceive to be a threat to traditional mores, have outlawed even sexual conduct between two consenting adults, where that sexual conduct is "nontraditional." And some courts have upheld the right of a state to punish those who choose to engage in nontraditional sexual activity.

For example, in 1976, without hearing arguments or giving reasons for its decision, the Supreme Court approved a lower-court ruling validating a Virginia antisodomy statute. Two male homosexuals had argued that the law could not be constitutionally applied to a male homosexual's "active and regular homosexual relations with another adult male, consensually and in private." The lower court refused to accept the argument that the right to privacy protected the men's conduct. It said that the Supreme Court's decisions on privacy dealt exclusively with "the privacy of the incidents of marriage," "the sanctity of the home," or "the nurture of family life." Homosexuality, in the lower court's view, was "obviously no portion of marriage, home or family life" and may be prohibited by the state "even when committed in the home" when "appropriate to the promotion of morality and decency." Even in light of the judicial affirmation of a state's right to outlaw sodomy, over the last fifteen years most states have repealed their antisodomy statutes. And, in 1985, the U.S. Court of Appeals for the Eleventh Circuit declared one of the remaining antisodomy statutes, Georgia's, unconstitutional—on the ground that homosexual relationships involve an "intimate association protected against state interference" by the Constitution. The court of appeals said that it did not believe the Supreme Court meant its summary action in 1976 to be the last word. We'll know soon if the U.S. Court of Appeals for the Eleventh Circuit was correct, because the Supreme Court is currently reviewing the court of appeals' decision.

Further evidence that a state can, to some degree, regulate freedom of sexual choice came in 1978, when a federal district court sustained the discharge of two employees of the Carnegie Free Library in Connellsville, Pennsylvania, for "living together in a state of 'open adultery.'" A male library custodian had left his wife and moved in with a female librarian after she became pregnant with his child. The library board fired both of them, saying that it did not want to appear to condone the extramarital affair and the child's birth out of wedlock. But not all courts have been willing to let the government intrude so far into the bedroom. Federal courts in Texas and Alabama have ruled that a school board that refused to hire an unwed parent as a teacher and one that fired an unwed pregnant teacher violated the constitutional freedom of those persons to conduct their sexual lives as they pleased. The Supreme Court's decision in the Georgia antisodomy case now before it may tell us more about the rights of couples to live in other kinds of nontraditional relationships like those in these cases.

◆◆◆ Can a State Prevent a Woman from Having an Abortion?

No, not unless the woman is more than six months pregnant. Her right to personal privacy—a right encompassed in the Fourteenth Amendment—protects her decision to have an abortion. The exception to that right comes in the last three months of her pregnancy, when it's possible that a fetus could live outside the womb. At that point, the state is considered to have a sufficient stake in protecting the fetus to justify its prohibiting an abortion unless the mother's life or health is at stake.

The landmark case in this controversial area came in 1973. Texas had passed a law making it a crime for a woman to have an abortion unless a doctor said that it was for the purpose of saving the mother's life. A pregnant single woman who was denied that permission sued the state. When the case—*Roe v. Wade*—eventually came before it, the Supreme Court declared the Texas statute unconstitutional. The Court based its decision on the Fourteenth Amendment, which says, "No State shall make or enforce any law which shall abridge the privileges or immunities of citizens of the United States; nor shall any State deprive any person of life, liberty, or property, without due process of law." The Court held that the term "liberty" encompasses a right to personal privacy and that this right guarantees personal rights that are "fundamental or implicit in the concept of ordered liberty." In a series of Court decisions dating from 1925 to 1972, the right to personal privacy had been extended to child rearing and education, procreation, family relations, marriage, and contraception. The Court's decision in *Roe v. Wade* in 1973 extended the right to cover a woman's choice to have an abortion.

In making its decision, the Court dealt with the thorny issue raised by those who later became known as Right to Life advocates. They insist that the fetus is a living being and has legal rights. The Court rejected that view, saying the fetus is not a person within the meaning of the Fourteenth Amendment and thus does not deserve protection under it.

Nevertheless, the Court did acknowledge that a state has the right to consider the health of the unborn child as well as the health of the mother, and can protect either, depending on when the abortion might be performed. According to its ruling, a state may not ban an abortion during the first three months of a pregnancy; the decision then is solely that of the woman and her doctor. But in the second three months, the state's interest in a mother's well-being becomes sufficiently compelling that a state may stipulate abortion procedures that "reasonably" relate to the preservation of her health. And during the last three months, a state—in the interest of protecting the unborn child—may actually forbid an abortion, unless the mother's life or health is in danger.

Thus far, the Court has resisted efforts by states or localities to impede a woman's right to an abortion. It has ruled that any law that "unduly burdens the right to seek an abortion" is unconstitutional. One such law was an Ohio statute that required a doctor to inform a woman seeking an abortion of the status of her pregnancy in anatomical and physiological detail, tell her about the possibility that the unborn child might live outside her womb after twenty-two weeks, cite the possible complications that could result from the abortion, and make available to her the names of agencies that provide information on birth control, adoption, and childbirth. In addition, the Ohio law required that all abortions performed after the first trimester be done in a hospital. The Supreme Court struck down all those provisions in 1983, saying that they set up significant obstacles that might prevent women who wanted abortions from getting them. The Court emphasized that a woman must be able to choose freely whether to have an abortion with the guidance of her doctor but without the interference of a state.

Moreover, the Court has ruled that a state may not require the consent of a parent or guardian even if the pregnant female is unmarried and a minor. (Who is a minor varies from state to state—from a child fourteen years old or under to a teenager who is eighteen or younger.) The state must allow her to have an abortion if she can prove to a court either that she is mature enough to make that decision or that the decision is in her best interest.

However, the Court has upheld as constitutional a Utah statute that requires a doctor to give notice to the parents of a fifteen-year-old girl before performing an abortion on her. In that case in 1981, the Court held that the teenager, who lived with her parents, was dependent on them and had not shown her maturity. Utah, it said, had a sufficiently compelling interest in requiring the girl's parents to be informed because that encouraged the girl to seek advice from them as well as gave them the opportunity to suggest possible medical advice.

As we go to press, the Supreme Court has before it two cases involving attempts by states to regulate abortions. In one, the justices are considering provisions of the Pennsylvania Abortion Control Act requiring (1) that women seeking abortions be given specific information describing what they are doing in having abortions, (2) that the abortion method most likely to result in a living fetus be used unless it would result in "significantly greater" risk to the mother, and (3) that insurers offer policies excluding abortion coverage at lower cost than comprehensive health-insurance policies. In the other case, the justices are considering sections of the Illinois Abortion Law requiring (1) that physicians who prescribe birth-control devices that (like the IUD) sometimes operate by inducing spontaneous abortions inform their patients that the device operates in that way, and (2) that the method of abortion used be that most likely to sustain the fetus without endangering the mother if the abortion is attempted at a time when the fetus has a reasonable possibility of survival. In both the Pennsylvania and the Illinois cases, the courts of appeals that reviewed the statutes found that they—like the Ohio statute that the Supreme Court invalidated in 1983—unconstitutionally put obstacles in the path of a woman seeking an abortion. The Supreme Court will now decide the issue itself.

◆◆◆ Does the Government Have to Pay for an Abortion If a Woman Cannot Afford One?

No. Although the Supreme Court has ruled that every woman has the right to have an abortion during the first six months of pregnancy, it has said that neither a state nor the federal government has to pay for abortions for financially needy pregnant women—even if the government would pay for the birth of the child.

Two key cases, decided within three years of each other, set the law in this area. In 1977, an indigent woman sued the state of Connecticut because its Medicaid legislation provided benefits for childbirth but none for abortions unless they were necessary to the mother's health. The woman said such discrimination encouraged poor people like herself to give birth rather than have an abortion. However, the Court found that encouraging childbirth over abortions was a legitimate state purpose. It also said that even though the Connecticut law did not remove economic barriers to having an abortion, it did not otherwise restrict having one: "Although the government may not place obstacles in the path of a woman's exercise of her freedom of choice, it need not remove those not of its own creation. Indigency falls into the latter category."

Three years later, in 1980, another indigent woman sued the federal government, charging that legislation known as the Hyde amendment (named for Henry Hyde, a conservative Republican representative from

New York, who sponsored the legislation) infringed on her right to have an abortion. The amendment withholds funds for certain medically necessary abortions, even in the case of rape or incest, unless carrying a child to term endangers a woman's life.

The Court rejected this woman's claim, too. In so doing, it drew two analogies: first, to a person's right to attend a private school versus state funding of private schools, and second, to a person's right to use contraceptives versus a state's supplying contraceptives. The Court declared:

> Although the liberty protected by the Due Process Clause [of the Fourteenth Amendment] affords protection against unwarranted government interference with freedom of choice in the context of certain personal decisions, it does not confer an entitlement to such funds as may be necessary to realize all the advantages of that freedom.

The Court also refused to support the woman's charge that the Hyde amendment was discriminatory because it prevented the subsidizing of medically necessary abortions while allowing the subsidizing of medically necessary services generally:

> [T]he fact remains that the Hyde Amendment leaves an indigent woman with at least the same range of choice in deciding whether to obtain a medically necessary abortion as she would have had if Congress had chosen to subsidize no health care costs at all.

Moreover, the Court said, abortion is sufficiently different from other medical procedures to justify a distinction in funding, because "no other procedure involves the purposeful termination of a potential life."

◆◆◆ Can a State Stop Me from Buying a Contraceptive If I'm Unmarried or a Minor?

If you're unmarried, no. If you're a minor, probably yes. The Supreme Court has made clear that the constitutional right to privacy guarantees the freedom of married and unmarried persons alike to purchase and use contraceptives. What is not yet clear is what right, if any, a minor has to purchase such devices.

A little over forty years ago the Court acknowledged that, because marriage and procreation were fundamental to the very existence and survival of the human race, decisions about them deserve protection.

While this declaration did not explicitly proclaim a right of privacy relating to sexual matters, it did lay the foundation for the idea that decisions concerning the issue of procreation possessed certain constitutional significance. Then, in 1965, in *Griswold* v. *Connecticut*, the Court held that statutes banning the use of contraceptive devices restricted the right of married couples to make their own decisions about whether to have children, and that the statutes were therefore unconstitutional. The ruling reflected the Court's general view that everyone has the right to make certain personal decisions free of governmental restrictions.

Subsequent decisions have made it clear that no adult—married or single—may be prohibited from purchasing and using contraceptive devices or otherwise be subjected to undue interference with his or her decisions about procreation.

For example, in 1972 the Court invalidated a Connecticut statute that banned the distribution of contraceptives to unmarried persons because, the Court said, treating them differently from married couples violated the Equal Protection Clause of the Fourteenth Amendment. And, in 1977, the Court also struck down a New York law that prohibited distribution of contraceptives to persons over sixteen by anyone other than a licensed pharmacist and that banned completely the advertisement or display of contraceptives. However, the Court has recognized the authority of states to pass laws ensuring that any contraceptive device meets health and safety standards.

It is not clear whether a state can prevent a minor from purchasing a contraceptive. A different provision of the New York law involved in the 1977 case prohibited the sale or distribution of contraceptives to minors under sixteen. The Court invalidated this provision of the New York law, but the justices did not produce a majority opinion in the issue. Justices William J. Brennan, Jr., Potter Stewart, Thurgood Marshall, and Harry A. Blackmun wrote a plurality opinion that implies that minors do have a right to purchase and use contraceptives. They voted to strike down the New York law. Justices Byron R. White, Lewis F. Powell, and John Paul Stevens also voted to strike down the law, but on more technical grounds. Both Chief Justice Warren E. Burger and Justice William H. Rehnquist, who dissented, were for upholding the law. Rehnquist, in fact, submitted a heated opinion, invoking with passion the memories of the Framers of the Constitution. His words give some sense of the breadth of the right of privacy that the Court has created:

> If those responsible for [the Bill of Rights and the post–Civil War amendments] could have lived to know that their efforts had en-

shrined in the Constitution the right of commercial vendors of contraceptives to peddle them to unmarried minors, [it] is not difficult to imagine their reaction. . . . There comes a point when endless and ill-considered extension of principles originally formulated in quite different cases produces such an indefensible result that no logic chopping can possibly make the fallacy of the result more obvious.

◆◆◆ Can a Law-Enforcement Officer Break into My Home to Search for Evidence without a Warrant?

Generally not. That is precisely the type of government action that violates the Fourth Amendment's provision: "The Right of the people to be secure in their persons, houses, papers, and effects, against unreasonable searches and seizures, shall not be violated, and no Warrants shall issue, but upon probable cause, supported by Oath or affirmation, and particularly describing the place to be searched, and the persons or things to be seized." However, there are a few, limited exceptions to the warrant requirement—so there are some times when an officer may be able to search your home without a warrant.

One of the causes of the American Revolution was the claim of British authorities to be able to search colonists' homes without warrants or with what were called general warrants, which permitted an officer to search any home for any reason and seize anything he thought should be seized. So, James Madison and the other members of the First Congress drafted, as part of the Bill of Rights, the Fourth Amendment.

Under the Fourth Amendment, law-enforcement authorities—whether city, state, or federal—are ordinarily forbidden to enter and search your home unless you permit them to come in or unless they have a search warrant. The warrant is issued by a judge or magistrate who must first determine that the search or seizure is not "unreasonable." He or she weighs the intrusiveness of the search against the community's interest in preventing evidence from being removed or destroyed. The magistrate also must determine whether the law-enforcement officers seeking the warrant have "probable cause" to believe that they will find a suspect or evidence on the premises. This finding has to be based on more than guesswork or instinct—for example, it could be based on a tip from an informant known to the officer to be reliable. And certain specific provisos must be met. The warrant has to include a description of the place to be searched and the persons or things to be seized.

There are some circumstances, however, when law-enforcement officers can search your home without a warrant—for example, if they are in "hot pursuit" of a dangerous criminal who runs into your home, or if they have reason to believe that the evidence inside will be destroyed if they wait to get a warrant. But because the Fourth Amendment expressly requires a warrant, these exceptions are interpreted very strictly when the search of a home is involved.

If a law-enforcement officer searches your home without a warrant and the search does not fit into any of the exceptions to the warrant requirement, any evidence he or she finds cannot be used against you in a trial. And, as the result of a 1971 Supreme Court decision and federal laws nearly one hundred years old, you often can sue a city, state, or federal officer for an improper search and collect money damages.

◆◆◆ Can Anyone Tell Me That I Can't Read Something Because It's Obscene?

No. The government cannot ban the possession of obscene materials in private places. It can ban the production and distribution of obscene material, and it can prohibit sending or receiving such material—even through the mail. But, if you can obtain one, you're perfectly free to read or look at an obscene magazine, book, tape, or film in the privacy of your home.

The Supreme Court has made it clear that obscenity is "not within the area of constitutionally protected speech or press." That's a position it first took in 1957 and which it holds to this day. The difficult part—which the Court has faced with increasing frequency as the result of the revolution in sexual mores in recent years—is in trying to define what is obscene.

A number of justices have tried to do so. Writing for the Court back in 1957, Justice William J. Brennan, Jr., proposed the following test: "whether to the average person, applying contemporary community standards, the dominant theme of the material taken as a whole appeals to prurient interest."

Three other justices tried their hand at it in 1964. Justice John Marshall Harlan described obscenity as "any material which, taken as a whole, has been reasonably found in state judicial proceedings to treat sex in a fundamentally offensive manner, under rationally established criteria for judging such material." Chief Justice Earl Warren said that material is obscene when three elements are found: "It must be established that (a) the dominant theme of the material taken as a whole appeals to a prurient interest in sex; (b) the material is patently offensive because it affronts contemporary community standards relating to the description or representation of sexual matters; and (c) the material is utterly without redeeming social value." On the other hand, Justice Potter Stewart took a more practical approach, saying, "I shall not today attempt further to define the kinds of material I understand to be embraced within that short-hand description ['hard-core pornography']; and perhaps I could never succeed in intelligently doing so. But I know it when I see it, and the motion picture involved in this case [*Les Amants*—"The Lovers"] is not it."

Faced with such diverse views even in cases where, for one reason or another, five justices agreed that the material was *not* obscene and that the criminal prosecution therefore was not appropriate, the Court in 1967 began the practice of reversing convictions for distributing obscene materials in *per curiam* decisions. When it issues a *per curiam* decision (from the Latin phrase meaning, "for the court"), the Court either issues no opinion or releases a brief, unsigned opinion stating the result and, sometimes, providing a sketch of the Court's reasoning. The justices issue *per curiam* opinions when they agree that a full opinion is either unnecessary or impossible to write. In the obscenity cases, the Court no doubt used the *per curiam* approach for the latter reason.

The *per curiam* approach was abandoned in 1973 when, in the case of *Miller v. California*, the Court, having despaired over its efforts to devise a national standard for judging what is obscene, decided to take a new tack—one emphasizing local community standards:

> [W]e now confine the permissible scope of . . . regulation [of obscenity] to works which depict or describe sexual conduct. That conduct must be specifically defined by the applicable state law, as written or authoritatively construed. A state offense must also be limited to works which, taken as a whole, appeal to the prurient interest in sex, which portray sexual conduct in a patently offensive way, and which, taken as a whole, do not have serious literary, artistic, political, or scientific value.
>
> The basic guidelines for the trier of fact must be: (a) whether "the average person, applying contemporary community standards," would find that the work, taken as a whole, appeals to the prurient interest, (b) whether the work depicts or describes, in a patently offensive way, sexual conduct specifically defined by the applicable state law, and (c) whether the work, taken as a whole, lacks serious literary, artistic, political, or scientific value. We do not adopt as a constitutional standard the "*utterly* without redeeming social value" test. . . .

[Our] Nation is simply too big and too diverse for this Court to reasonably expect that such standards [for defining obscenity] could be articulated for all 50 States in a single formation, even assuming the prerequisite consensus exists. [To] require a State to structure obscenity proceedings around evidence of a *national* "community standard" would be an exercise in futility. . . . It is neither realistic nor constitutionally sound to read the First Amendment as requiring that the people of Maine or Mississippi accept public depiction of conduct found tolerable in Las Vegas, or New York City. [People] in different States vary in their tastes and attitudes, and this diversity is not to be strangled by the absolutism of imposed uniformity.

But this "community standard" approach has not freed the Court from the burden of defining obscenity. The following year, for example, a Georgia jury convicted a film distributor for showing the film *Carnal Knowledge*—which the jury had found to be obscene. The trial judge in the Georgia court did not upset the jury's verdict, because he believed that, under the ruling in *Miller* v. *California*, the jury spoke for the community. The Supreme Court said that he was wrong, and it reversed the conviction—holding that the film was not obscene (and that, therefore, showing it could not be a crime). Writing for the Court, Justice William H. Rehnquist noted the following:

"Carnal Knowledge" could not be found under the *Miller* standards to depict sexual conduct in a patently offensive way. . . . While the subject matter of the picture is, in a broader sense, sex, and there are scenes in which sexual conduct including "ultimate sexual acts" is to be understood to be taking place, the camera does not focus on the bodies of the actors at such times. There is no exhibition whatever of the actors' genitals, lewd or otherwise, during these scenes. There are occasional scenes of nudity, but nudity alone is not enough to make material legally obscene under the *Miller* standards.

Although the Supreme Court has made clear that the production and distribution of obscene materials—however defined—may be banned, it also has said that the First Amendment prohibits making the private possession of obscene material a crime. The Court made that clear in a Georgia case in which the search of a home for bookmaking evidence had uncovered the obscene films that were used to convict the homeowner of possession of obscene material. The Court reversed the conviction, saying that the "right to receive information and ideas, regardless of their social worth, [is] fundamental to our free society"—especially when the right is exercised in the privacy of a person's home. The Court added: "Whatever may be the justification for other statutes regulating obscenity, we do not think they reach into the privacy of one's own home."

But the Court has refused to extend this principle very far. For example, it has rejected the argument that if a person has the right to possess obscene materials, then someone must have the right to deliver such materials to him or her. The Court therefore upheld a federal law prohibiting the mailing of obscene materials.

◆◆◆ Can I Carry a Gun If I Want To?

Only if the government permits you to do so. The Second Amendment's promise that "the right of the people to keep and bear Arms, shall not be infringed" does not bar local, state, and (for most weapons) even federal gun-control legislation. And many such laws exist and have been upheld.

One thing is clear: The Second Amendment does not limit *in any way* state and local gun-control laws. In an 1886 case, the Supreme Court said that the Second Amendment "is one of the amendments that has no effect other than to restrict the powers of the National government." And that is still the law. So states and local governments have passed a host of bills regulating guns. They have imposed conditions on the purchase, possession, or carrying of a weapon. They have said that certain classes of people—such as minors, aliens, convicted felons, ex-convicts, and intoxicated persons—cannot carry guns. They have even barred guns altogether. And all these laws are acceptable under the Constitution.

For example, in 1981, the city of Morton Grove, Illinois, banned all handguns that were not rendered permanently inoperable. Residents challenged the ordinance, but both a federal district court and, in 1982, the U.S. Court of Appeals for the Seventh Circuit upheld the prohibition. Both courts said that the Second Amendment did not limit the city's right to outlaw guns and that the ban was permissible under the Illinois constitution.

The Second Amendment also does not impose much of a limit on the right of the federal government to regulate guns.

In 1939, the Supreme Court held that the words "the right to . . . bear Arms" are inextricably connected to the preservation of a militia. Therefore, the Court said that the right to keep and bear arms extends only to those arms that are necessary to maintain a well-regulated militia—weapons that normally would be used by soldiers and are carried openly, such as rifles. Thus, the Court made it clear that even the federal government could also regulate handguns.

Thus far, there's only been limited federal regulation of such weapons. Congress did impose rules on the transport, shipping, and receiving of firearms in interstate or foreign commerce in the Gun Control Act of 1968—enacted after the assassinations that year of the Reverend Martin Luther King, Jr., and Senator Robert F. Kennedy of New York. But because the Supreme Court has interpreted the Second Amendment as protecting only a *collective* right to bear certain weapons *collectively*—that is, more as a matter of state sovereignty than as one of individual rights—the federal government could do much more to regulate firearms if it wished.

◆◆◆ Does My Child Enjoy the Same Rights I Do?

To some extent, yes. And to some extent, no.

In many different ways the federal, local, and state governments treat children differently from adults—and the Constitution does not prevent them from doing so. We have minimum-age limits for driving and drinking—and even for working. We compel persons below a certain age to go to school. We have limited the movies that children can see. And we have special juvenile-delinquency rules that treat youngsters who commit crimes differently from adult offenders. All these rules are perfectly permissible under the Constitution. Unless a government makes some inappropriate distinction *among* young adults—as Oklahoma once did in forbidding the sale of beer to young men under the age of twenty-one while permitting its sale to young women over eighteen—the government is free to treat age as a factor in setting down rules where it can be said that age makes a difference.

Nonetheless, your child does enjoy most of the same rights as you do. As the Supreme Court declared in 1976: "Minors, as well as adults, are protected by the Constitution and possess constitutional rights." Thus, your child can protest in school against war by wearing a black armband—as some in Des Moines, Iowa, did during the Vietnam War. That activity, the Court found in 1969, is protected by the First Amendment. Your child can refuse to salute the flag in school—as did several young members of the Jehovah's Witnesses in West Virginia. That, the Court found in 1943—at the height of World War II—is protected by the First Amendment as well.

The Court's ruling in the 1976 case just quoted made it clear that females under eighteen have a right to an abortion. "Constitutional rights," it declared, "do not mature and come into being magically only when one attains the state-defined age of majority." The Court therefore struck down a Missouri law requiring an unmarried woman under eighteen to obtain the consent of her parents before she could have an abortion. Justice Harry A. Blackmun, the architect of the 1973 decision in *Roe v. Wade* that first recognized a woman's right to an abortion, insisted for the Court that a state could not "give a third party an absolute, and possibly arbitrary, veto over the decision of the physician and his patient to terminate the patient's pregnancy."

On the other hand, the Court has also made it clear that a minor does not have the *same* right to an abortion as does an adult. For example, a 1981 case upheld a Utah law requiring a doctor who was about to perform an abortion on a minor to notify her parents—unless she could prove that she was mature enough to decide for herself or that her parents were hostile to her.

Equality ================================

◆◆◆ Can a Law Treat Different Groups Differently?

Yes, it can, but only if it does not violate the Equal Protection Clause of the Fourteenth Amendment, which prevents the government from denying "to any person within its jurisdiction the equal protection of the laws." The Supreme Court's decisions interpreting this clause are complex, but it is clear that the clause guarantees that similar people must be dealt with in a similar way by the government.

The word *equality* does not appear in the Constitution that was written in 1787, although the Declaration of Independence drafted eleven years earlier affirms that "all Men are created equal." This statement simply means that all people are equal before the law. With the end of the Civil War in 1865, the Republicans in Congress sought to make permanent in the Constitution their victory over states' rights, secession, and slavery. As part of this effort, they proposed the so-called Civil War amendments—the Thirteenth, which abolished slavery; the Fifteenth, which prohibited discrimination on account of race against those who seek to vote, and the Fourteenth.

The Fourteenth Amendment, which Congress required former Confederate states to ratify before their representatives could be readmitted to Congress, has proved to be the most important of the three amendments in the development of constitutional law. It constituted a fundamental reworking of the American political system. Not only did it establish the federal government as the focus of power in our system of government, but it also transformed equality from a nebulous goal into a pivotal doctrine of American constitutional law. That happened as the Supreme Court took the seed planted in the Equal Protection Clause and molded it into the doctrine as it is known today.

The clause comes into play whenever a government—city, state, or federal—passes a law or adopts a rule or regulation that classifies persons or "draws lines" by what is called a "scheme of classification." In reviewing a classification, courts must decide whether it is permitted or forbidden by the clause.

In many circumstances, a government *can* classify or draw lines. Most courts uphold classification schemes as long as a government can show some rational basis for the rule of thumb it has adopted. For example, Congress can divide the nation's taxpayers into income groups and charge those with higher incomes a higher rate of tax. Such a distinction does not violate the Constitution because it distinguishes between persons, or groups, to advance a legitimate interest of society. A graduated income tax distributes the burden of taxes according to the ability to pay. There is a "rational basis" for the law.

But a government rarely can use some classification schemes—such as those based on race or nationality. The courts call such classification schemes "suspect" classifications—and subject them to a much tougher test, "strict scrutiny." This means that before the government can employ the suspect classification, it must show a *compelling* purpose that the scheme will achieve or promote—and that there is no other, "less suspect" way to achieve or promote that interest. For example, a school board cannot separate students by race, because there is no compelling purpose to do so. But Congress can require aliens to carry certain identification papers that American citizens are not required to carry because the government's control over illegal immigration cannot be handled in any other way.

The Supreme Court listed the classification schemes that are "suspect" in a 1938 case, *United States* v. *Carolene Products Co.* In the now-famous Footnote 4 to the Court's opinion, Justice Harlan Fiske Stone wrote that, while the Court would defer to policy decisions by legislatures on social and economic affairs, the Court would take a closer and more skeptical look at (1) statutes that on their face appear to violate specific prohibitions of the Bill of Rights and the rest of the Constitution; (2) statutes restricting the democratic political process; and (3) statutes directed at "discrete and insular minorities"—particular religious groups, nationalities, or racial minorities, for example.

Recently, the Court has begun to employ a third method of review for some classifications—a level of review that demands more than a "rational basis" to justify a classification but that is not as demanding as "strict scrutiny." The Court has used this "middle tier" standard when the classification at issue is based on illegitimacy, noncitizenship, sex, or age. The Court will uphold a classification in this middle group only if a government can show that it is related to an *important* (as distinct from a compelling) state interest. This standard was first set forth in a 1976 decision striking down an Oklahoma law that banned the sale of 3.2 percent beer to males under twenty-one years old and females under eighteen. The Court refused to accept the view that distinguishing between the sexes in setting the drinking age advanced an important interest of the state.

Of all areas of American constitutional law, equal-protection doctrine is the most intricate and controversial. The Court's and the nation's ongoing struggles to define when a law may or may not treat different groups differently reflects a never-ending quest to combat injustice and to fulfill Thomas Jefferson's vision of a society in which all persons are indeed equal before the law.

◆◆◆ Are "Separate-But-Equal" Facilities for Different Races Allowed under the Constitution?

At one time they were, but not any more. Racial equality is guaranteed by the Equal Protection Clause of the Fourteenth Amendment.

The separate-but-equal concept was approved by the Supreme Court in the case of *Plessy v. Ferguson* in 1896, when it upheld a Louisiana statute calling for separate-but-equal accommodations for "white" and "colored" passengers on trains. At that time, the Equal Protection Clause did little more than protect blacks from being slaves.

In adopting the doctrine, the Court asserted that the Fourteenth Amendment "could not have been intended to abolish distinctions based upon color, or to enforce social as distinguished from political equality, or a commingling of the two races upon terms unsatisfactory to either." Writing for the majority, Justice Henry B. Brown also noted the long-standing pattern of segregated facilities in many areas of the country. He cited an 1850 case that upheld segregation in the Boston public school system. Brown conceded that a legislature must promote the public good and not be oppressive. But he also said that it was not obliged to integrate: Separate-but-equal facilities were just that—separate but equal—and did not mark the black race with a "badge of inferiority." In real life, he added, the races would not and could not be forced to mix; consequently, social prejudice could not be overcome by law.

The only dissent in the *Plessy* case came from Justice John Marshall Harlan, a Kentuckian who, ironically, had owned slaves before the Civil War. Harlan argued the government ought not to be allowed to use a person's color to determine that person's rights because "the Constitution is color blind."

Although the *Plessy* case only dealt with separate accommodations on railroads and other public carriers, later courts relied on the decision to uphold segregation in public schools and many other public areas. It was not until nearly sixty years later that a full-fledged reconsideration of the validity of the separate-but-equal doctrine came with the landmark decision in *Brown v. Board of Education.* In that 1954 case, the Court, in an opinion by Chief Justice Earl Warren, unanimously declared that segregation had no place in American education because separate schools for the races were not and never could be "equal."

The Court based its electrifying decision in part on several cases from the late 1940s and early 1950s that had disapproved segregation in higher education. In one case, the University of Texas Law School had refused to admit blacks because the state had established a separate law school for them. Writing for the Court in 1950, Chief Justice Fred M. Vinson found no "substantial equality in the educational opportunities offered white and Negro law students by the State." As he put it: "In terms of the number of faculty, variety of courses and opportunity for specialization, size of the student body, scope of the library, availability of law review and similar activities, the University of Texas Law School is superior. What is more important, the University of Texas Law School possesses to a far greater degree those qualities which are incapable of objective measurement but which make for greatness in a law school. Such qualities, to name a few, include reputation of the faculty, experience of the administration, position and influence of the alumni, standing in the community, traditions and prestige."

In a second 1950 case, in another opinion written by Vinson, the Court insisted that a black student who had been admitted to a graduate program be allowed to take classes with white students; the school, Oklahoma State University, had insisted that the student sit in separate sections in or adjoining the classrooms, library, and cafeteria. In rejecting the argument that the student might be ostracized by his fellow students anyway, Vinson said, "There is a vast difference—a constitutional difference—between restrictions imposed by the state [and] the refusal of individuals to commingle."

The Texas and Oklahoma higher-education cases did not repudiate the separate-but-equal doctrine. Instead, the Court found that the separate facilities *were not* equal. In *Brown v. Board of Education,* the Court took the next step: Separate facilities *could never be equal.*

As a technical matter, the Court's ruling in the *Brown* case did not reject the possibility of separate-but-equal treatment for all places and all times. The decision dealt only with segregation in the public schools.

However, by 1964 the Court had held that the doctrine was invalid with regard to a wide variety of public facilities, including buses, public parks and golf courses, public beaches and bathhouses, and seating in courtrooms, airport restaurants, and municipal auditoriums. And it is now well settled that separate cannot be equal—anywhere.

The Equal Protection Clause of the Fourteenth Amendment bans only unequal treatment by the government. It does not outlaw segregation or discrimination by private clubs, groups, or individuals. However, the Civil Rights Act enacted by Congress in 1964 bars discrimination in many private institutions, businesses, and social activities as well.

◆◆◆ **Is School Busing Constitutional?**

Yes. In fact, in some circumstances it is even required as a means to correct discrimination.

In the landmark case of *Brown* v. *Board of Education* in 1954, the Supreme Court ruled that any law or policy that served to segregate public schools violated the Equal Protection Clause of the Fourteenth Amendment. The Court said that, "because of their proximity to local conditions and the possible need for further hearings," federal district courts should have the responsibility to supervise the "transition to a system of public education freed of racial discrimination." The district courts were to ensure that school officials make a "prompt and reasonable start toward full compliance" with the Court's ruling and that the transition should occur "with all deliberate speed." However, the Court did not outline a specific plan for achieving desegregation.

There was a tremendous outcry about implementing the Court's decision, especially in the South, where states had previously been able to provide segregated schools under the separate-but-equal doctrine upheld in 1896. The matter came to a head in Arkansas in 1957, when Governor Orval Faubus ordered the state's National Guard to stand "shoulder to shoulder at the school grounds and thereby forcibly prevent" black students from entering a Little Rock school under a desegregation program approved by a district court. President Dwight D. Eisenhower ordered army troops to break up the blockade. He later placed the Arkansas National Guard under his own command and ordered it to enforce the desegregation plan.

Faced with continuing resistance to implementing its decision, however, the Court attempted to define broad guidelines for the district courts in the hope of expediting the process. Emphasizing that "the transition to a unitary, nonracial system of public education was and is the ultimate end to be brought about," the Court put the "burden on [each] school board . . . to come forward with a plan that promises realistically to work, and promises realistically to work *now.*" In 1971, it held that mathematical ratios could serve as "a useful starting point in shaping a remedy to correct past constitutional violations." The Court also empowered the district courts to take "affirmative action" by altering attendance zones, and it ruled that local authorities could use busing as "a tool of school desegregation." (At the same time, the Court struck down a North Carolina statute that prohibited the busing of students who objected.)

The Court has imposed some limits on the extent to which school districts may bus students to achieve racial balance. For example, in 1974 it forbade the busing of children from districts in which there had not been a policy of segregation into one where there was segregation—even though the purpose of the busing plan was to achieve racial balance. And in 1976, the Court held that a school district that had initially complied with a court desegregation order and balanced the racial composition of its schools could not be forced to redraw its attendance zones each year to account for population shifts.

In two 1982 cases, one from Seattle, Washington, the other from Los Angeles, California, the Court considered state measures designed to curb mandatory busing programs adopted by school districts. In the Seattle case, the Court struck down a state law that had been enacted after it was placed on the state ballot by citizens. The law, Initiative 350, forbade school boards from requiring students to attend a school that was not geographically "nearest or next nearest" to their homes. Writing for the Court, Justice Harry A. Blackmun condemned Initiative 350 because "it uses the racial nature of an issue to define the government's decisionmaking structure." In his view, it was "beyond reasonable dispute [that] the initiative was enacted because of, not merely in spite of, its adverse effects on busing for integration."

In the Los Angeles case, however, the Court upheld an amendment to the state constitution that made provisions of it conform to those of the Fourteenth Amendment. The effect was to cut back on busing throughout California. Prior to the amendment, California courts had invoked the state constitution to order busing in situations where the federal Constitution would not have required it. After the amendment, California courts were required to do no more than what is required under the federal Constitution.

_____

◆◆◆ Why Is an Affirmative-Action Program Necessary If Everyone Is Supposed to Be Equal?

_____

Because the Supreme Court has realized that to wipe out nearly two centuries of discrimination, it has to support programs that create special opportunities for minorities, particularly blacks, in areas such as schooling and jobs. Otherwise, the condition of such groups cannot be bettered or the effects of the years of discrimination cannot be remedied.

The consequences of the centuries of unequal treatment are stark: the average black has a life expectancy five years less than the average white; black families have a median income that is 60 percent that of white families; unemployment among blacks is twice as high as it is among whites; and blacks, who represent 11.5 percent of the population, constitute less than 2.5 percent of the lawyers, doctors, dentists, engineers, and college professors. Considering the Constitution "color blind" cannot obscure the reality that adopting a "color-blind" approach to all manner of political, economic, and social action serves to make permanent the effects of discrimination. As Justice Harry A. Blackmun put it in 1978, "In order to get beyond racism, we must first take account of race. There is no other way. And in order to treat persons equally, we must treat them differently. We cannot—we dare not—let the Equal Protection Clause perpetuate racial supremacy."

The civil-rights struggle of the 1960s focused the attention of the nation on the plight of blacks. The Court's decision in *Brown* v. *Board of Education* in 1954 outlawing segregation in public schools had expressed the goal of equal opportunity for all without regard to race. Soon, affirmative-action programs were developed to help the nation achieve that goal. Such programs—which ordinarily would be considered discriminatory because they treat people differently because of race or sex—are now considered "benign."

At issue is the conflict created between two goals of the Equal Protection Clause of the Fourteenth Amendment: the removal of barriers to full racial equality, and the requirement that government treat individuals on the basis of personal merit or achievements, not their race.

The Supreme Court first made clear that affirmative-action programs could play a role in redressing discrimination when, in 1978, it said that race could be a factor, though not a determining one, in granting a student admission to a college or university. The next year, in a case involving a steel company, it held that private employers could volunteer to set up affirmative-action programs. And, in 1980, it upheld a federal law that requires 10 percent of the money spent on federal public-works projects to be spent on bids from businesses owned by members of minority groups.

On the other hand, in 1984, the Court ruled—in a case involving firefighters—that when budget cuts require layoffs, a city may follow its seniority system without regard to whether the firefighters are white or black. That holds true even though doing so erases many of the gains that blacks had achieved in being hired under an affirmative-action program. The Court reasoned that seniority rights could not be violated unless the seniority system itself had been adopted in the first place with an intent to discriminate or there was an identifiable member of a minority group who had been deprived of a higher seniority ranking because of discrimination.

The Supreme Court has before it two cases—one out of New York, the other out of Cleveland—involving affirmative-action plans where non-minority workers are seeking to invalidate the plans by invoking the Court's 1984 decision. In each case, a federal court of appeals held that the affirmative-action plan at issue was valid because it did not compromise any of the seniority rights of nonminority workers. The courts of appeals said that the Supreme Court's 1984 decision held only that such seniority rights took precedence over affirmative-action schemes. The Supreme Court will now decide the issue.

◆◆◆ Can Race Be a Factor When I Apply to College or Graduate School?

Yes, but only if it is not the sole determining factor. This unusual and highly controversial principle was established in 1978 when a white pre-medical student complained that he had been discriminated against because he was white.

The case involved the medical school of the University of California at Davis, which had opened in 1968. That year, although racial and ethnic minorities made up over 23 percent of the population of California, there were no blacks, Mexican Americans, or Native Americans, and only three Asian-Americans in the entering class of fifty students. To increase the representation of minorities, the medical school faculty created a special admissions program that operated parallel to the regular admissions process. Sixteen seats in each entering class were reserved for candidates accepted through a special admissions program administered by a separate committee composed mainly of faculty and students from minority groups. For the medical school, the term *minority group* apparently covered blacks, Mexican Americans, Native Americans, and Asian Americans.

The special admissions program increased the number of minority students in the medical school. Between 1970 and 1974, of the 452 applicants admitted to Davis, 27 were black and 39 were Mexican American; without the special admissions program, only 1 black and 6 Mexican Americans would have been accepted.

Allan Bakke, a white, applied unsuccessfully to the medical school in 1973 and again in 1974. In both years, applicants with significantly lower scores were accepted through the special admissions program. Bakke sued, claiming that he had been denied admission because of his race, in violation of both the Fourteenth Amendment of the Constitution and the Civil Rights Act of 1964.

The *Bakke* decision was in fact two 5-to-4 rulings, with Justice Lewis F. Powell, Jr., the only justice participating in both majorities. He was part of one group, consisting of Chief Justice Warren E. Burger and Justices Potter Stewart, William H. Rehnquist, and John Paul Stevens, that invalidated the school's special admissions program and ordered Bakke admitted. He was also a member of a second group, composed of Justices William J. Brennan, Jr., Byron R. White, Thurgood Marshall, and Harry A. Blackmun, that held that race can be a consideration in a constitutionally acceptable admissions program.

Justice Stevens—writing for himself, the chief justice, and Justices Stewart and Rehnquist—concluded that the Civil Rights Act settled the case. In his view, that law's prohibition on the use of racial classifications outlawed a program such as the one at Davis. Stevens emphasized that because the Davis program—the only one before the Court—was in his view illegal, it was unnecessary for him to decide whether it, or any alternative admissions program, was constitutional under the Equal Protection Clause. As a result, he and the three other justices for whom he wrote did not address the constitutional issue at all.

Justice Brennan—in an opinion joined by Justices White, Marshall, and Blackmun—found that the Civil Rights Act of 1964 and the Equal Protection Clause forbid (or permit) precisely the same things—and neither forbids the use of racial criteria to advance the position of minorities, as in a minority admissions program. In his view, if a state institution detects that its actions will have an unequal racial impact resulting from its own or society's past discriminatory acts, it can adopt a race-conscious program. Thus, to Justice Brennan and the three justices who joined him, the Davis plan in all of its details was acceptable.

The split between the Brennan and Stevens groups left it to Powell to cast the deciding vote. He took a middle position. He agreed with the Brennan group that universities may take race into account when admitting students, but he did not agree with them that race could be the single determining factor, as it was in Bakke's case. Accordingly, although he accepted the principle of affirmative action, he voted with the Stevens group to invalidate the specific plan used at the Davis medical school. Instead, as a model of an acceptable affirmative-action admissions program, Powell offered the Harvard College admissions program, which uses race as a "plus factor" for minorities in an effort to ensure a diversified class.

The bottom line is that the specific program at issue was illegal. However, by joining the second group of justices on the issue of affirmative-action programs in general, Powell created a second ruling that some such programs may still be valid. An example would be one that takes race into account as one of many other factors as part of an attempt to create a diversified student body.

◆◆◆ What Rights Did the Framers Intend Women to Have?

The Framers probably intended women to enjoy all the protections provided by the Constitution: the right to a trial by jury, freedom of religion, free speech—all the safeguards men enjoyed. But they made no attempt to change existing common-law traditions regarding women in American society or their role vis-à-vis husbands. And women did not vote. So the rights they enjoyed in the late eighteenth century were severely circumscribed.

The law then was that married women could not own property in their own right, make contracts, or otherwise conduct business on their own. Single women fared better; they could engage in economic activity. But all women—married and single—were barred from voting. When Mercy Otis Warren wrote the only contribution by a woman to the ratification campaign of 1788, she published the pamphlet, the Anti-Federalist *Observations on the Constitution,* under the pseudonym "A Columbian Patriot" because she believed the nation's leaders would not pay attention to it if they knew a woman had written it.

Starting in 1848, the climate of opinion began, ever so slowly, to change. That year, New York passed a Married Women's Property Act in an attempt to rectify some of the inequalities, and other states soon followed suit. That same year, a vigorous campaign for women's rights was launched by Lucretia Coffin Mott, Elizabeth Cady Stanton, and other feminists who gathered at Seneca Falls, New York, and issued what was called the Seneca Falls Declaration, a manifesto to secure equal rights for women, especially the right to vote, throughout the nation.

The legal system at this time consistently rebuffed women's attempts to seek advancement, basing decisions against them on the time-honored understanding that a woman's role in society was that of nurturer, home-maker, mother, and guardian of the feminine virtues of tenderness, affection, and mercy. For all these reasons, the Supreme Court in 1873 rejected the attempt of Myra Bradwell to become a member of the Illinois bar. It held that Illinois could forbid women to assume roles, such as that of an attorney, that were not consistent with their "nature." As Justice Joseph P. Bradley noted in his concurring opinion in that case, "Man is, or should be, woman's protector and defender . . . . The paramount destiny and mission of woman are to fulfill the noble and benign offices of wife and mother. This is the law of the Creator." (Within a year after the *Bradwell* case, the Illinois legislature repealed the law restricting membership in the legal profession to men.)

A similar fate befell Belva Lockwood, a leader of the women's movement, who was denied her law-school diploma from National Law School in Washington, D.C., and finally asked President Ulysses S. Grant, the school's honorary president, for help in securing it. Like Bradwell, Lockwood was at first denied membership in the U.S. Supreme Court Bar. In 1879, however, she finally became the first woman to be admitted to practice before the Supreme Court as the result of legislation enacted by Congress that year.

The suffragist movement spread rapidly at the turn of the century, as more and more women began working in newly created or expanding industries. The Nineteenth Amendment, by which women gained the right to vote, was finally ratified in 1920. But although some barriers subsequently came down—women were finally admitted to the bar and certain other professions—it was not until the 1960s that women finally began to organize to demand and win equal rights.

During that decade, the civil rights movement inspired many Americans to grapple with the ideal of equality and the difficulty of achieving it. By the late 1960s many women had rethought the strategy of the women's movement and applied the lessons of the civil rights and antiwar movements to win equal rights for themselves at long last. The Civil Rights Act of 1964 had outlawed sex discrimination in many contexts, and some state antidiscrimination laws had also been enacted, but the promise of equality had still not been realized for women (any more than for racial minorities). An equal-rights amendment, first proposed by Susan Anthony (who tried to have a clause recognizing the equal rights of men and women added to the Fourteenth Amendment) and her colleagues, became the centerpiece of the women's rights movement. (By 1982, it had failed to be ratified by enough states.)

Meanwhile, in 1971, the Supreme Court began what would be a modest effort to apply the Fourteenth Amendment's guarantee of equality to the problem of discrimination based on sex. That year, the Court struck down an Idaho law that gave men a blanket preference over women as administrators of estates. However, the Court has been more willing to tolerate discrimination based on sex than discrimination based on race. Therefore, not surprisingly, its effort to provide constitutional protection against sex discrimination has been less successful than its effort to eradicate racial discrimination. So, in many ways, women still do not enjoy all the rights that men do.

◆◆◆ Would an Equal-Rights Amendment Affect the Rights Women Already Have?

Yes. The amendment would provide more protection for women with regard to federal and state laws. It might also bar certain traditional privileges granted only to women (such as exemption from military service), and it certainly would prohibit the practice of imposing certain burdens only on men (such as the payment of child support, which is still an exclusively male obligation in some states).

The equal-rights amendment (or ERA) that Congress proposed and sent to the states for ratification in 1972 stated, "Equality of rights under the law shall not be denied or abridged by the United States or by any State on account of sex." It ultimately was ratified by only thirty-five of the necessary thirty-eight states before a statutory time limit ran out—so it never became part of the Constitution. The overall effect that the amendment would have had on women's rights is difficult to define. Like any other provision of the Constitution, the ERA undoubtedly would have been the subject of Supreme Court interpretations, which are hard to predict.

Women do enjoy legal protections under a wide variety of federal and state laws against discrimination based on sex. For example, there are federal antidiscrimination laws such as Title VII of the Civil Rights Act of 1964, which protects against job discrimination, and Title IX of the same act, which entitles women to equal education opportunities at institutions receiving federal funds. Moreover, seventeen states have added equal-rights amendments to their state constitutions.

On top of those laws, the Equal Protection Clause of the Fourteenth Amendment, as interpreted by the Supreme Court, offers women some protection against discriminatory laws. The Court ruled in 1976, for example, that laws that discriminate on the basis of sex, while not deserving of the "strict scrutiny" reserved for discrimination on the basis of race, religion or national origin, still require "intermediate scrutiny." The Court in the previous year had struck down a Utah statute that established a lower age of majority for females than for males. And, in 1979, it struck down an Alabama statute that required only husbands to pay alimony in a divorce.

However, the Court has not rejected all laws that discriminate on the basis of sex. In 1974, for example, it upheld a Florida statute granting widows, but not widowers, an annual $500 property-tax exemption. And, in 1981, it upheld a federal law requiring only males to register for the draft. It is likely that if the ERA had been ratified, such statutes would not have been upheld: Florida would have to grant widowers a tax exemption, too, and both males and females would be subject to the draft.

Many people believe that the ERA would have strengthened existing state and federal antidiscrimination laws. It certainly would have given women a federal constitutional basis for fighting some forms of paternalistic sex discrimination that they may not fight now on that ground.

◆◆◆ Can Pregnancy and Childbirth Benefits Be Omitted from a Health-Insurance Plan?

No. In response to several Supreme Court decisions saying that federal law did not prevent discrimination against pregnant women, Congress amended the laws expressly to forbid such discrimination.

In what is considered an unusual decision—especially in light of other recent Court rulings that upset sex-discrimination laws—the Court in 1974 upheld a California disability-insurance plan that covered all disabilities except maternity and hospital costs resulting from a normal pregnancy.

The majority in the case, *Geduldig* v. *Aiello*, concluded that a state health plan could be limited to only those medical problems that men and women share in common. Obviously, pregnancy is not one of them. The Court also maintained that California had acted reasonably because, by excluding pregnancies, the state saved a considerable amount of money. (The finding was surprising because the Court had earlier denied to several other states the right to make certain presumptions based on sex that would have resulted in cheaper and more efficient administration.)

In the *Geduldig* case, the Court said that the exclusion of pregnancy benefits raised no constitutional problem because there was no evidence that the risks covered in the health plan harmed one sex but not the other. According to the Court, women were treated evenhandedly because coverage was limited to risks that both sexes share in common. The Court believed that in denying pregnancy benefits the insurance plan merely drew a line between pregnant and nonpregnant persons, and the latter group could include women. This, it said, was not discrimination against women.

The Court reached the same result in later cases, among them a 1976 case involving the insurance plan of a private employer that also excluded pregnancy benefits. This time, interpreting Title VII of the Civil Rights Act of 1964, the Court concluded that a private employer was free to choose not to take the needs of pregnant workers into account in an insurance-disability plan. The Court said again that the distinction between pregnant women and nonpregnant persons made sense; to prove a claim of discrimination, a worker must show that distinctions made on the basis of a pregnancy were used simply as a pretext to discriminate against one sex or the other.

However unintentionally, the Court appeared to be saying that, for women, the price of equality in the workplace is that they be childless. Realizing this, Congress in 1978 amended the Civil Rights Act of 1964 so that any employer who in any way—including the distribution of health benefits—maintains a policy that treats pregnant employees differently from nonpregnant employees is guilty of discrimination—unless the employer can show that there is some bona fide reason for doing so.

Subsequently, in 1983, the Court ruled that if pregnancy coverage is given to female workers, it must also be extended to the spouses of male workers. The Court said that failure to extend the coverage to the spouses of the males would give married male workers a benefit package for their families that is less inclusive than the family coverage provided to married female workers. This, the Court said, would be illegal discrimination.

In addition, the agency charged with enforcing the federal law—the Equal Employment Opportunity Commission—has taken the position that an employer may not deny unmarried workers pregnancy benefits. The Supreme Court has not yet ruled on this issue.

◆◆◆ Is It Legal to Discriminate against Homosexuals?

Probably yes. Gays and lesbians presently enjoy very little protection from discrimination. There is no federal law prohibiting discrimination against them. Many states, in fact, still have laws on their books that make homosexual conduct a crime, and most states refuse to allow homosexuals to marry. But two states and about thirty cities have passed ordinances forbidding discrimination against homosexuals, and some courts have suggested that the Constitution may in some circumstances forbid the government from treating gays and lesbians differently because of their sexual preference.

For most of American history, those (including homosexuals) who engaged in sexual activity different from that practiced by most people have been the targets of restrictive and even savagely harsh criminal laws. For example, the report of the commissioners appointed in 1776 by the Virginia legislature to review that state's laws after the Declaration of Independence (Thomas Jefferson was one of them) included in its proposed "Bill for Proportioning Crimes and Punishments" the following provision:

> Whosoever shall be guilty of rape, polygamy, or sodomy with man or woman, shall be punished; if a man, by castration; if a woman, by boring through the cartilage of her nose a hole of one half inch in diameter at the least.

The commissioners pointed out in footnotes to their report that most European countries, and most legal commentators of the time, imposed or supported the death penalty for sodomy, which they defined as including homosexuality. (Many states still have in force criminal statutes forbidding private, consensual sodomy.)

In the United States, as in England, homosexuality was publicly denounced as immoral and unnatural. It was not until the 1960s that three factors combined to stimulate the rise of the gay rights movement. One was the civil rights movement by blacks, which provided a model for minority groups to campaign publicly and peaceably to achieve certain rights. Another was the women's rights movement, which paralleled the civil rights movement but emphasized issues related to sexual identity and behavior. The third was the development in law of the constitutional right of privacy, particularly with regard to sexual conduct, as exemplified in the Supreme Court's 1965 decision protecting the right of married couples to use contraceptives.

Most courts have ruled that federal and state antidiscrimination laws that prohibit discrimination on the basis of sex do not apply to homosexuals. In most parts of the country, therefore, governments, employers, and other persons who choose to do so are legally free to treat homosexuals differently. However, Wisconsin and approximately thirty cities have statutes outlawing discrimination on the basis of sexual preference, and California has a law that says gays and lesbians may not be denied public accommodations because of their sexual preference. Such laws make it illegal to treat gays and lesbians differently from others.

Some federal and state courts have suggested that the First and Fourteenth amendments may in some circumstances forbid the government from treating gays and lesbians differently because of their sexual preference. Emphasizing the fundamental importance of sexuality to the individual and the relative unimportance of the state's interest in regulating private conduct, such courts have said that the federal government or a state government may not take adverse action against a gay or lesbian merely because he or she is a homosexual. But, where the government can make a connection between the person's homosexuality and some government interest, courts have upheld adverse action against gays and lesbians. Thus, a federal appellate court has said that the navy could discharge a petty officer on the ground that private gay sexual activity constituted conduct unbecoming an officer. Pentagon regulations state that homosexuality is "incompatible" with military service. The Supreme Court currently has before it a case involving a Georgia antisodomy statute that, depending on how it is decided, may shed new light on the constitutional rights of homosexuals.

A related issue is discrimination against someone who has contracted the disease known as Acquired Immune Deficiency Syndrome, or AIDS. Most courts have been unwilling to provide protection for victims of AIDS under job-discrimination statutes. On the other hand, many courts have read state statutes outlawing discrimination against the disabled to forbid discrimination against a person with AIDS. These courts reason that the disease is a disability, and to discriminate against someone who has it is to treat that person differently because he or she is disabled.

◆◆◆ Do I Have to Be a Citizen to Get Welfare Assistance, Medicare, a Civil Service Job, or a Free Public Education?

Generally speaking, no. There are certain categories of government jobs and benefit programs that may legally be available only to American citizens, but, by and large, the Constitution forbids discrimination against aliens in employment and other matters.

The Supreme Court has expanded the rights of aliens on the same basis that it has expanded the rights of minorities generally: through the Equal Protection Clause of the Fourteenth Amendment. But this was not always the case. In decisions made early in this century, the Court upheld the constitutionality of laws like the New York statute that forbade the employment of noncitizens in public works projects and the Pennsylvania law that barred noncitizens from hunting game or possessing any hunting weapon. As recently as 1948, the Court also upheld a California statute that prohibited noncitizens from owning land.

As the doctrine of equal protection of the laws matured and evolved, the Court began to reassess the validity of discriminatory laws regarding aliens. In a series of cases in the early 1970s, it struck down a number of them, including statutes in Arizona and Pennsylvania discriminating against aliens in the distribution of welfare benefits, a New York law barring aliens from all state civil service jobs, and laws that required citizenship for the certification of civil engineers and for admission to the bar.

But the rights of aliens are not the same as those of citizens. Thus, for example, in 1978 the Court held that New York could refuse to permit aliens to be state troopers. Writing for the Court, Chief Justice Warren E. Burger distinguished this narrow ban from the general one the Court had struck down earlier: "In the enforcement and execution of the laws the police function is one where citizenship bears a rational relationship to the special demands of the particular position." Using the same logic, the Court in 1979 held that a state may refuse to employ aliens as elementary and secondary school teachers. But, in 1984, the Court refused to allow Texas, on that basis, to prevent aliens from serving as notaries public.

Because Congress has the power to regulate immigration (in Article I, Section 8), it has considerably more power than the states to enact legislation affecting aliens. For example, in 1976 the Court upheld a federal law limiting Medicare benefits to aliens who had been in the country for five years. In doing so, the Court noted that in exercising its "broad power over naturalization and immigration," Congress necessarily made rules affecting aliens that, by their very nature, treated aliens differently from citizens.

Illegal aliens also have rights under the Constitution—but they are limited. In 1984, the Supreme Court held that a Texas statute that authorized local school districts to refuse admission to the children of illegal aliens, and that withheld state funds to local school districts which admitted the children of illegal aliens, violated the Equal Protection Clause of the Fourteenth Amendment. In striking down the statute, the Court stopped short of adopting a legal principle that would provide illegal aliens with the same protection that legal aliens enjoy. And, it is difficult from this case to generalize about the rights of illegal aliens in other situations. In striking down the Texas statute, the Court emphasized the unfairness of punishing children—by depriving them of an education—because their parents illegally brought them to this country: "Even if the State found it expedient to control the conduct of adults by acting against their children, legislation directing the onus of a parent's misconduct against his children does not comport with fundamental conceptions of justice."

◆◆◆ Can a State Deny Welfare to Me If I Haven't Lived There for at Least a Year?

No. That kind of requirement for benefits such as welfare aid is not constitutional. The Supreme Court has repeatedly held that laws cannot prevent an individual from exercising certain fundamental rights—in this case, the right to move to another state whenever he or she wants.

That right was cited in the Court's ruling in *Shapiro* v. *Thompson* in 1969. The decision invalidated those statutes of Connecticut, Pennsylvania, and the District of Columbia that denied welfare benefits to residents who had not lived within their borders for at least one year. The Court said that a state may not, without good reason, treat newly arrived residents less favorably than those who have lived in the state longer. The one-year waiting period, it said, denied newcomers aid "upon which may depend the ability of families to obtain the very means to subsist—food, shelter and other necessities of life." In other words, the statutes were struck down because they interfered with the right to travel and impinged on fundamental constitutional rights.

Other statutes have been invalidated on this theory, too. For example, an Arizona law that denied free non-emergency medical treatment to indigent people who had not resided in the state for at least a year was struck down in 1974. The Court declared that the penalty inherent in the law was very severe: "Diseases, if untreated for a year, may become all but irreversible paths to pain, disability, and even loss of life."

On the other hand, the Court has held that there are circumstances when a waiting period is all right. For example, it has upheld laws in both

Minnesota and Washington that require a year of residence as a condition for paying lower tuition at their state-run universities.

The Court has also made it clear that a state may insist that those who benefit from its services actually be residents. In 1983, it upheld a Texas law that denied a free public-school education to a child who had left his home in Mexico to live with a brother in Texas in order to attend a public school there. The Constitution, the Court said, does not prevent Texas from insisting that free education be available only to bona fide residents of the state.

Criminal Justice ═══════════════════

◆◆◆ Why Is an "Obviously Guilty" Person Entitled to a Fair Trial?

For many reasons. For one thing, an "obviously guilty" person may actually be innocent or not responsible for his or her actions. Frequently, an innocent person is wrongly identified and arrested for a crime he or she did not commit. Also, witnesses sometimes lie, and a government agent may have actually enticed the defendant to commit the crime. Moreover, occasionally a person who does commit a crime is not legally responsible because of his or her mental state. But underlying all these reasons is a fundamental principle of our legal system, going back to the beginnings of the common law in medieval England: that a person's guilt or innocence is to be determined only according to the law, not by the untested opinion of law-enforcement officers or the community. That is the essence of our system's presumption that every person is innocent until proved guilty—and the essence of the constitutional value known as "due process of law."

The Fifth and Fourteenth amendments prohibit the federal and state governments from depriving any person of life, liberty, or property without due process of law. Even if someone commits a crime on nationwide television in front of millions of viewers, he or she is still entitled under the Constitution to a fair trial to determine whether he or she is guilty under the law.

The Constitution—in scattered places throughout the original document and in the first ten amendments—spells out the critical features of what our legal system means by due process of law. Article I, Section 9, forbids Congress either to pass a law imposing a punishment on a particular person (a bill of attainder) or to make a given act punishable as a crime after that act has been committed (an *ex post facto* law). Article I, Section 10, imposes the same prohibitions on the states. Article III, Section 2, provides that the trials of all federal crimes, except those of impeachment, are to be by jury and to be held in the state where the crime was committed (except if it was committed on federal territory; in such cases, the trial is to be conducted only where Congress previously has specified by law that it should take place). Article III, Section 3, narrowly defines the crime of treason, sets standards of proof, and limits the punishments that Congress can establish for it—the only section of the Constitution to define a crime.

In addition, the Fourth Amendment establishes standards governing searches and seizures and the issuing of search warrants, which must be based, among other things, on probable cause. The Fifth Amendment recognizes a person's right not to be a witness against himself or herself, directs that persons charged with federal crimes must be charged by a grand jury, forbids trying a person twice for the same offense, and directs that no person can be deprived of life, liberty, or property without due process of law. The Sixth Amendment establishes standards for criminal trials, including a defendant's right to counsel, to a speedy and public trial, to know the charges made against him or her, to be tried by an impartial jury, to be able to subpoena witnesses against him or her, and to have a lawyer to assist in his or her defense. Finally, the Eighth Amendment prohibits the imposition of excessive bail or fines and cruel and unusual punishments.

For the last fifty years or so, the Supreme Court has also, in effect, been framing a constitutional standard of due process for state criminal proceedings by deciding which guarantees of the Bill of Rights should be applied to the states under the Due Process Clause. And, indeed, most have been applied to the states under that clause.

In criminal law, the right to a fair trial often involves the right to trial by a jury rather than by a judge. In a 1968 decision, Justice Byron R. White summed up the reasons for that right:

> The guarantees of jury trial in the Federal and State Constitutions reflect a profound judgment about the way in which law should be enforced and justice administered. A right to jury trial is granted to criminal defendants in order to prevent oppression by the Government. . . . Beyond this, the jury trial provisions . . . reflect a fundamental decision about the exercise of official power—a reluctance to entrust plenary powers over the life and liberty of the citizen to one judge or to a group of judges. Fear of unchecked power, so typical of our State and Federal Governments in other respects, found expression in the criminal law in this insistence upon community participation in the determination of guilt or innocence.

And the trial must take place in the right atmosphere. A classic example occurred in 1966 in a case involving the conviction of Dr. Sam Sheppard for murdering his wife. In the course of the trial, the news media had conducted what the Court described as a "Roman holiday," rendering the trial a farce and a guilty verdict a foregone conclusion. The Court granted Sheppard a writ of *habeas corpus*, setting aside the conviction as hopelessly tainted by the circus atmosphere of the trial. (The writ of *habeas corpus*, which translates literally as "you shall have the body," is used to release a person unlawfully imprisoned or detained.) Sheppard was acquitted in a second trial.

The presumption of innocence means that the government must prove its case against a defendant beyond a reasonable doubt, a standard far stricter than that applied in civil suits. If there is any doubt in the minds of the jury as to the defendant's guilt, the jury is instructed to acquit the defendant. The purpose of the trial is to assess the government's charges against the standards of proof established by law with regard to evidence and due process. That is why, on occasion, the Supreme Court or other courts reverse convictions of defendants whom everyone believes to be guilty.

◆◆◆ Why Is Evidence Seized by the Police Sometimes Held Inadmissible in Court Because of a "Technicality"?

The reason is one of the most complex and controversial principles in American constitutional law: the exclusionary rule. It bars the government from breaking the law to punish a lawbreaker—specifically, from using as evidence in a trial any material that law-enforcement officers find and take in violation of the Fourth Amendment's protection against unreasonable searches and seizures.

Evidence is material—whether oral or written testimony, or objects such as papers, fingerprints, and marijuana—that a jury or trial judge considers in reaching a verdict. The law governing whether it may be introduced involves an intricate collection of rules and guidelines, most of which were established by judges in England and the United States over the centuries. The rules test the material's reliability, believability, and whether it can be made available for cross-examination. If evidence fails to satisfy these standards, it ordinarily is not admitted in court.

However, the Supreme Court has developed one rule of evidence that prohibits the government from using evidence that is concededly reliable and believable—often the most reliable and believable evidence available, such as illegal drugs, counterfeit money, or stolen property found on the person of the accused. That rule, the exclusionary rule, says that evidence *illegally* obtained by the police *must be excluded* at a trial—no matter how reliable it is.

The exclusionary rule is intended to serve several purposes: to deter unreasonable searches and seizures; to preserve the integrity of the judicial process, guarding against the courts becoming "accomplices in the willful disobedience of a Constitution they are sworn to uphold;" and to bolster public confidence that the government will not benefit from lawless behavior on the part of its agents.

Unlike the Fifth Amendment—which specifically forbids the government from compelling people to be witnesses against themselves—the Fourth Amendment does not explicitly bar the use of illegally seized material as evidence. However, the Supreme Court said in 1886 that it was "unable to perceive that the seizure of a man's private books and papers to be used in evidence against him is substantially different from compelling him to be a witness against himself." The Court reaffirmed this exclusionary rule in 1914, though it refused then to hold that the rule applied to the states as well as the federal government. It wasn't until 1952—in a case known as the "stomach pump" case—that the justices began to think otherwise. In that case, *Rochin v. California,* police had forced a suspect in a narcotics case to take an emetic in order to recover drug capsules that he had swallowed as he was being arrested. Writing for the Court, Justice Felix Frankfurter said that the Due Process Clause of the Fourteenth Amendment barred the introduction into evidence of material gathered by "conduct that shocks the conscience." Eventually, in 1961, the Court—citing the Due Process Clause—held that states were also subject to the exclusionary rule.

Since then, there has been a significant increase in the use of search warrants, in efforts to train police officers in the law and in the development of closer working relations between prosecutors and the police. At the same time, case law concerning the exclusionary rule has evolved with bewildering speed, expanding to cover police searches of suspects, their homes, cars, boats, purses, and luggage. As a result, the rule has grown extremely complicated and the Court at times has reversed itself abruptly. Perhaps the most important development, however, was the Court's recognition in 1984 of a "good faith" exception to the exclusionary rule that permits the government to introduce into evidence material seized by law-enforcement officers who reasonably believe that they are acting under a valid search warrant that, in fact, may turn out to be defective in minor ways.

◆◆◆ What Happens If I Can't Afford a Lawyer?

That depends on the kind and seriousness of the case. In a civil suit, you can either serve as your own lawyer or try to persuade a lawyer to take your case for a percentage of the damages you win, if you win. In a criminal case, you can also serve as your own lawyer, or—if the crime involved calls for a sentence of more than six months—ask the court to appoint an attorney to represent you for free.

The guarantee of counsel in criminal cases is based on the Sixth Amendment, which declares, "In all criminal prosecutions, the accused shall enjoy the right . . . to have the Assistance of Counsel for his defence." Even though this seems a clear-cut guarantee, it took almost two hundred years for the Court to decide—in a case involving a convicted felon and a future justice—that the Sixth Amendment means that the state must provide a lawyer to a criminal defendant who cannot afford one.

The decision was based on a case involving an indigent, Clarence Earl Gideon, who was arrested in 1961 for breaking and entering a poolroom in a small Florida town. Gideon wanted to be represented by a lawyer but couldn't afford one. He asked the trial judge to appoint one, but under Florida law only defendants charged with capital offenses had the right to the assistance of counsel. So Gideon had to argue his own case. He made an opening statement to the jury, cross-examined the prosecution's witnesses, called witnesses to testify for him, and made a brief closing argument to the jury "about as well as could be expected from a layman." He was convicted and sentenced to five years in state prison.

Gideon believed that, because he hadn't had a lawyer, he hadn't had a fair trial and that he had been unjustly convicted. He asked Florida's supreme court to overturn his conviction, but it refused. Convinced that his constitutional rights had been violated, Gideon filed a handwritten petition asking the U.S. Supreme Court to review his case—which it did in 1963.

For the hearing, Gideon was represented by Abe Fortas, a noted Washington, D.C., lawyer who was later appointed to the Supreme Court. Fortas, who volunteered his services, convinced the Court that one of its earlier rulings—a 1942 decision that said a defendant did not have the right to counsel—had been wrong, and the Gideon had been right all along. Agreeing, the Court held that the Sixth Amendment was binding on the states as well as on the federal government and that its guarantee of the assistance of counsel was a fundamental right. "In our adversary system of criminal justice," the Court declared, "any person haled into court, who is too poor to hire a lawyer, cannot be assured a fair trial unless counsel is provided for him . . . [because] lawyers in criminal courts are necessities, not luxuries."

In reaching its decision, the Court took into account not only the difference between a rich person and a poor one, but also the difference between a layman and a lawyer. It found that both discrepancies pose a threat to the fundamental belief that all persons are equal before the law: A poor man unable to afford a lawyer, like the layman unskilled in legal advocacy, though not guilty, "faces the danger of conviction because he does not know how to establish his innocence." (At a second trial in which he was represented by a state-appointed counsel, Gideon was acquitted.)

The Court's decision in Gideon's case considerably broadened the right to counsel. However, it is by no means as sweeping as it appears. According to a subsequent Court ruling in 1979, it does not mean that a defendant must always have a lawyer. One who stands only to pay a fine or who faces a very brief prison sentence need not have counsel. Nor, according to a decision in 1974, does the *Gideon* decision prevent a state from trying to get a convicted felon to repay the state for the services rendered by a court-appointed lawyer. And, according to another ruling in 1974, a defendant who is entitled to be represented at some stage of a criminal prosecution is not necessarily entitled to representation at every stage of the proceeding. The defendant must be provided with counsel at all "critical" stages prior to an appeal and then only through the first appeal to which he or she is entitled by law. The right of counsel does not extend, for example, to an appeal to the Supreme Court.

◆◆◆ Can I Defend Myself in a Criminal Case If I Want To?

Yes. It doesn't matter whether a state or federal crime is involved—you can be your own lawyer. But a judge will question you to make sure you know what you're doing—that you're acting voluntarily and intelligently in deciding to defend yourself. And, if the judge thinks the case is serious enough that you need some protection, he or she may appoint an attorney anyway to stand on the sidelines, ready to jump in if you get into trouble during the court proceedings.

A defendant who represents himself or herself is called a *pro se* defendant, from the Latin phrase meaning "for oneself." Such a defendant can control the conduct of his or her own defense, make motions, argue points of law, participate in selecting the jury, question witnesses, and address the judge and the jury.

The leading case in this area, a 1975 decision of the Supreme Court, involved Anthony Faretta, who had been charged in California with grand theft. Faretta requested that he be permitted to represent himself. He said that he had a high-school diploma, had represented himself in a previous criminal trial, and did not want a court-appointed public defender to represent him because of his concern about the public defender's heavy caseload. However, after conducting a second pretrial hearing and after questioning Faretta in detail about his understanding of law and trial procedures, the judge ruled that Faretta had not knowingly and intelligently given up his right to counsel and had no constitutional right to conduct his own defense. He reappointed the public defender and denied Faretta any role in the conduct of his defense. A jury subsequently found Faretta guilty.

When Faretta's appeal finally reached the Supreme Court, it ruled that he did indeed have a right to represent himself and conduct his own defense—a protection reflecting the other side of the coin of the Sixth Amendment's right to have "the Assistance of Counsel." The Court based its ruling on an examination of English and American law and on the recognition of personal choice. It declared:

> It is undeniable that in most criminal prosecutions defendants could better defend with counsel's guidance than by their own unskilled efforts. But where the defendant will not voluntarily accept representation by counsel, the potential advantage of a lawyer's training and experience can be realized, if at all, only imperfectly. To force a lawyer on a defendant can only lead him to believe that the law contrives against him. Moreover, it is not inconceivable that in some rare instances, the defendant might in fact present his case more effectively by conducting his own defense. Personal liberties are not rooted in the law of averages. The right to defend is personal. The defendant, and not his lawyer or the State, will bear the personal consequences of a conviction. It is the defendant, therefore, who must be free personally to decide whether in his particular case counsel is to his advantage. And although he may conduct his own defense ultimately to his own detriment, his choice must be honored out of "that respect for the individual which is the lifeblood of the law."

In a brief aside, the Court acknowledged that it might be permissible for a trial judge to appoint an attorney as an *amicus curiae*—"a friend of the court" or "standby" counsel—in case a defendant gets into difficulty or needs advice.

The Court's decision was by no means unanimous. One of three justices who dissented, Harry A. Blackmun, said, "If there is any truth to the old proverb that 'one who is his own lawyer has a fool for a client,' the Court by its opinion today now bestows a *constitutional* right on one to make a fool of himself."

The right to represent yourself is not absolute, however, as the Court made clear in a 1984 decision that explored in detail the aside in Faretta's case about the appointment of a standby counsel. This decision involved Carl Wiggins, whose first trial for robbery in Texas had ended in a mistrial. At both it and a second trial, Wiggins tried to represent himself, but each time the judge appointed two lawyers to act as standby counsel to assist Wiggins if he desired it. Wiggins objected both times, but at the first trial he agreed to let them raise objections on his behalf without first consulting him. In preparing for the second trial, Wiggins at first asked to have counsel appointed to represent him, but he changed his mind by the time of the trial, saying he would do so himself and repeating his objection to having standby counsel appointed. Nonetheless, Wiggins at first consulted with both lawyers and even allowed one to examine a prospective juror without his help—although during the *voir dire* ("to see and to speak," that part of the trial proceeding when lawyers on both sides question prospective jurors) a heated argument broke out between the two in which the lawyer finally told Wiggins, "Goddamit, sit down and shut up." As the trial progressed, Wiggins and this lawyer frequently clashed over the conduct of his defense, at times in the presence of the jury. The judge rejected Wiggins's repeated appeals to order the standby counsel to let him conduct his own defense. Wiggins's second trial resulted in his conviction.

After the Texas Supreme Court rejected Wiggins's appeal, he filed a petition for a writ of *habeas corpus* with the federal district court in Texas, seeking his release from jail. The Court of Appeals for the Fifth Circuit granted the writ, but the Supreme Court reversed the court of appeals' ruling in 1984. The Court held that the *Faretta* case merely required that a defendant who chooses to represent himself should be given a fair chance to present his defense in his own way. Wiggins, it said, had been given that opportunity. Besides which, the Court said, Wiggins had eventually waived his right to represent himself and had asked for the assistance of the standby counsel. The Court said that a standby attorney "must generally respect" a defendant's preference to conduct his own defense, but "counsel need not be excluded altogether, especially when the participation is outside the presence of the jury or is with the defendant's express or tacit consent. The defendant in this case was allowed to make his own appearance as he saw fit. In our judgment counsel's unsolicited involvement was held within reasonable limits."

◆◆◆ Does a Person Who Pleads the Fifth Amendment Necessarily Have Something Criminal to Hide?

Not at all. Despite the stigma attached to pleading the Fifth Amendment that arose in the 1950s as the result of investigations into Communist subversion during the McCarthy Era, there are many justifiable reasons for invoking the Fifth Amendment's protection against self-incrimination. For example, you may not agree with the goals of a particular congressional investigation. Or you may want to keep embarrassing facts about your past from being thrust into the headlines or you could be concerned about the reaction of relatives, friends, or an employer to, say, your past or present association with a radical political organization.

Even if you do have something criminal to hide, there is nothing wrong with "taking the Fifth." The men who wrote the Fifth Amendment made a deliberate decision—based on their experience with English legal practice—to take away from government the power to make criminal suspects or witnesses at inquiries convict themselves out of their own mouths. The history of England was filled with instances of persons being coerced into confessions so that they could be convicted of crimes against the state. But the Fifth Amendment guarantees, among other things, that the government cannot take a shortcut to convict someone of a crime or gather evidence to be used against him or her at a later date. The amendment states, "No person . . . shall be compelled in any criminal case to be a witness against himself."

Many of the most sensational Fifth Amendment claims have arisen not in court but in Congress. Ever since the first one convened in 1789, one of the principal functions of Congress has been to serve as the "grand inquest of the nation" to gather information concerning proposed legislation or to determine how the executive branch is carrying out legislation already enacted. In the 1930s, the House of Representatives created the Committee on Un-American Activities. For the next two decades, the committee—joined in 1950 by Senator Joseph R. McCarthy of Wisconsin and his special investigating subcommittee of the Senate Committee on Government Operations—conducted what they called a "crusade" to uncover

Communists in government and many other fields. Many persons were subpoenaed by the two committees and questioned about their connections with the Communist party. Many of these hearings took place in front of television cameras, solely to embarrass and humiliate the witnesses in the hope that they would be more forthcoming with facts not only about their own activities but those of friends as well. The individuals involved did not have a number of the normal protections that are enjoyed in a criminal proceeding. For example, many of them were not allowed to have an attorney present to advise them.

At first some witnesses tried to plead the First Amendment as a defense, claiming that the investigations infringed upon or violated their rights under the First Amendment to associate with anyone they chose. But the committees threatened to hold such witnesses in contempt of Congress, so the Fifth Amendment became the only refuge remaining from the loaded questions and accusations of the committee investigators.

In criminal cases, the Fifth Amendment is the centerpiece of the so-called Miranda warnings that police must give to persons suspected of a crime—suspects are told they have the right to remain silent, because otherwise anything they say can be used in court against them. Constitutional questions arise, however, over what self-incrimination entails. For example, the Supreme Court ruled in 1966 that you cannot cite the privilege against self-incrimination to avoid taking a blood test that might be introduced in evidence against you. The decision made a distinction between "testimonial" evidence and other forms of evidence that do not force a person to actually speak evidence against himself or herself. It has subsequently been extended to cover voice prints and being asked to stand in a lineup, to wear certain clothing in that lineup, and to repeat certain words, used by the criminal, while in the lineup.

The only time you cannot plead the Fifth Amendment and refuse to testify against yourself is when the government grants you immunity. There are two kinds of immunity: "Use immunity," by far the more common of the two, simply means that the government cannot use your own testimony against you; "transaction immunity" means that the government cannot prosecute you for any crime about which you are questioned or which you happen to mention after being granted immunity.

◆◆◆ What Is Double Jeopardy?

Double jeopardy is a legal term that derives from the Fifth Amendment, which declares that no person "shall . . . be subject for the same offence to be twice put in jeopardy of life or limb." It means that you cannot be tried for the same crime twice. However, simple as that sounds, the ban on double jeopardy has produced several complicated questions.

The right against double jeopardy governs only criminal cases. Its purpose is to protect a person from the harassment, frustration, inconvenience, and the expense of repeated trials for the same crime, as well as from the possibility of being held in jail awaiting retrial while the state pursues its case until it gets the result it wants.

Clearly, you cannot be tried again if your first trial results in your being acquitted or the charges against you being dismissed. And the state cannot try you again if it gets a conviction in a first trial for a "lesser included offense"—for example, if you're convicted of manslaughter, you cannot be tried subsequently for first-degree murder for the same act.

But what happens if you're convicted but the verdict is set aside by a higher court of appeal? Usually, the state can put you on trial again on the same charge, unless the higher court declared that the evidence against you was not enough to justify a conviction in the first place.

Sometimes you can be retried when a judge declares a mistrial. A mistrial means that the trial is over, as if it had never taken place at all. A judge will order a mistrial when a jury is unable to agree on a verdict (a "hung jury"), when material that should not have been entered in evidence was actually presented to the jury, or when the prosecutor is guilty of misconduct, such as interfering in the relationship between a defendant and his or her counsel by telling the former not to trust the latter.

But retrial after a mistrial is not automatic. The defendant has a Fifth Amendment right to have his or her guilt or innocence decided in one proceeding, if possible. However, that interest must be balanced against society's interest in affording the prosecutor one full and fair opportunity to present his or her evidence to the jury. When a mistrial is declared even though the defendant objects and wants to continue, the defendant can ordinarily be retried only if the mistrial was absolutely necessary—as for example, in the case of a hung jury. When a mistrial is declared with a defendant's consent, he or she ordinarily can be reprosecuted. For example, after a federal judge in Florida dismissed a defendant's lawyer for misconduct, the judge asked the defendant if he wanted to continue the trial with a new attorney or have a mistrial declared. The defendant chose a mistrial, but then objected to being tried again on the ground that it placed him in double jeopardy. The Supreme Court ruled in 1976 that he could be tried again.

◆◆◆ What Is Meant by "Cruel and Unusual Punishment"?

The phrase—from the Eighth Amendment's injunction against "cruel and unusual punishments" being "inflicted"—has had a long, complex, and controversial history. For most of the past two hundred years, courts have thought that the phrase only barred torture, other barbaric or inhumane punishment, and punishment out of all proportion to the seriousness of a crime. In our own time, the injunction has become the focus of a bitter—and as yet unresolved—debate over whether to eliminate the death penalty.

The Eighth Amendment—which bars "excessive" bail and fines as well as cruel and unusual punishments—was interpreted throughout the nineteenth century and well into the twentieth as meaning only that the government could not torture defendants or convicts, or impose penalties that were "unnecessarily cruel." For example, in 1879 the Supreme Court held that execution by shooting was not a cruel or unusual form of the death penalty. Similarly, in 1947, in a case in which a Louisiana convict sentenced to die in the electric chair was not executed at the first attempt because of a wiring defect, the Court ruled that it was not cruel and unusual punishment for the warden to order the executioner to fix the problem and try again. Writing the plurality opinion, Justice Stanley F. Reed noted that in an earlier, 1890 decision the Court had cited as examples of cruel and unusual punishment "burning at the stake, crucifixion, breaking on the wheel, or the like." Reed then quoted the following from that decision:

> Punishments are cruel when they involve torture or a lingering death; but the punishment of death is not cruel, within the meaning of that word as used in the Constitution. It implies there something inhuman and barbarous, something more than the mere extinguishment of life.

Thus, it came as a surprise to many when the Court ruled in 1972 that in certain instances the death penalty amounted to cruel and unusual punishment and was unconstitutional. At issue then was a Georgia statute that allowed the jury in a capital case to decide whether to impose the death penalty. What troubled the justices was the potential for arbitrary and discriminatory sentencing—for example, the concern that more blacks would be executed than whites. At one stroke, all existing capital-punishment statutes—which thirty-seven of the fifty states had enacted—were no longer valid.

Subsequently, thirty-five states amended their death penalty statutes or wrote new ones. Inevitably, convicts sentenced to death under the new laws challenged them, citing the 1972 Court ruling. In 1976, the Court considered a number of these challenges. It struck down a North Carolina statute that required that the death penalty be automatically imposed in murder convictions. In the Court's eyes, the across-the-board penalty, with no possibility of any lesser punishment based on the facts of the case, was as arbitrary as the Georgia penalty.

On the other hand, the Court upheld in 1976 a Georgia law requiring the jury to consider the absence or presence of specified aggravating and mitigating circumstances in deciding whether to impose the death penalty. The Court, though, was badly divided. The "opinion of the Court" was actually a "plurality opinion"—that is, an opinion representing the largest number of votes, but not a majority of the Court. It was written by Justice Potter Stewart, who explained: "We may not require the legislature to select the least severe penalty possible so long as the penalty selected is not cruelly inhumane or disproportionate to the crime involved." The death penalty does not offend society's standards of decency, Stewart continued, noting that—according to public-opinion polls—an increasing majority of Americans favored restoring it.

Since 1976, the Court has consistently upheld the use of the death penalty in all cases coming before it, despite charges by critics that the Court has chosen to ignore a large body of evidence showing that the sentence is still administered in many states in an arbitrary and discriminatory manner. Two facts have added to the controversy. First, of the hundreds of prisoners now in death-row cells awaiting execution are some thirty who committed murders in their youth. The laws of twenty-nine states permit such executions. Indiana, for one, permits the death penalty for murderers who were ten years old. Others, such as New Jersey and Connecticut, set the minimum age at fourteen and eighteen, respectively. Second, throughout the country wherever the death penalty exists, it falls far more frequently on blacks than it does on whites. In particular, a black person who kills a white person is far more likely to be sentenced to death than any other convicted murderer.

The Eighth Amendment has also been invoked by convicts challenging the severity of their prison sentences. The Court's decisions in this area are based on the principle that a prison term is considered cruel and unusual if it is grossly out of proportion to the severity of the crime or imposes unnecessary pain and suffering. In the past few years, in three cases, the Court has established three factors for a judge to consider before sentencing: (1) the gravity of the crime and the harshness of the penalty, (2) a comparison of the sentences imposed on other criminals in the same jurisdiction, and (3) a comparison of the sentences imposed for the same crime in other jurisdictions.

Notwithstanding this test, the Court has often been willing to grant states broad discretion in imposing penalties and has upheld severe punishments. For example, in 1980 the Court upheld a Texas statute governing repeat offenders that mandates a sentence of life for a criminal's third felony conviction. In this particular case, the man's conviction was for fraudulently obtaining money. His previous convictions were for credit-card fraud and for passing a forged check. The Court said the life sentence was not out of proportion to his crime.

Then, in 1982, the Court held that Virginia could impose a penalty of forty years in prison and a $20,000 fine for the possession of less than nine ounces of marijuana. In doing so, the Court reversed a lower court's decision that said the penalty was unconstitutional under the Eighth Amendment.

On the other hand, in 1983 the Court struck down a South Dakota statute that resulted in a sentence of life imprisonment without parole for a repeat offender's seventh felony offense. The Court said the sentence was grossly out of proportion to the crimes the man had committed, which included three convictions for third-degree burglary and convictions for obtaining money under false pretenses, grand larceny, and driving while intoxicated.

Occasionally, the Court has held that certain prison conditions amount to the imposition of cruel and unusual punishment. For example, in 1978 it held that the imprisonment in Arkansas of ten to eleven inmates in a cell eight feet by ten feet for more than thirty days was cruel and unusual. Moreover, in 1976, in a Texas case, the Court said that a state cannot withhold medical treatment from a prisoner.

The Schools

◆◆◆ Can My Child Express Any Political Views He or She Wants To While in School?

Yes, just as long as he or she doesn't substantially disrupt school discipline.

The leading case on this question arose in December 1965, when a group of adults and students in Des Moines, Iowa, got together to discuss ways of expressing their opposition to the Vietnam War. They agreed to wear black armbands during the holiday season and to fast on New Year's Eve. When local school principals learned of the plan, they adopted a policy that students wearing armbands in school would be asked to remove them or face suspension until the armbands were removed, even though students in some of the schools had previously worn the buttons of presidential candidates, and some even wore the Iron Cross, a symbol sometimes connected with Nazism.

Despite the ban, John Tinker, a fifteen-year-old, and Christopher Eckhardt, a sixteen-year-old, who attended high schools in Des Moines, and John's sister Mary Beth Tinker, a thirteen-year-old student in junior high school, wore armbands to school. When they refused to take them off, they were suspended. The students stayed home until after New Year's Day. They then sought an injunction against the disciplinary action, but neither a federal district court nor the U.S. Court of Appeals for the Eighth Circuit would grant one. The courts refused to follow an earlier Fifth Circuit decision that said the wearing of "freedom buttons" in a Mississippi high school could not be banned because the buttons did not "materially and substantially interfere with the requirements of appropriate discipline in the operation of the school."

However, the Supreme Court accepted the reasoning of the Fifth Circuit and ruled in favor of the Des Moines students. Writing for the Court, Justice Abe Fortas pointed out that wearing armbands presented no analogy with dress codes or rules against fighting or disrupting classes. The wearing of armbands, he wrote, is not "speech or action that intrudes upon the work of the school or the rights of other students." Moreover, the mere possibility of a disturbance could not justify the ban. Any word spoken in school that "deviates from the views of another person may start an argument or cause a disturbance," Fortas continued. "But our Constitution says we must take this risk . . . and our history says that it is this sort of hazardous freedom—this kind of openness—that is the basis of our national strength and of the independence and vigor of Americans who grow up and live in this relatively permissive, often disputatious society." State-operated schools, Fortas concluded, may not be "enclaves of totalitarianism."

◆◆◆ Can a Public School Expel or Suspend My Child without a Hearing?

No. Under the Due Process Clause of the Fourteenth Amendment, if your child is threatened with even a brief suspension, he or she generally must receive a hearing before being suspended or expelled from school. But the exact form of the hearing is pretty much up to the school authorities, and tough penalties for drug or alcohol abuse are perfectly permissible under the Constitution.

The Supreme Court first faced this issue in 1975 in a case that had begun four years earlier when public schools in Columbus, Ohio, faced frequent outbreaks of student unrest. Under an Ohio statute, school officials suspended ten high-school students for ten days without a hearing. The students filed suit to have the suspensions removed from their records and to have the Ohio statute declared unconstitutional under the Due Process Clause, which forbids depriving any person of life, liberty, or property without due process of law. A three-judge federal district court agreed with the students and declared the Ohio law unconstitutional.

On appeal, the Supreme Court backed the lower court's decision by a five-to-four vote. Writing for the Court, Justice Byron R. White noted that the students had a legitimate claim under Ohio law to a public education that could not be taken away because of alleged misconduct without providing "fundamentally fair procedures to determine whether the misconduct has occurred." Ohio, White continued, was not constitutionally required to provide and maintain a public-school system, but its decision to do so obligated it to recognize that students do not "shed their constitutional rights at the schoolhouse door."

At the same time, the Court pointed out that it was both difficult and inappropriate to say what kind of hearing process was required under the Due Process Clause. However, following many of its own earlier interpretations of the Clause, the Court said that a student must at least be given notice of the charges against him or her and an opportunity to answer them. And, it added, as a general rule the hearing should precede the suspension or expulsion, although the justices acknowledged that in certain circumstances—which they did not spell out—this would not always be possible. The justices did specify, however, that students did not have to be represented at the hearing by counsel, nor was it required to give them an opportunity to confront and cross-examine witnesses or call their own witnesses. The justices pointed out that imposing such requirements would overwhelm the resources of school systems.

Critics of the Court's decision—beginning with the four justices who dissented—have argued that the Court was leading the federal judiciary into an impossible thicket of "judicial intervention in the operation of our public schools that may affect adversely the quality of education." But lower courts have largely deferred to school authorities in evaluating hearings that are conducted before students are suspended or expelled. For example, in a 1979 case, a United States district court held that the principal of a North Carolina high school had satisfied the due process requirement when he suspended a student for ten days. The principal had informed the student that he was accused of stealing a wallet, showed him the wallet—which had been found among the student's belongings—gave him the chance to answer the charge and discussed the matter with the student's father. Similarly, in 1981 another federal district court upheld disciplinary actions taken against five Indiana students for distributing leaflets calling for a walkout by their fellow students to protest several earlier suspensions. The students had an opportunity to discuss the charges against them with the principal before they were suspended for three days, and a full hearing was held before a school-board examiner before they were expelled for the semester.

Most states take a firm stand against the possession, sale, and use of drugs—and courts have sustained the stiff penalties that states and their school districts impose for violations of antidrug rules. In 1981 a federal district court upheld the expulsion of a Kentucky student for the rest of the school year for smoking marijuana on school grounds, rejecting the student's argument that so severe a punishment was a violation of the Due Process Clause. Similarly, federal district courts in Maine and Ohio upheld the suspensions of students on drug charges in 1982 and 1983. And, in 1982, the Supreme Court upheld the decision of an Arkansas school board to act under an antidrug regulation in suspending a student caught drunk during school hours. The Court ruled that alcohol could be considered a drug for purposes of enforcing the rule and that the suspension—for the rest of the semester—was not an excessive penalty under the Due Process Clause.

◆◆◆ Does My Child Have to Take Sex-Education Classes in Public School?

Yes, if the school or state policy requires it. But most school districts now permit students to elect not to take the course.

Many parents and parents' groups—usually religious fundamentalists—have sued in many parts of the nation either to have sex-education classes halted or to allow their children to choose not to attend them. When they do so, they generally make two constitutional arguments: first, that requiring students to take the classes violates the students' constitutional right to privacy and the right of parents to direct the sexual education of their children; second, that such classes interfere with their children's ability to engage in the "free exercise" of their religion and its moral teachings.

Although this issue has never reached the Supreme Court, a number of lower federal and state courts have examined the parents' claims and all have ruled against them. Although the courts have recognized a child's right to privacy and a parent's authority over the child, they have carefully weighed those rights against a school board's interest in a balanced curriculum and a state's interest in informing its citizens about matters of sexual health. All the courts have found that the offering of sex-education classes is a reasonable way for a school board to achieve such state interests. The classes, the courts have concluded, do not involve any coercion directed at the practice of one's religion and so do not violate the Free Exercise Clause of the First Amendment. This argument is made even stronger in school districts where the classes are not compulsory.

◆◆◆ Can a Local School Board Remove Books from the Library of My Child's School?

It depends on the board's reason for doing so. Ordinarily a school board has great latitude in deciding curriculum and related matters, such as what books go into a library. But there's a serious question whether the board can *remove* books as part of an effort to push some point of view—either because the books contain ideas the board dislikes or because they do not conform to the board's view of what is acceptable in politics, religion, or other matters of opinion. What is involved in this kind of situation is a fundamental conflict between the interest of a community—acting through its school board—to decide what values to teach its children and the First Amendment right of children to learn a diversity of ideas.

The Supreme Court confronted but did not resolve this issue in a 1982 suit brought against the school board of the Island Trees Union Free School District on Long Island, New York, for removing nine books from its high-school and junior-high-school libraries: Kurt Vonnegut's *Slaughterhouse Five*; Bernard Malamud's *The Fixer* (which won the 1967 Pulitzer Prize for fiction); Piri Thomas's *Down These Mean Streets*; Alice Childress's *A Hero Ain't Nothin' but a Sandwich*; Desmond Morris's *The Naked Ape*; Jerome Archer's *A Reader for Writers: A Critical Anthology of Prose Readings*; Eldridge Cleaver's *Soul on Ice*; Langston Hughes's compilation, *The Best Short Stories by Negro Writers*; and *Go Ask Alice*, by an anonymous author. The books appeared on a list compiled by an organization called Parents of New York United, a politically conservative organization that considered the books to be anti-Christian, anti-Semitic, and just plain "filthy." After getting the list, the local school board ordered the books removed from the shelves, declaring that it was the board's duty to protect schoolchildren from what it saw as the moral dangers of this kind of literature.

The Supreme Court was unable to resolve the issue because the justices were sharply divided and no single opinion commanded a majority. There was agreement that local school boards have broad powers in the management of school affairs, including a legitimate and substantial interest in promoting respect for authority and inculcating values necessary to the maintenance of a democratic political system. However, Justice William J. Brennan, Jr., and three of his colleagues found that the courts have a responsibility to ensure that school boards perform this delicate function within the limits set by the First Amendment. For them, the amendment itself sets a national educational policy in favor of students' having access to a diversity of ideas. The school library, no less than a local library, in the view of Brennan and his colleagues, is a "locus of understanding, a place where students must always remain free to inquire, to study and to evaluate, and to gain new maturity and understanding." The school library, moreover, is a place where a student can explore the unknown and discover ideas and develop interests that are not part of the standard curriculum. Brennan concluded that whether or not the school board could remove the books depended on its reasons for doing so, and that its action would be unconstitutional if a court found that the members of the board had acted to impose the kind of "officially prescribed orthodoxy" condemned by the First Amendment.

The Supreme Court remanded the case to the federal district court for an inquiry as to whether political or partisan considerations had motivated the board's decision, but the case was dismissed after the Island Trees Board of Education decided to return the nine books to the libraries' shelves.

◆◆◆ Can My Child's Locker Be Searched?

Yes, if the child's principal or teachers have reasonable grounds to suspect that their search will turn up evidence that the youngster has violated or is violating either the law or school regulations. The Supreme Court, in a six-to-three decision in 1985, ruled that although the Fourth Amendment requires that a search conducted by public-school authorities be reasonable, it does not require that they have a warrant or need to show probable cause that they'll uncover some criminal evidence.

The case involved a high-school teacher in Piscataway, New Jersey, who discovered two girls smoking cigarettes in the school bathroom and took them to the principal's office, where they met with an assistant vice principal. One girl admitted that she had violated the school's rule against smoking. However, the other claimed that she had never smoked. The assistant vice principal asked her to step into his office and demanded to see her purse. When he opened it, he found a package of cigarettes. As he reached into the purse for it, he also saw a package of cigarette rolling papers. In his experience, they were closely associated with the use of marijuana. Seeking more evidence to justify his suspicion that the girl was using the drug, he then searched the purse thoroughly, finding a small amount of marijuana, a pipe, a number of empty plastic bags, a large number of dollar bills, an index card that appeared to be a list of students who owed her money, and two letters that indicated that she was involved in marijuana dealing.

The assistant vice principal notified the girl's mother. He also turned over to the police the materials he found. Later that day at the police station, the girl confessed that she had been selling marijuana at the school. Based on this confession and on the evidence implicating her in drug dealing, the state brought delinquency charges against her in juvenile court. The girl's attorney moved to suppress the evidence on the ground that the school administrator's search of her purse violated the Fourth Amendment.

When the case reached the Supreme Court, the Court sought to strike a balance between a student's legitimate expectations of privacy and a school's equally strong need to maintain a safe, orderly environment. Noting the recent increase in drug use and violence in the nation's schools, the Court held that the interest of public-school officials in maintaining order outweighed the student's interest. However, the justices carefully emphasized that their decision did not mean that students were required to give up all their rights to privacy. For example, they said, school officials, like police officers, are bound by the Fourth Amendment and may not arbitrarily search such "nondisruptive yet highly personal items as photographs, letters, and diaries." On the other hand, the justices also declared that the school environment requires some easing of the restrictions usually limiting searches by law-enforcement officers. For example, requiring a principal or teacher to obtain a warrant before searching a student would, the Court said, significantly interfere with the "maintenance of the swift and informal disciplinary procedures needed in the schools."

The Court also held that although ordinarily the police must have probable cause to believe that a person has committed a crime before carrying out a search, school officials need not. The search, it said, should depend simply on its "reasonableness"—that is, whether it was justified at its beginning and whether, when the search was actually carried out, it "was reasonably related in scope to the circumstances which justified the interference in the first place."

The Court said two separate searches had taken place in the case of the New Jersey girl. The first was for the cigarettes. That search provided the suspicion that prompted the second search, when the marijuana was discovered. Applying its "reasonableness" test, the Court concluded that both searches were valid under the Fourth Amendment.

The Workplace ═══════════════════════

◆◆◆ Does the Constitution Tell My Boss When He or She Can or Cannot Fire Me?

That depends on whether you work for the government or a private company. Federal, state, and municipal employees enjoy extensive protections derived from both the Constitution and state and local statutes. Employees of private companies generally are not protected against their employers by the Constitution—but private companies now are bound by state and federal laws dealing with discrimination in the workplace that regulate when a person can be fired.

Government workers fall under the protective umbrella of the Fifth and Fourteenth amendments, which provide that the government cannot deprive any person of "life, liberty, or property, without due process of law." Courts have said that this protection against arbitrary action applies to both hirings and firings by government at all levels—local, state, and federal.

As for workers in private industry, Congress has enacted many laws to protect them from being fired arbitrarily or for an inappropriate reason—for example, because a worker is black. Title VII of the Civil Rights Act of 1964 prevents workers from being fired because of race, color, religion, sex, or national origin. Similarly, the Age Discrimination Act of 1967 bars employers from firing workers because of how old they are. Many other state and federal laws also make it illegal to fire an employee because of his or her political beliefs—and, in some localities, his or her sexual preference.

Also, under common law—that is, law made by judges in deciding cases as opposed to statutes passed by legislatures—some courts have recently held that an implied contract exists between an employee and his or her boss and that, after a certain number of years, the employee can be fired only for cause. That's quite a change from the previous common-law rule, which said that in most cases a worker could be fired at any time for any reason.

◆◆◆ Does the Constitution Give Workers the Right to Join a Union?

Yes and no. The First Amendment protects the freedom of individuals "peaceably to assemble" or associate together. This means that neither Congress nor a state can pass a law outlawing labor unions. However, the right of assembly does not extend so far as to give an unqualified right to workers to unionize on any terms they choose.

At the beginning of the republic, American courts followed English common law and custom regarding unions—which were antilabor. Starting with the English Statute of Labourers in 1349, English law imposed harsh penalties on workers who tried to organize to secure better wages and working conditions. In 1721, for example, the Court of King's Bench held that a union of tailors seeking wage increases amounted to a criminal conspiracy. And in 1800 Parliament enacted a law that prohibited workers "to enter any combination to obtain an advance of wages, or to lessen or alter the hours of work."

In the United States, the first major prosecution for criminal conspiracy involving workers—a shoemakers' union in this instance—occurred in 1806 in Philadelphia. Nevertheless, American workers continued to try to organize. A major break came in 1842, when a bootmakers' union in Boston fined one of its members for doing extra work without pay and then expelled him for refusing to pay the fine and tried to get his employer to fire him. The union and its president were prosecuted for criminal conspiracy, and when they appealed their conviction, the case reached the Massachusetts Supreme Judicial Court. Chief Justice Lemuel Shaw ruled that a labor union was not a criminal conspiracy or even a conspiracy in restraint of trade. His decision did away almost completely with criminal-conspiracy prosecutions of labor unions because of the nearly universal respect in which Shaw was held. In the 1880s, employers tried to revive the doctrine of criminal conspiracy but soon abandoned it because of the lengthy and costly trials it required and sought instead to obtain injunctions against strikes and other union activities. This was especially so after the Sherman Antitrust Act, which was sometimes interpreted to cover labor unions, was passed in 1890.

The Norris-LaGuardia Anti-Injunction Act of 1932, sponsored by Senator George W. Norris of Nebraska and Representative Fiorello LaGuardia of New York, barred courts from issuing injunctions in most labor disputes. In 1935, the Wagner-Connery Act first spelled out, in federal law, that workers "shall have the right to self-organization, to form, join, or assist labor organizations." But that right is heavily regulated by federal law under the authority of the Commerce Clause of the Constitution (in Article I, Section 8). Much of this regulation stems from the Taft-Hartley Labor Relations Act of 1947, which established a comprehensive system of federal labor law.

Under federal law, the National Labor Relations Board oversees most union activity. It monitors the establishment of a union in a factory or office. If a majority of workers vote to join, the union becomes the sole representative and bargaining agent for all the workers. Typically—if the workers so choose—this also establishes what is called a union shop, which means that anyone who is subsequently hired must join the union (or at least pay dues to support the collective-bargaining activities of the union) whether they want to or not. However, the Taft-Hartley Act has provisions that permit a state to pass a so-called right-to-work statute effectively outlawing the union shop. Such a statute mandates an open shop, where union and nonunion employees work side by side and union membership is not required. Those who want to join a union may still do so in a right-to-work state. The purpose of such a law is to grant anyone who chooses *not* to join a union the right to refuse to do so. Nineteen states have adopted right-to-work laws.

◆◆◆ Can I Be Fired from a City, State, or Federal Job Because I Do Not Belong to the Same Political Party as My Boss?

No. The First and Fourteenth amendments protect you from being fired, unless you're a policymaker such as a cabinet officer, presidential adviser, or head of a state agency—positions that obviously require that your political views jibe with those of your boss.

However, in deciding whether a particular worker who has been dismissed because of political affiliation is one of those who can be fired consistent with the Constitution, courts do not look at job titles. Instead, under principles developed by the Supreme Court, they look at the purpose and duties of the person's job itself. The idea is to determine whether the worker's affiliation with a political party different from that of his or her boss will hamper the worker in carrying out his or her duties and responsibilities.

The Supreme Court laid out the basic rules in a 1976 case in which it held that a newly elected Democratic sheriff of Cook County, Illinois, could not discharge several Republican employees—three process servers and a juvenile-court bailiff and security guard. Justice William J. Brennan, Jr., writing for himself and Justices Byron R. White and Thurgood Marshall, concluded that patronage dismissals must be limited to "policymaking positions." Justices Potter Stewart and Harry A. Blackmun concurred, providing the crucial fourth and fifth votes for the result, but expressed the reasons for doing so a bit differently. As Stewart put it, "a nonpolicymaking, nonconfidential government employee [cannot be discharged] from a job that he is satisfactorily performing upon the sole ground of his political beliefs."

Four years later, in a case involving two Republican assistant public defenders who were dismissed by Manhattan's newly appointed Democratic public defender, the Court reconsidered the question and expanded the protection of non-civil-service workers against being fired for patronage reasons. Writing for a solid majority of six justices, Justice John Paul Stevens said: "[T]he ultimate inquiry is not whether the label 'policymaker' or 'confidential' fits a particular position; rather, the question is whether the hiring authority can demonstrate that party affiliation is an appropriate requirement for the effective performance of the public office involved." Applying this new version of the rule, the Court decided that, because the assistant public defenders were considered "competent attorneys" and because they were not involved in policymaking or confidential activities, they should be reinstated.

In 1982, the U.S. Court of Appeals for the Third Circuit applied the new rule to say that a Pennsylvania district attorney could fire an assistant district attorney because of his political affiliation. The court agreed with a federal district court that the duties of the assistant district attorney were "consonant" with those of the district attorney; indeed, it noted that the assistant might have to assume his superior's duties if the district attorney were absent. Earlier that year, the same appellate court had used similar reasoning to determine that, as a matter of law, the positions of city solicitor and assistant city solicitor in York, Pennsylvania, were those for which party affiliation was an appropriate requirement for effective performance and therefore the mayor's dismissal of those attorneys because of their political affiliation did not violate the First Amendment.

The Military ════════════════════

◆◆◆ Who Decides Whether We Go to War?

That's a matter of debate, but it seems to be the president—at least for the first sixty days, under the War Powers Resolution of 1973. After that, Congress plays a stronger role and the decision to go to war becomes a more equal partnership.

The Framers of the Constitution purposely rejected the virtually unrestrained war-making authority of the British monarchy. Instead, they delicately balanced the war powers of the United States between the president and Congress. Congress is given exclusive authority to raise an army and declare war (Article I, Section 8), but the president is designated the commander in chief of the armed forces (Article II, Section 2). Like a pendulum, the exact scope of authority that each branch of government has in a given situation has swung back and forth since the earliest days of the nation and has been a continuing subject of controversy.

One early draft of the Constitution gave Congress the power to "make war." However, on the motion of James Madison of Virginia and Elbridge Gerry of Massachusetts, the Constitutional Convention substituted the phrase "declare war." According to Madison's notes, the change was designed to give the president the power to repel sudden attacks against the nation.

The first test of this authority came in 1801 when President Thomas Jefferson sent navy ships out to protect commercial shipping from the so-called Barbary pirates of North Africa. In a letter to Congress detailing the exploits of the *Enterprise,* which had captured a vessel from one of the Barbary states, rendered it harmless, and then released it, Jefferson wrote:

> Unauthorized by the Constitution, without the sanction of Congress, to go beyond the line of defense, the vessel, being disabled from committing further hostilities, was liberated with its crew. The

legislature will doubtless consider whether, by authorizing measures of offense also, they will place our force on an equal footing with that of its adversaries.

Jefferson's letter seems to indicate that he believed *defensive* actions were within a president's war powers, but that *offensive* actions needed the approval of Congress. As the role of the United States in world affairs increased, this distinction between offensive and defensive action began to deteriorate. In 1844, President John Tyler committed troops to defend Texas, then an independent republic, from possible invasion by Mexico. Ten years later, President Franklin Pierce approved the bombardment of Greytown, Nicaragua, in retaliation for violence against American citizens there.

The early twentieth century was marked by an even greater expansion of unilateral presidential war-making power. In 1900, President William McKinley sent 5,000 soldiers to China to help quell the Boxer Rebellion, and Presidents Theodore Roosevelt, William Howard Taft, and Woodrow Wilson, among others, sent troops or intervened in several nations in the Caribbean and in Central America. These presidents, however, were careful to describe their actions as "neutral interpositions" limited to the protection of American lives and property. Outright foreign intervention was still thought to require congressional approval. Moreover, both World War I and World War II were formally declared by Congress.

The modern view of the president's powers as commander in chief began with President Harry S Truman's decision to rush 50,000 troops to South Korea to repel an invasion by North Korea in 1950. This was the first time that a president offered only his constitutional powers as commander in chief as justification for a substantial troop deployment. Truman's conception of those powers was endorsed by his successor, President Dwight D. Eisenhower, who sent 15,000 marines to Lebanon to defend a newly established government and stave off civil war in 1958, and by subsequent presidents during the Vietnam War and other international incidents involving military force.

This expansion of the president's war-making powers has largely been held valid by federal courts. As early as 1800, the Supreme Court recognized that the Constitution allowed Congress to authorize the president to take limited actions without an explicit declaration of war.

The president's authority to involve American forces in Vietnam was granted by the Gulf of Tonkin Resolution adopted by Congress in 1964. The resolution empowered the president "to take all necessary steps, including the use of armed forces, to assist any member or protocol state [of the South-East Asia Treaty Organization] requesting assistance in defense of its freedom."

The repeal of the Gulf of Tonkin Resolution in 1971 led to a series of lawsuits challenging the constitutionality of the war because, it was argued, continuing the war without the sanction was illegal. In approaching them, the federal courts faced two issues. The first was the question of implicit consent: Did Congress tacitly authorize the conflict by passing military appropriation bills, extension of the draft, and other related legislation? The second was the question of the courts' "competency": Was this strictly a political question outside the province of the courts and solely the province of Congress and the president, or was there a legal issue that the court could decide? Most courts that had to rule on these questions held that Congress had given its consent by passing the military-aid measures. Nearly all of them indicated that they believed the issue was not justiciable—that is, that the issue was outside their jurisdiction.

In an effort to check the war powers of the president and assert more control over the deployment of troops—the result chiefly of bitterness engendered by the Vietnam War—Congress enacted the War Powers Resolution in 1973 over President Richard M. Nixon's veto. This law requires that the president report to Congress within forty-eight hours after American military units have been sent to an area where they face hostilities or imminent hostilities. If Congress has not explicitly authorized the use of soldiers within sixty days, the armed forces must be withdrawn.

Every president since Nixon has resisted complying with its provisions. When President Ronald W. Reagan signed an eighteen-month authorization to employ troops in Lebanon in 1982, he became the first president actually to sign a war-powers resolution. However, he purposely included in his accompanying statement a disclaimer saying that he did not feel constitutionally bound by its troop-withdrawal provision.

The next year, nearly ten years to the day after the adoption of the War Powers Resolution, the Grenada incident raised new and troubling questions about the balance of authority between Congress and the president over control of the United States armed forces. A coup had overthrown Grenada's Marxist premier, Maurice Bishop. On the evening of October 24, 1983, President Reagan summoned Speaker of the House Thomas P. O'Neill, Jr., and the majority and minority leaders of the House and Senate to the White House to give them confidential advance notice that U.S. armed forces would invade Grenada the next day. In his official letter to the House and Senate informing them of the invasion, the president asserted as reasons for the invasion his concern that the complete collapse of the island's government endangered the lives of 1,100 Americans (mostly students at a medical school) and posed a "threat to the peace and security of the region." The president announced that he was committing the United States to assist the expeditionary force of the Organization of Eastern Caribbean States in restoring order and tranquility to Grenada. "This deployment of United States Armed Forces," he added, "is being undertaken pursuant to my constitutional authority with respect to the conduct of foreign relations and as Commander-in-Chief of the United States Armed Forces." The president's sole acknowledgment of the War Powers Resolution was his declaration: "In accordance with my desire that the Congress be informed on this matter, and consistent with the War Powers Resolution, I am providing this report on this deployment of the United States Armed Forces."

Congressional response was quick, as members of the House and Senate argued over whether the president had complied with the War Powers Resolution. On November 6, the House adopted a resolution demanding the withdrawal of American armed forces by December 25—that is, within sixty days after their original deployment in Grenada. The Senate's companion resolution was lost in parliamentary maneuvering. By December 15, 1983, forty-eight days after the original deployment and well within the sixty-day limit of the War Powers Resolution, all American combat forces had been removed from Grenada, leaving only three hundred military police. While members of the House and Senate claimed that their actions under the Resolution had compelled the Reagan administration to comply with the sixty-day limit, others pointed out that the War Powers Resolution was supposed to be self-activating—that is, that it should not have required special actions by the House and Senate to set a limit to the president's use of armed forces in Grenada.

The Grenada operation involved 5,500 American soldiers, of whom 18 were killed and 116 were wounded. Grenadian casualties were 45 soldiers killed and 337 wounded; also, 24 Cuban soldiers were killed and 59 were wounded. Actual fighting lasted three days.

As a result of the War Powers Resolution, if, after the expiration of a congressional troop authorization or the initial sixty-day cut-off provision, a president refused to withdraw the troops, he would undoubtedly face a battle with Congress over funding the operation, and possibly court action as well. If the latter occurs, the courts again would be confronted with the question of their competency to judge such an issue.

In 1983 the U.S. Court of Appeals for the District of Columbia Circuit decided the only suit brought to date under the War Powers Resolution: *Crockett* v. *Reagan*, in which twenty-nine members of the House of Representatives sued for an injunction directing President Reagan to withdraw all American military aid and personnel from El Salvador and prohibiting any further aid. A district judge had dismissed the suit because it presented a political question that could not be resolved by the courts. The court of appeals upheld the decision, though it did not comment on the district judge's suggestion that "were Congress to pass a resolution to the effect that a report was required under the [War Powers Resolution], or to the effect that the forces should be withdrawn, and the President disregarded it, a constitutional impasse appropriate for judicial resolution would be presented." The lower court's decision seems to indicate that in certain circumstances the federal courts may be willing to enforce the Resolution. This, in turn, raises the possibility that a court might attempt to order the president to comply with the statutory provisions.

◆◆◆ What Gives the Government the Right to Run a Draft?

The Constitution—in several clauses of Article I, Section 8—grants Congress the power "[t]o raise and support Armies," "[t]o provide and maintain a Navy," and "[t]o make Rules for the Government and Regulation of the land and naval Forces." Even given these constitutional provisions, however, the question is not an idle one. Military conscription by the North during the Civil War sparked riots. In our own times, there was widespread resistance to conscription by opponents of the Vietnam War and, more recently, by young men protesting laws requiring them to register for the draft.

A draft was first instituted in 1814, during the War of 1812, and covered all men between the ages of twenty and forty-five years. (The Revolutionary War had been fought by volunteer forces, in which men enlisted for one- or two-year tours of duty and then returned home after the tours were up if their officers could not persuade them to reenlist.) There were several drafts in 1863 and 1864 for the Civil War, as well as calls for volunteers and enlistments for which cash bounties were offered. The 1863 draft prompted antidraft riots in several Northern cities, the most serious of which took place in New York City. Its mayor sympathized with the Confederacy and repeatedly urged that the city should secede from the Union and from New York State, either joining the Confederacy or going it alone. In four days of rioting in New York City, more than one hundred persons were killed.

The government did not use the draft in the Spanish-American War of 1898, but revived it for World War I, initially calling up men between twenty-one and thirty. Though the draft was favorably received in general, there were some protests that led to court challenges in 1918. However, the Supreme Court rejected them.

The draft was reinstituted in 1940, after the outbreak of war in Europe. It was the first peacetime draft in American history, but under the law anyone drafted could serve only in the United States or in its Western Hemisphere possessions. The restriction was quickly removed after the Japanese bombing of Pearl Harbor on December 7, 1941. Neither the 1940 draft nor its wartime successor prompted any widespread protests or resistance.

After a three-year gap, the draft was reinstated with enactment of the Universal Military Training and Service Act of 1951 and continued throughout the Korean War and the Vietnam War. After four extensions—in 1955, 1959, 1963, and 1967—the draft finally expired on June 30, 1973, and registration was suspended from 1975 to 1980. Although there is no draft now—the army is an all-volunteer one—since 1980 young men have had to register with the Selective Service System within a year after their eighteenth birthday.

Whether a peacetime draft or a wartime one, courts have always upheld the right of the federal government to conscript men for military service. As was recently stated by the Supreme Court: "Few interests can be more compelling than a nation's need to insure its own security. It is well to remember that freedom as we know it has been suppressed in many countries. Unless a society has the capability and will to defend itself from the aggressions of others, constitutional protections of any sort have little meaning."

In 1980, after President Jimmy Carter ordered the reestablishment of draft registration, several young men challenged the exclusion of women. The Supreme Court, however, rejected the challenge, holding that the exclusion of women did not deny men the equal protection of the law. According to Justice William H. Rehnquist, who wrote the Court's majority opinion, Congress believed that any future draft would be used to obtain combat forces, and because women in the armed forces are excluded from combat assignments, Congress could reasonably exclude them from the draft. Three dissenting justices found that Congress's exclusion of women grossly undervalued the role that women in the military could play in a national emergency and reflected the traditional stereotypes that relegate women to an inferior status.

Not only does the federal government have the power to draft men, but your state government does, too, according to interpretations of the phrase "the Militia of the several States" in Article II, Section 2, of the Constitution. Although no state has done so in more than a century, in the early days of the republic many states had mandatory militia service for all men.

◆◆◆ What Makes a Person a Traitor?

Despite what some people who call their critics traitors say, treason— the only crime specifically defined in the Constitution—"consist[s] only in levying War" against the United States "or in adhering to their Enemies, giving them Aid and Comfort." Moreover, according to Article III, Section 3, no one can be convicted of treason "unless on the Testimony of two Witnesses to the same overt Act, or on Confession in open Court." The Framers of the Constitution deliberately refused to make criticism of the government or of its elected and appointed officials punishable as treason, as it was in England for most of its history.

In medieval times, just about any act against the "king's peace" was considered treason because it threatened his authority. Any criticism of government policies could also be considered treason for the same reason. And any new threat to the authority of the Crown was quickly defined as treason, with the result that a large number of acts were punishable as treason by the middle of the fourteenth century. In 1350, Parliament enacted what came to be known as the Statute of Edward III, named after the king who was then on the throne. It severely reduced the kinds of acts that could be punished as treason, leaving only three categories of offenses—levying war against the king; adhering to his enemies, or giving them aid and comfort; and plotting or imagining the death of the king. The last category became known as "constructive treason," and was used to punish critics of government policy as well as those who, like Guy Fawkes in 1605, actually plotted to murder the king.

Most colonial statutes defining treason were based on the Statute of Edward III, and during the Revolution the states enacted treason laws based on it as well. But the states, sensitive to the abuse of treason prosecutions under English rule, omitted the offense of constructive treason, and the Constitutional Convention of 1787 ultimately confirmed this view of treason prosecutions in the narrow definition it placed in Article III.

James Willard Hurst, author of the most respected book on the subject, has identified thirty-three cases of prosecutions for treason between 1790 and the early 1950s. The most famous were the trial of the leaders of the Whiskey Rebellion for resisting enforcement of federal tax laws in 1794;

the attempt to prosecute Aaron Burr for conspiring to separate the western territories from the United States and establish his own empire; the prosecution of Iva Ikoku Toguri d'Aquino for her radio broadcasts as "Tokyo Rose" during World War II; and the attempt to prosecute the noted poet Ezra Pound for his pro-Fascist broadcasts for the Italian government during the same war. The leaders of the Whiskey Rebellion were convicted and sentenced to prison, but later pardoned. Burr was acquitted. Mrs. d'Aquino was convicted and served several years in prison. (Long after she was released, the government continued to press her for the $10,000 fine imposed along with her sentence, until President Gerald R. Ford pardoned her in January 1977.) Pound was never tried because he successfully pleaded that he was insane and thus incompetent to stand trial. (He was released after twelve years of confinement in a mental hospital.)

Nazi Germany's attempt to send saboteurs to the United States in 1942 produced two differing Supreme Court rulings on treason. The first involved Anthony Cramer, a naturalized American who had been born in Germany. He befriended two saboteurs, met with them, ate with them, and talked with them, unaware that he was under surveillance by agents of the Federal Bureau of Investigation. The government argued that his activities satisfied the constitutional requirement of an "overt Act," and that the FBI agents' surveillance satisfied the need to have two witnesses. The Court, however, disagreed, saying that an overt act must demonstrate a defendant's intent to commit treason. The government, it said, could not show treason by citing the context and circumstances of an act innocent in itself. In addition, the Court said that the evidence of two witnesses must establish the traitorous intent of the act beyond a reasonable doubt, which the case against Cramer did not.

The second case concerned Hans Haupt, the father of one of the saboteurs, who gave shelter to his son, tried to get a job for him in a factory manufacturing the Norden bombsight, and helped him to buy a car. On the surface, it seemed that those acts were just as innocent as those at issue in the Cramer case, but the Court thought otherwise. In an opinion written by Justice Robert H. Jackson—who had also written the Cramer opinion—the Court argued that the acts at issue in Haupt's case clearly were "helpful to an enemy agent." The difference between the two cases is that Haupt's actions could reasonably be interpreted as giving aid and comfort to an enemy, while Cramer's could not.

The Court also held, in 1952, that an American citizen can commit treason even when he is not inside the United States. The defendant in this case, Tomoya Kawakita, held joint American and Japanese citizenship and was visiting Japan as a student at the time that war broke out between Japan and the United States in 1941. He remained in Japan and worked as a civilian interpreter in a Japanese factory manufacturing war materials. He also beat American prisoners of war assigned to work in the factory and its mines.

Since the early 1950s, the government has not prosecuted anyone for treason. Instead, it has brought charges under specific laws that make certain acts illegal, such as espionage laws or the Atomic Energy Act, as in the case of Julius and Ethel Rosenberg, who were convicted in 1951 of passing nuclear secrets to the Russians during World War II. The government chose to prosecute Daniel Ellsberg for releasing the top-secret *Pentagon Papers* to the *New York Times* under the espionage laws. Yet despite demands by right-wing representatives, the government—without giving any reason—chose *not* to prosecute actress Jane Fonda or former Attorney General Ramsey Clark for their visits to North Vietnam during the Vietnam War.

◆◆◆ Do I Enjoy the Same Rights in Wartime As I Do in Peacetime?

Not quite. In the past, the federal and state governments have imposed harsh restrictions on individual rights during wartime. Since World War II, however, the Supreme Court has greatly expanded its interpretation of civil liberties and civil rights, so that it probably would be far more skeptical of and hostile to proposed restrictions than it was during both World War I and World War II. Nonetheless, courts have given and probably will continue to give greater weight to government arguments for restrictions in wartime than in peacetime.

Such restrictions date back to the American Revolution, when state governments persecuted the Loyalists as well as those who refused to swear loyalty oaths merely because they wanted to remain neutral. In 1798, the Federalists adopted the Alien and Sedition Acts to suppress criticism of the undeclared naval war between the United States and France.

In the 1860s President Abraham Lincoln claimed vast emergency powers to enable him to conduct the Civil War. He suspended the writ of *habeas corpus* in 1861. At the same time, he ordered military authorities to arrest and detain citizens suspected of engaging in or planning "treasonable practices." Although Chief Justice Roger B. Taney denounced Lincoln's actions in a circuit court opinion, his decision had no effect. Congress dutifully authorized Lincoln's suspension of *habeas corpus* in

1863, thus removing a major safeguard against illegal detentions and imprisonments.

The Civil War proved an especially fruitful source of authority for sweeping presidential and congressional war powers. By far the most striking violation of individual rights then was the government's institution of martial law and the trial of civilians by military courts. Ultimately, in 1866, the Supreme Court ruled that the president could not authorize military courts to try civilians in areas remote from battle lines when civilian courts were still available. The decision came in a case involving a man who had been sentenced to death by a military commission in Indianapolis for conspiring to aid Confederate prisoners. Writing for the Court, Justice David Davis declared: "The Constitution of the United States is a law for rulers and people, equally in war and peace."

Nevertheless, the government once more sought to suppress dissent and prevent interference with the war effort during World War I—and the Court went along. It upheld the Espionage Act of 1917, which made it a crime to, among other things, "willfully cause or attempt to cause disloyalty, insubordination, mutiny, or refusal of duty in the armed forces," or to "willfully obstruct the recruitment" of soldiers and sailors. At issue was the conviction of a man and a woman for sending letters to prospective draftees opposing the draft. The Court declared that the letters posed a "clear and present danger" that they would "bring about substantive evils that Congress has a right to prevent." The Court also upheld in 1919 a 1918 federal ban on drinking, justifying it as a wartime measure. In addition, in 1919 the Court upheld the conviction of labor leader Eugene Debs for attempting to call a railroad strike during the war. (While serving his sentence, Debs ran for president in 1920 on the Socialist ticket and received a million votes.) During the war—both by congressional enactment and presidential action—the government marshalled its powers to commit the entire energy and resources of the nation to the war effort. Under the Lever Act of 1917, Congress empowered the president to create new agencies or to carry out emergency domestic functions through whatever established agency he chose. Under that law, President Woodrow Wilson (through the Council of National Defense headed by Secretary of War Newton D. Baker) exercised control over wages and prices (especially food and fuel), operated the nation's railroads, established censorship of the mail in order to enforce espionage and sedition acts passed in 1917 and 1918, and created the Committee on Public Information, which effectively controlled the American press. All these measures were quickly repealed after the war ended.

During World War II, Congress enacted legislation authorizing, among other things, federal control of prices and rents as well as rationing of other resources such as food and fuel. Still other laws allowed the government to recover excess profits from individuals. The Court upheld these measures in 1944 as valid exercises of the government's war powers. In addition, to guard against interruptions in the production of critical war material, the government invoked its inherent executive authority as well as a specially enacted statute (the Labor Disputes Act of 1942) to justify the seizure of factories or industries beset by strikes. By executive order, President Franklin D. Roosevelt nationalized the railroads from December 1942 through January 1944. Overall coordination of the nation's resources and industrial capacity was the responsibility of the War Production Board.

The greatest infringement of civil liberties during World War II was Executive Order 9066, which Roosevelt signed on February 19, 1942. It authorized the secretary of war and other government officials to identify military areas from which any person might be excluded, and granted them extraordinary discretion to decide which persons would be permitted to enter, travel in, and leave those areas. Under these provisions, the War Department ordered the removal of all persons of Japanese ancestry from the Pacific Coast area. "Relocation centers" were set up to house 112,000 men, women, and children of Japanese descent, 70,000 of whom were American citizens. In 1944, in an appeal brought by one of them, Fred Korematsu, the Supreme Court upheld the executive order and the relocation measures as valid exercises of war powers in an opinion written by Justice Hugo L. Black, ordinarily one of the court's fiercest defenders of civil liberties. The decision left terrible scars on those who were detained, and only in recent years has the government begun an effort to make amends for this flagrant violation of the Bill of Rights. In 1984, the Japanese-American Citizens' League obtained a writ to reopen Korematsu's case.

The one bright spot for civil liberties during that war was the Court's 1943 ruling that overturned a previous decision and prohibited making schoolchildren salute the American flag. The prior decision, made only three years earlier, had rejected the claims of members of the Jehovah's Witnesses who, as a matter of religious principle, didn't want to be forced to say the Pledge of Allegiance. That decision had provoked bitter criticism, and the Court quickly reconsidered its position.

Since World War II, Court decisions on civil liberties have established a number of general principles: Statutes, regulations, or other government actions that infringe on freedom of speech, press, religion, and assembly, or restrict the rights of defendants and suspects in criminal cases, or classify individuals based on race, are now carefully examined. They are upheld only if the government can show a compelling interest that justifies them and can also show that less restrictive measures would not achieve the same result. However, the paradox is that although the government may tend mostly to exercise such restrictions during times of national emergency, the courts are far less likely to question them then. Besides which, courts realize that they have few if any powers to enforce their decisions against an executive and a legislative body determined to limit rights in time of war.

◆◆◆ Does a Member of the Armed Forces Have the Same Constitutional Rights as a Civilian?

Yes and no. The Supreme Court has ruled that the Constitution, including all its amendments, applies to members of the armed forces. However, various rights—such as that of free speech—have a different meaning and a narrower scope when applied to servicemen and servicewomen.

As early as 1858, in cases dealing with constitutional safeguards for soldiers and sailors, the Court denied that the Bill of Rights applied *at all* to military personnel. However, the Court reversed that position in 1974 in a case in which it nonetheless upheld the court-martial conviction of an officer who had advised his men to refuse to serve in Vietnam. Although "the different character of the military community and of the military mission require a different application of [the Constitution's] protections," the Court ruled that "members of the military are not excluded from the protection granted by the First Amendment." The captain had challenged his court-martial on the ground that the section of the Uniform Code of Military Conduct barring "conduct unbecoming an officer" under which he was charged was far too broad and vague. The Court, however, found that his conduct fell well within the scope of acts that could be permissibly punished under the code.

In a number of ways, the constitutional rights of a member of the armed forces are not as extensive as those of a civilian. For example, the right to free speech does not allow military personnel in uniform to demonstrate against United States foreign policy. However, in 1973 a federal district court ruled that the U.S. Air Force cannot prevent off-duty military personnel from collecting signatures for a petition opposing foreign policy.

And the Court of Military Review, the Army's final court of appeal, has ruled that the right to complain to a commanding officer is also protected by the First Amendment.

Courts have also ruled that a member of the armed forces cannot be dishonorably discharged for extremist political beliefs. As Department of Defense Directive 1325.6 states, "The service member's right of expression should be preserved to the maximum extent possible, consistent with good order and discipline and the National Security." Service members also enjoy a constitutional right to privacy. The courts have ruled that they may not be searched without cause or randomly interrogated about their conduct.

The Supreme Court, in a 1955 decision that greatly expanded the judicial rights of members of the armed forces, ruled that a former service member cannot be tried in a military court if he or she is no longer part of the military. Furthermore, a crime committed by a service member while off duty and not connected to his or her military duties must be tried in a civilian court and the defendant must be given all his or her constitutional rights. Nonmilitary personnel living on military bases, such as dependents or civilian employees, also cannot be tried in a military court. This was established in 1957, when the Supreme Court ruled that a woman accused of killing her husband, an army sergeant, while on a military base had to be tried by a civilian court.

Appendix A ══════════
The Constitution of the United States of America

WE THE PEOPLE *of the United States, in Order to form a more perfect Union, establish Justice, insure domestic Tranquility, provide for the common defence, promote the general Welfare, and secure the Blessings of Liberty to ourselves and our Posterity, do ordain and establish this Constitution for the United States of America.*

ARTICLE I.

SECTION 1. All legislative Powers herein granted shall be vested in a Congress of the United States, which shall consist of a Senate and House of Representatives.

SECTION 2. The House of Representatives shall be composed of Members chosen every second Year by the People of the several States, and the Electors in each State shall have the Qualifications requisite for Electors of the most numerous Branch of the State Legislature.

No Person shall be a Representative who shall not have attained to the Age of twenty-five Years, and been seven Years a Citizen of the United States, and who shall not, when elected, be an Inhabitant of that State in which he shall be chosen.

*[Representatives and direct Taxes shall be apportioned among the several States which may be included within this Union, according to their respective Numbers, which shall be determined by adding to the whole Number of free Persons, including those bound to Service for a Term of Years, and excluding Indians not taxed, three fifths of all other Persons.][1] The actual Enumeration shall be made within three Years after the first Meeting of the Congress of the United States, and within every subsequent Term of ten Years, in such Manner as they shall by Law direct. The Number of Representatives shall not exceed one for every

---

Courtesy: U.S. Government Printing Office.
*[NOTE: Items that have since been amended or superseded, as identified in the footnotes, are bracketed.]
[1]Changed by Section 2 of the Fourteenth Amendment.

thirty Thousand,[2] but each State shall have at Least one Representative; and until such enumeration shall be made, the State of New Hampshire shall be entitled to chuse three, Massachusetts eight, Rhode-Island and Providence Plantations one, Connecticut five, New-York six, New Jersey four, Pennsylvania eight, Delaware one, Maryland six, Virginia ten, North Carolina five, South Carolina five, and Georgia three.

When vacancies happen in the Representation from any State, the Executive Authority thereof shall issue Writs of Election to fill such Vacancies.

The House of Representatives shall chuse their Speaker and other Officers; and shall have the sole Power of Impeachment.

SECTION 3. The Senate of the United States shall be composed of two Senators from each State, [chosen by the Legislature thereof,][3] for six Years; and each Senator shall have one Vote.

Immediately after they shall be assembled in Consequence of the first Election, they shall be divided as equally as may be into three Classes. The Seats of the Senators of the first Class shall be vacated at the Expiration of the second Year, of the second Class at the Expiration of the fourth Year, and of the third Class at the Expiration of the sixth Year, so that one-third may be chosen every second Year; [and if Vacancies happen by Resignation, or otherwise, during the Recess of the Legislature of any State, the Executive thereof may make temporary Appointments until the next Meeting of the Legislature, which shall then fill such Vacancies.][4]

No Person shall be a Senator who shall not have attained to the Age of thirty Years, and been nine Years a Citizen of the United States, and who shall not, when elected, be an Inhabitant of that State for which he shall be chosen.

The Vice President of the United States shall be President of the Senate, but shall have no Vote, unless they be equally divided.

The Senate shall chuse their other Officers, and also a President pro tempore, in the absence of the Vice President, or when he shall exercise the Office of President of the United States.

The Senate shall have the sole Power to try all Impeachments. When sitting for that Purpose, they shall be on Oath or Affirmation. When the President of the United States is tried, the Chief Justice shall preside: And no Person shall be convicted without the Concurrence of two thirds of the Members present.

Judgment in Cases of Impeachment shall not extend further than to removal from Office, and disqualification to hold and enjoy any Office of honor, Trust or Profit under the United States: but the Party convicted shall nevertheless be liable and subject to Indictment, Trial, Judgment and Punishment, according to Law.

SECTION 4. The Times, Places and Manner of holding Elections for Senators and Representatives, shall be prescribed in each State by the Legislature thereof;

---

[2]Ratio in 1965 was one to over 410,000.
[3]Changed by Section I of the Seventeenth Amendment.
[4]Changed by Clause 2 of the Seventeenth Amendment.

but the Congress may at any time by Law make or alter such Regulations, except as to the Place of Chusing Senators.

The Congress shall assemble at least once in every Year, and such Meeting shall [be on the first Monday in December,][5] unless they shall by Law appoint a different Day.

SECTION 5. Each House shall be the Judge of the Elections, Returns and Qualifications of its own Members, and a Majority of each shall constitute a Quorum to do Business; but a smaller number may adjourn from day to day, and may be authorized to compel the Attendance of absent Members, in such Manner, and under such Penalties as each House may provide.

Each House may determine the Rules of its Proceedings, punish its Members for disorderly Behavior, and, with the Concurrence of two thirds, expel a Member.

Each House shall keep a Journal of its Proceedings, and from time to time publish the same, excepting such Parts as may in their Judgment require Secrecy; and the Yeas and Nays of the Members of either House on any question shall, at the Desire of one fifth of those Present, be entered on the Journal.

Neither House, during the Session of Congress, shall, without the Consent of the other, adjourn for more than three days, nor to any other Place than that in which the two Houses shall be sitting.

SECTION 6. The Senators and Representatives shall receive a Compensation for their Services, to be ascertained by Law, and paid out of the Treasury of the United States. They shall in all Cases, except Treason, Felony and Breach of the Peace, be privileged from Arrest during their Attendance at the Session of their respective Houses, and in going to and returning from the same; and for any Speech or Debate in either House, they shall not be questioned in any other Place.

No Senator or Representative shall, during the Time for which he was elected, be appointed to any civil Office under the Authority of the United States, which shall have been created, or the Emoluments whereof shall have been encreased during such time; and no Person holding any Office under the United States, shall be a Member of either House during his Continuance in Office.

SECTION 7. All Bills for raising Revenue shall originate in the House of Representatives; but the Senate may propose or concur with Amendments as on other Bills.

Every Bill which shall have passed the House of Representatives and the Senate, shall, before it become a Law, be presented to the President of the United States; If he approve he shall sign it, but if not he shall return it, with his Objections to that House in which it shall have originated, who shall enter the Objections at large on their Journal, and proceed to reconsider it. If after such Reconsideration two thirds of that House shall agree to pass the Bill, it shall be sent, together with the Objections, to the other House, by which it shall likewise be reconsidered, and if approved by two thirds of that House, it shall become a Law. But in all such Cases the Votes of both Houses shall be determined by Yeas and Nays, and the Names of

---

[5] Changed by Section 2 of the Twentieth Amendment.

the Persons voting for and against the Bill shall be entered on the Journal of each House respectively. If any Bill shall not be returned by the President within ten days (Sundays excepted) after it shall have been presented to him, the Same shall be a Law, in like Manner as if he had signed it, unless the Congress by their Adjournment prevent its Return, in which Case it shall not be a Law.

Every Order, Resolution, or Vote to which the Concurrence of the Senate and House of Representatives may be necessary (except on a question of Adjournment) shall be presented to the President of the United States; and before the Same shall take Effect, shall be approved by him, or being disapproved by him, shall be passed by two thirds of the Senate and House of Representatives, according to the Rules and Limitations prescribed in the Case of a Bill.

SECTION 8. The Congress shall have Power To lay and collect Taxes, Duties, Imposts and Excises, to pay the Debts and provide for the common Defence and general Welfare of the United States; but all Duties, Imposts and Excises shall be uniform throughout the United States;

To borrow money on the credit of the United States;

To regulate Commerce with foreign Nations, and among the several States, and with the Indian Tribes;

To establish an uniform Rule of Naturalization, and uniform Laws on the subject of Bankruptcies throughout the United States;

To coin Money, regulate the Value thereof, and of foreign Coin, and fix the Standard of Weights and Measures;

To provide for the Punishment of counterfeiting the Securities and current Coin of the United States;

To establish Post Offices and post Roads;

To promote the Progress of Science and useful Arts, by securing for limited Times to Authors and Inventors the exclusive Right to their respective Writings and Discoveries;

To constitute Tribunals inferior to the supreme Court;

To define and punish Piracies and Felonies committed on the high Seas, and Offenses against the Law of Nations;

To declare War, grant Letters of Marque and Reprisal, and make rules concerning Captures on Land and Water;

To raise and support Armies, but no Appropriation of Money to that Use shall be for a longer Term than two Years;

To provide and maintain a Navy;

To make Rules for the Government and Regulation of the land and naval Forces;

To provide for calling forth the Militia to execute the Laws of the Union, suppress Insurrections and repel Invasions;

To provide for organizing, arming, and disciplining the Militia, and for governing such Part of them as may be employed in the Service of the United States, reserving to the States respectively, the Appointment of the Officers, and the Authority of training the Militia according to the discipline prescribed by Congress;

To exercise exclusive Legislation in all Cases whatsoever, over such District (not exceeding ten Miles square) as may, by Cession of particular States, and the acceptance of Congress, become the Seat of the Government of the United States, and to exercise like Authority over all Places purchased by the Consent of the Legislature of the State in which the Same shall be, for the Erection of Forts, Magazines, Arsenals, dock-Yards, and other needful Buildings;—And

To make all Laws which shall be necessary and proper for carrying into Execution the foregoing Powers, and all other Powers vested by this Constitution in the Government of the United States, or in any Department or Officer thereof.

SECTION 9. The Migration or Importation of such Persons as any of the States now existing shall think proper to admit, shall not be prohibited by the Congress prior to the Year one thousand eight hundred and eight, but a tax or duty may be imposed on such Importation, not exceeding ten dollars for each Person.

The privilege of the Writ of Habeas Corpus shall not be suspended, unless when in Cases of Rebellion or Invasion the public Safety may require it.

No Bill of Attainder or ex post facto Law shall be passed.

No capitation, or other direct, Tax shall be laid, unless in Proportion to the Census or Enumeration herein before directed to be taken.[6]

No Tax or Duty shall be laid on Articles exported from any State.

No Preference shall be given by any Regulation of Commerce or Revenue to the Ports of one State over those of another: nor shall Vessels bound to, or from, one State, be obliged to enter, clear, or pay Duties in another.

No Money shall be drawn from the Treasury, but in Consequence of Appropriations made by Law; and a regular Statement and Account of the Receipts and Expenditures of all public Money shall be published from time to time.

No Title of Nobility shall be granted by the United States: And no Person holding any Office of Profit or Trust under them, shall, without the Consent of the Congress, accept of any present, Emolument, Office, or Title, of any kind whatever, from any King, Prince, or foreign State.

SECTION 10. No State shall enter into any Treaty, Alliance, or Confederation; grant Letters of Marque and Reprisal; coin Money; emit Bills of Credit; make any Thing but gold and silver Coin a Tender in Payment of Debts; pass any Bill of Attainder, ex post facto Law, or Law impairing the Obligation of Contracts, or grant any Title of Nobility.

No State shall, without the Consent of the Congress, lay any Imposts or Duties on Imports or Exports, except what may be absolutely necessary for executing its inspection Laws: and the net Produce of all Duties and Imposts, laid by any State on Imports or Exports, shall be for the Use of the Treasury of the United States; and all such Laws shall be subject to the Revision and Controul of the Congress.

No State shall, without the Consent of Congress, lay any duty of Tonnage, keep Troops, or Ships of War in time of Peace, enter into any Agreement or Compact

_____

[6] But see the Sixteenth Amendment.

with another State, or with a foreign Power, or engage in War, unless actually invaded, or in such imminent Danger as will not admit of delay.

ARTICLE II.

SECTION 1. The executive Power shall be vested in a President of the United States of America. He shall hold his Office during the Term of four Years, and, together with the Vice-President, chosen for the same Term, be elected, as follows.

Each State shall appoint, in such Manner as the Legislature thereof may direct, a Number of Electors, equal to the whole Number of Senators and Representatives to which the State may be entitled in the Congress: but no Senator or Representative, or Person holding an Office of Trust or Profit under the United States, shall be appointed an Elector.

[The Electors shall meet in their respective States, and vote by Ballot for two persons, of whom one at least shall not be an Inhabitant of the same State with themselves. And they shall make a List of all the Persons voted for, and of the Number of Votes for each; which List they shall sign and certify, and transmit sealed to the Seat of the Government of the United States, directed to the President of the Senate. The President of the Senate shall, in the Presence of the Senate and House of Representatives, open all the Certificates, and the Votes shall then be counted. The Person having the greatest Number of Votes shall be the President, if such Number be a Majority of the whole Number of Electors appointed; and if there be more than one who have such Majority, and have an equal Number of Votes, then the House of Representatives shall immediately chuse by Ballot one of them for President; and if no Person have a Majority, then from the five highest on the List the said House shall in like Manner chuse the President. But in chusing the President, the Votes shall be taken by States, the Representation from each State having one Vote; a quorum for this Purpose shall consist of a Member or Members from two thirds of the States, and a Majority of all the States shall be necessary to a Choice. In every Case, after the Choice of the President, the Person having the greatest Number of Votes of the Electors shall be the Vice President. But if there should remain two or more who have equal Votes, the Senate shall chuse from them by Ballot the Vice-President.][7]

The Congress may determine the Time of chusing the Electors, and the Day on which they shall give their Votes; which Day shall be the same throughout the United States.

No person except a natural born Citizen, or a Citizen of the United States, at the time of the Adoption of this Constitution, shall be eligible to the Office of President; neither shall any Person be eligible to that Office who shall not have attained to the Age of thirty-five Years, and been fourteen Years a Resident within the United States.

[In Case of the Removal of the President from Office, or of his Death, Resignation, or Inability to discharge the Powers and Duties of the said Office, the

_____

[7]Superseded by the Twelfth Amendment.

same shall devolve on the Vice President, and the Congress may by Law, provide for the Case of Removal, Death, Resignation or Inability, both of the President and Vice President, declaring what Officer shall then act as President, and such Officer shall act accordingly, until the Disability be removed, or a President shall be elected.][8]

The President shall, at stated Times, receive for his Services, a Compensation, which shall neither be encreased nor diminished during the Period for which he shall have been elected, and he shall not receive within that Period any other Emolument from the United States, or any of them.

Before he enter on the Execution of his Office, he shall take the following Oath or Affirmation:—"I do solemnly swear (or affirm) that I will faithfully execute the Office of President of the United States, and will to the best of my Ability, preserve, protect and defend the Constitution of the United States."

SECTION 2. The President shall be Commander in Chief of the Army and Navy of the United States, and of the Militia of the several States, when called into the actual Service of the United States; he may require the Opinion in writing, of the principal Officer in each of the executive Departments, upon any subject relating to the Duties of their respective Offices, and he shall have Power to Grant Reprieves and Pardons for Offenses against the United States, except in Cases of Impeachment.

He shall have Power, by and with the Advice and Consent of the Senate, to make Treaties, provided two-thirds of the Senators present concur; and he shall nominate, and by and with the Advice and Consent of the Senate, shall appoint Ambassadors, other public Ministers and Consuls, Judges of the supreme Court, and all other Officers of the United States, whose Appointments are not herein otherwise provided for, and which shall be established by Law: but the Congress may by Law vest the Appointment of such inferior Officers, as they think proper, in the President alone, in the Courts of Law, or in the Heads of Departments.

The President shall have Power to fill up all Vacancies that may happen during the Recess of the Senate, by granting Commissions which shall expire at the End of their next Session.

SECTION 3. He shall from time to time give to the Congress Information of the State of the Union, and recommend to their Consideration such Measures as he shall judge necessary and expedient; he may, on extraordinary Occasions, convene both Houses, or either of them, and in Case of Disagreement between them, with Respect to the Time of Adjournment, he may adjourn them to such Time as he shall think proper; he shall receive Ambassadors and other public Ministers; he shall take Care that the Laws be faithfully executed, and shall Commission all the Officers of the United States.

SECTION 4. The President, Vice President and all civil Officers of the United States, shall be removed from Office on Impeachment for, and Conviction of, Treason, Bribery, or other high Crimes and Misdemeanors.

---

[8] This clause has been affected by the Twenty-fifth Amendment.

SECTION 1. The judicial Power of the United States, shall be vested in one supreme Court, and in such inferior Courts as the Congress may from time to time ordain and establish. The Judges, both of the supreme and inferior Courts, shall hold their Offices during good Behaviour, and shall, at stated Times, receive for their Services, a Compensation, which shall not be diminished during their Continuance in Office.

SECTION 2. The judicial Power shall extend to all Cases, in Law and Equity, arising under this Constitution, the Laws of the United States, and Treaties made, or which shall be made, under their Authority;—to all Cases affecting Ambassadors, other public Ministers and Consuls;—to all Cases of admiralty and maritime Jurisdiction;—to Controversies to which the United States shall be a Party;—to Controversies between two or more States;—between a State and Citizens of another State;—between Citizens of different States;—between Citizens of the same State claiming Lands under Grants of different States, and between a State, or the Citizens thereof, and foreign States, Citizens or Subjects.

In all Cases affecting Ambassadors, other public Ministers and Consuls, and those in which a State shall be Party, the supreme Court shall have original Jurisdiction. In all the other Cases before mentioned, the supreme Court shall have appellate Jurisdiction, both as to Law and Fact, with such Exceptions, and under such Regulations as the Congress shall make.

The trial of all Crimes, except in Cases of Impeachment, shall be by Jury; and such Trial shall be held in the State where the said Crimes shall have been committed; but when not committed within any State, the Trial shall be at such Place or Places as the Congress may by Law have directed.

SECTION 3. Treason against the United States, shall consist only in levying War against them, or in adhering to their Enemies, giving them Aid and Comfort. No Person shall be convicted of Treason unless on the Testimony of two Witnesses to the same overt Act, or on Confession in open Court.

The Congress shall have Power to declare the Punishment of Treason, but no Attainder of Treason shall work Corruption of Blood, or Forfeiture except during the Life of the Person attainted.

ARTICLE IV.

SECTION I. Full Faith and Credit shall be given in each State to the public Acts, Records, and judicial Proceedings of every other State. And the Congress may by general Laws prescribe the Manner in which such Acts, Records and Proceedings shall be proved, and the Effect thereof.

SECTION 2. The Citizens of each State shall be entitled to all Privileges and Immunities of Citizens in the several States.

A Person charged in any State with Treason, Felony, or other Crime, who shall flee from Justice, and be found in another State, shall on demand of the executive

Authority of the State from which he fled, be delivered up, to be removed to the State having Jurisdiction of the Crime.

[No Person held to Service or Labour in one State, under the Laws thereof, escaping into another, shall, in Consequence of any Law or Regulation therein, be discharged from such Service or Labour, but shall be delivered up on Claim of the Party to whom such Service or Labour may be due.]⁹

Section 3. New States may be admitted by the Congress into this Union; but no new State shall be formed or erected within the Jurisdiction of any other State; nor any State be formed by the Junction of two or more States, or parts of States, without the Consent of the Legislatures of the States concerned as well as of the Congress.

The Congress shall have Power to dispose of and make all needful Rules and Regulations respecting the Territory or other Property belonging to the United States; and nothing in this Constitution shall be so construed as to Prejudice any Claims of the United States, or of any particular State.

Section 4. The United States shall guarantee to every State in this Union a Republican Form of Government, and shall protect each of them against Invasion; and on Application of the Legislature, or of the Executive (when the Legislature cannot be convened) against domestic Violence.

ARTICLE V.

The Congress, whenever two-thirds of both Houses shall deem it necessary, shall propose Amendments to this Constitution, or, on the Application of the Legislatures of two-thirds of the several States, shall call a Convention for proposing Amendments, which, in either Case, shall be valid to all Intents and Purposes, as part of this Constitution, when ratified by the Legislatures of three-fourths of the several States, or by Conventions in three-fourths thereof, as the one or the other Mode of Ratification may be proposed by the Congress: Provided that no Amendment which may be made prior to the Year One thousand eight hundred and eight shall in any Manner affect the first and fourth Clauses in the Ninth Section of the first Article; and that no State, without its Consent, shall be deprived of its equal Suffrage in the Senate.

ARTICLE VI.

All Debts contracted and Engagements entered into, before the Adoption of this Constitution, shall be as valid against the United States under this Constitution, as under the Confederation.

This Constitution, and the Laws of the United States which shall be made in Pursuance thereof; and all Treaties made, or which shall be made, under the

---

⁹Superseded by the Thirteenth Amendment.

Authority of the United States, shall be the supreme Law of the Land; and the Judges in every State shall be bound thereby, any Thing in the Constitution or Laws of any State to the Contrary notwithstanding.

The Senators and Representatives before mentioned, and the Members of the several State Legislatures, and all executive and judicial Officers, both of the United States and of the several States, shall be bound by Oath or Affirmation, to support this Constitution; but no religious Test shall ever be required as a Qualification to any Office or public Trust under the United States.

ARTICLE VII.

The Ratification of the Conventions of nine States shall be sufficient for the Establishment of this Constitution between the States so ratifying the Same.

DONE in Convention by the Unanimous Consent of the States present the Seventeenth Day of September in the Year of our Lord one thousand seven hundred and Eighty seven and of the Independence of the United States of America the Twelfth.

In Witness whereof We have hereunto subscribed our Names.

Go Washington
Presidt and deputy from Virginia

New Hampshire.
JOHN LANGDON
NICHOLAS GILMAN

Massachusetts.
NATHANIEL GORHAM
RUFUS KING

New Jersey.
WIL: LIVINGSTON
DAVID BREARLEY.
WM PATERSON.
JONA: DAYTON

Pennsylvania.
B FRANKLIN
ROBT. MORRIS
THOS. FITZSIMONS
JAMES WILSON
THOMAS MIFFLIN
GEO. CLYMER
JARED INGERSOLL
GOUV MORRIS

Delaware.
GEO: READ
JOHN DICKINSON
JACO: BROOM
GUNNING BEDFORD jun
RICHARD BASSETT

Connecticut.
WM SAML JOHNSON
ROGER SHERMAN

New York.
ALEXANDER HAMILTON

Maryland.
JAMES MCHENRY
DANL CARROL
DAN: of ST THOS JENIFER

Virginia.
JOHN BLAIR
JAMES MADISON Jr.

North Carolina.
WM BLOUNT
HU WILLIAMSON
RICHD DOBBS SPAIGHT.

Georgia.
WILLIAM FEW
ABR BALDWIN

South Carolina.
J. RUTLEDGE
CHARLES PINCKNEY
CHARLES COTESWORTH PINCKNEY
PIERCE BUTLER

Attest:

WILLIAM JACKSON, *Secretary.*

ARTICLES IN ADDITION TO, AND AMENDMENT OF, THE CONSTITUTION OF THE UNITED STATES OF AMERICA, PROPOSED BY CONGRESS, AND RATIFIED BY THE LEGISLATURES OF THE SEVERAL STATES, PURSUANT TO THE FIFTH ARTICLE OF THE ORIGINAL CONSTITUTION.[10]

[*THE FIRST 10 AMENDMENTS WERE RATIFIED DECEMBER 15, 1791, AND FORM WHAT IS KNOWN AS THE "BILL OF RIGHTS"*]

AMENDMENT I

Congress shall make no law respecting an establishment of religion, or prohibiting the free exercise thereof; or abridging the freedom of speech, or of the press; or the right of the people peaceably to assemble, and to petition the Government for a redress of grievances.

AMENDMENT II

A well regulated Militia, being necessary to the security of a free State, the right of the people to keep and bear Arms, shall not be infringed.

AMENDMENT III

No Soldier shall, in time of peace be quartered in any house, without the consent of the Owner, nor in time of war, but in a manner to be prescribed by law.

---

[10] Amendment XXI was not ratified by state legislatures, but by state conventions summoned by Congress.

The right of the people to be secure in their persons, houses, papers, and effects, against unreasonable searches and seizures, shall not be violated, and no Warrants shall issue, but upon probable cause, supported by Oath or affirmation, and particularly describing the place to be searched, and the persons or things to be seized.

AMENDMENT V

No person shall be held to answer for a capital, or otherwise infamous crime, unless on a presentment or indictment of a Grand Jury, except in cases arising in the land or naval forces, or in the Militia, when in actual service in time of War or public danger; nor shall any person be subject for the same offence to be twice put in jeopardy of life or limb; nor shall be compelled in any criminal case to be a witness against himself, nor be deprived of life, liberty, or property, without due process of law; nor shall private property be taken for public use, without just compensation.

AMENDMENT VI

In all criminal prosecutions, the accused shall enjoy the right to a speedy and public trial, by an impartial jury of the State and district wherein the crime shall have been committed, which district shall have been previously ascertained by law, and to be informed of the nature and cause of the accusation; to be confronted with the witnesses against him; to have compulsory process for obtaining witnesses in his favor, and to have the Assistance of Counsel for his defence.

AMENDMENT VII

In suits at common law, where the value in controversy shall exceed twenty dollars, the right of trial by jury shall be preserved, and no fact tried by a jury, shall be otherwise reexamined in any Court of the United States, than according to the rules of the common law.

AMENDMENT VIII

Excessive bail shall not be required, nor excessive fines imposed, nor cruel and unusual punishments inflicted.

AMENDMENT IX

The enumeration in the Constitution, of certain rights, shall not be construed to deny or disparage others retained by the people.

AMENDMENT X

The powers not delegated to the United States by the Constitution, nor prohibited by it to the States, are reserved to the States respectively, or to the people.

AMENDMENT XI
[Ratified February 7, 1795]

The Judicial power of the United States shall not be construed to extend to any suit in law or equity, commenced or prosecuted against one of the United States by Citizens of another State, or by Citizens or Subjects of any Foreign State.

AMENDMENT XII
[Ratified June 25, 1804]

The Electors shall meet in their respective states and vote by ballot for President and Vice-President, one of whom, at least, shall not be an inhabitant of the same state with themselves; they shall name in their ballots the person voted for as President, and in distinct ballots the person voted for as Vice-President, and they shall make distinct lists of all persons voted for as President, and of all persons voted for as Vice-President, and of the number of votes for each, which lists they shall sign and certify, and transmit sealed to the seat of the government of the United States, directed to the President of the Senate;—The President of the Senate shall, in presence of the Senate and House of Representatives, open all the certificates and the votes shall then be counted;—The person having the greatest number of votes for President, shall be the President, if such number be a majority of the whole number of Electors appointed; and if no person have such majority, then from the persons having the highest numbers not exceeding three on the list of those voted for as President, the House of Representatives shall choose immediately, by ballot, the President. But in choosing the President, the votes shall be taken by states, the representation from each state having one vote; a quorum for this purpose shall consist of a member or members from two-thirds of the states, and a majority of all the states shall be necessary to a choice. [And if the House of Representatives shall not choose a President whenever the right of choice shall devolve upon them, before the fourth day of March next following, then the Vice-President shall act as President, as in the case of the death or other constitutional disability of the President.—][11] The person having the greatest number of votes as Vice-President, shall be the Vice-President, if such number be a majority of the whole number of Electors appointed, and if no person have a majority, then from the two highest numbers on the list, the Senate shall choose the Vice-President; a

----

[11] Superseded by Section 3 of the Twentieth Amendment.

quorum for the purpose shall consist of two-thirds of the whole number of Senators, and a majority of the whole number shall be necessary to a choice. But no person constitutionally ineligible to the office of President shall be eligible to that of Vice-President of the United States.

AMENDMENT XIII
[Ratified December 6, 1865]

Section 1. Neither slavery nor involuntary servitude, except as a punishment for crime whereof the party shall have been duly convicted, shall exist within the United States, or any place subject to their jurisdiction.

Section 2. Congress shall have power to enforce this article by appropriate legislation.

AMENDMENT XIV
[Ratified July 9, 1868]

Section 1. All persons born or naturalized in the United States, and subject to the jurisdiction thereof, are citizens of the United States and of the State wherein they reside. No State shall make or enforce any law which shall abridge the privileges or immunities of citizens of the United States; nor shall any State deprive any person of life, liberty, or property, without due process of law; nor deny to any person within its jurisdiction the equal protection of the laws.

Section 2. Representatives shall be apportioned among the several States according to their respective numbers, counting the whole number of persons in each State, excluding Indians not taxed. But when the right to vote at any election for the choice of electors for President and Vice-President of the United States, Representatives in Congress, the Executive and Judicial officers of a State, or the members of the Legislature thereof, is denied to any of the male inhabitants of such State, being twenty-one years of age,[12] and citizens of the United States, or in any way abridged, except for participation in rebellion, or other crime, the basis of representation therein shall be reduced in the proportion which the number of such male citizens shall bear to the whole number of male citizens twenty-one years of age in such State.

Section 3. No person shall be a Senator or Representative in Congress, or elector of President and Vice-President, or hold any office, civil or military, under the United States, or under any State, who, having previously taken an oath, as a member of Congress, or as an officer of the United States, or as a member of any State legislature, or as an executive or judicial officer of any State, to support the Constitution of the United States, shall have engaged in insurrection or rebellion against the same, or given aid or comfort to the enemies thereof. But Congress may by a vote of two-thirds of each House, remove such disability.

---

[12] Changed by Section 1 of the Twenty-sixth Amendment.

SECTION 4. The validity of the public debt of the United States, authorized by law, including debts incurred for payment of pensions and bounties for services in suppressing insurrection or rebellion, shall not be questioned. But neither the United States nor any State shall assume or pay any debt or obligation incurred in aid of insurrection or rebellion against the United States, or any claim for the loss or emancipation of any slave; but all such debts, obligations and claims shall be held illegal and void.

SECTION 5. The Congress shall have power to enforce, by appropriate legislation, the provisions of this article.

AMENDMENT XV
[Ratified February 3, 1870]

SECTION 1. The right of citizens of the United States to vote shall not be denied or abridged by the United States or by any State on account of race, color, or previous condition of servitude—

SECTION 2. The Congress shall have power to enforce this article by appropriate legislation.

AMENDMENT XVI
[Ratified February 3, 1913]

The Congress shall have power to lay and collect taxes on incomes, from whatever source derived, without apportionment among the several States, and without regard to any census or enumeration.

AMENDMENT XVII
[Ratified April 8, 1913]

The Senate of the United States shall be composed of two Senators from each State, elected by the people thereof, for six years; and each Senator shall have one vote. The electors in each State shall have the qualifications requisite for electors of the most numerous branch of the State legislatures.

When vacancies happen in the representation of any State in the Senate, the executive authority of such State shall issue writs of election to fill such vacancies: *Provided,* That the legislature of any State may empower the executive thereof to make temporary appointments until the people fill the vacancies by election as the legislature may direct.

This amendment shall not be so construed as to affect the election or term of any Senator chosen before it becomes valid as part of the Constitution.

[Ratified January 16, 1919]

[SECTION 1. After one year from the ratification of this article the manufacture, sale, or transportation of intoxicating liquors within, the importation thereof into, or the exportation thereof from the United States and all territory subject to the jurisdiction thereof for beverage purposes is hereby prohibited.

[SECTION 2. The Congress and the several States shall have concurrent power to enforce this article by appropriate legislation.

[SECTION 3. This article shall be inoperative unless it shall have been ratified as an amendment to the Constitution by the legislatures of the several States as provided in the Constitution, within seven years from the date of the submission hereof to the States by the Congress.][13]

AMENDMENT XIX
[Ratified August 18, 1920]

The right of citizens of the United States to vote shall not be denied or abridged by the United States or by any State on account of sex.

Congress shall have power to enforce this article by appropriate legislation.

AMENDMENT XX
[Ratified January 23, 1933]

SECTION 1. The terms of the President and Vice President shall end at noon on the 20th day of January, and the terms of Senators and Representatives at noon on the 3d day of January, of the years in which such terms would have ended if this article had not been ratified; and the terms of their successors shall then begin.

SECTION 2. The Congress shall assemble at least once in every year, and such meeting shall begin at noon on the 3d day of January, unless they shall by law appoint a different day.

SECTION 3. If, at the time fixed for the beginning of the term of the President, the President elect shall have died, the Vice President elect shall become President. If a President shall not have been chosen before the time fixed for the beginning of his term, or if the President elect shall have failed to qualify, then the Vice President elect shall act as President until a President shall have qualified; and the Congress may by law provide for the case wherein neither a President elect nor a Vice President elect shall have qualified, declaring who shall then act as President, or the manner in which one who is to act shall be selected, and such person shall act accordingly until a President or Vice President shall have qualified.

SECTION 4. The Congress may by law provide for the case of the death of any of the persons from whom the House of Representatives may choose a President

---

[13]Repealed by Section 1 of the Twenty-first Amendment.

whenever the right of choice shall have devolved upon them, and for the case of the death of any of the persons from whom the Senate may choose a Vice President whenever the right of choice shall have devolved upon them.

SECTION 5. Sections 1 and 2 shall take effect on the 15th day of October following the ratification of this article.

SECTION 6. This article shall be inoperative unless it shall have been ratified as an amendment to the Constitution by the legislatures of three-fourths of the several States within seven years from the date of its submission.

AMENDMENT XXI
[Ratified December 5, 1933]

SECTION 1. The eighteenth article of amendment to the Constitution of the United States is hereby repealed.

SECTION 2. The transportation or importation into any State, Territory, or possession of the United States for delivery or use therein of intoxicating liquors, in violation of the laws thereof, is hereby prohibited.

SECTION 3. This article shall be inoperative unless it shall have been ratified as an amendment to the Constitution by conventions in the several States, as provided in the Constitution, within seven years from the date of the submission hereof to the States by the Congress.

AMENDMENT XXII
[Ratified February 27, 1951]

SECTION 1. No person shall be elected to the office of the President more than twice, and no person who has held the office of President, or acted as President, for more than two years of a term to which some other person was elected President shall be elected to the office of the President more than once. But this Article shall not apply to any person holding the office of President when this Article was proposed by the Congress, and shall not prevent any person who may be holding the office of President, or acting as President, during the term within which this Article becomes operative from holding the office of President or acting as President during the remainder of such term.

SECTION 2. This article shall be inoperative unless it shall have been ratified as an amendment to the Constitution by the legislatures of three-fourths of the several States within seven years from the date of its submission to the States by the Congress.

AMENDMENT XXIII
[Ratified March 29, 1961]

SECTION 1. The District constituting the seat of Government of the United States shall appoint in such manner as the Congress may direct:

A number of electors of President and Vice President equal to the whole number of Senators and Representatives in Congress to which the District would be entitled if it were a State, but in no event more than the least populous State; they shall be in addition to those appointed by the States, but they shall be considered, for the purposes of the election of President and Vice President, to be electors appointed by a State; and they shall meet in the District and perform such duties as provided by the twelfth article of amendment.

SECTION 2. The Congress shall have power to enforce this article by appropriate legislation.

AMENDMENT XXIV
[Ratified January 23, 1964]

SECTION 1. The right of citizens of the United States to vote in any primary or other election for President or Vice President, for electors for President or Vice President, or for Senator or Representative in Congress, shall not be denied or abridged by the United States or any State by reason of failure to pay any poll tax or other tax.

SECTION 2. The Congress shall have power to enforce this article by appropriate legislation.

AMENDMENT XXV
[Ratified February 10, 1967]

SECTION 1. In case of the removal of the President from office or of his death or resignation, the Vice President shall become President.

SECTION 2. Whenever there is a vacancy in the office of the Vice President, the President shall nominate a Vice President who shall take office upon confirmation by a majority vote of both Houses of Congress.

SECTION 3. Whenever the President transmits to the President pro tempore of the Senate and the Speaker of the House of Representatives his written declaration that he is unable to discharge the powers and duties of his office, and until he transmits to them a written declaration to the contrary, such powers and duties shall be discharged by the Vice President as Acting President.

SECTION 4. Whenever the Vice President and a majority of either the principal officers of the executive departments or of such other body as Congress may by law provide, transmit to the President pro tempore of the Senate and the Speaker of the House of Representatives their written declaration that the President is unable to discharge the powers and duties of his office, the Vice President shall immediately assume the powers and duties of the office as Acting President.

Thereafter, when the President transmits to the President pro tempore of the Senate and the Speaker of the House of Representatives his written declaration that no inability exists, he shall resume the powers and duties of his office unless the Vice President and a majority of either the principal officers of the executive department or of such other body as Congress may by law provide, transmit within four days to the President pro tempore of the Senate and the Speaker of the House of Representatives their written declaration that the President is unable to discharge the powers and duties of his office. Thereupon Congress shall decide the issue, assembling within forty-eight hours for that purpose if not in session. If the Congress, within twenty-one days after receipt of the latter written declaration, or, if Congress is not in session, within twenty-one days after Congress is required to assemble, determines by two-thirds vote of both Houses that the President is unable to discharge the powers and duties of his office, the Vice President shall continue to discharge the same as Acting President; otherwise, the President shall resume the powers and duties of his office.

AMENDMENT XXVI
[*Ratified July 1, 1971*]

Section 1. The right of citizens of the United States, who are eighteen years of age or older, to vote shall not be denied or abridged by the United States or by any State on account of age.

Section 2. The Congress shall have power to enforce this article by appropriate legislation.

Appendix B

Calendar of Commemorative Dates for the Celebration of the Bicentennial of the United States Constitution

The following list is adapted from Report No. 85-100 of the Congressional Research Service of the Library of Congress. The list was compiled by Project '87 of the American Political Science Association and the American Historical Association.

March 25–28, 1785: Mount Vernon Conference. George Washington hosted a meeting at Mount Vernon of four commissioners from Maryland and four from Virginia to discuss problems relating to the navigation of the Chesapeake Bay and the Potomac River. After negotiating agreements, the commissioners recommended to their respective legislatures that annual conferences be held on commercial matters, and that Pennsylvania be invited to join Maryland and Virginia to discuss linking the Chesapeake and the Ohio River.

January 16, 1786: Virginia's legislature adopted a statute for religious freedom, originally drafted by Thomas Jefferson and introduced by James Madison. The measure protected Virginia's citizens against compulsion to attend or support any church, and against discrimination based upon religious belief. The law served as a model for the First Amendment to the United States Constitution.

January 21, 1786: Virginia's legislature invited all the States to a September meeting in Annapolis to discuss commercial problems.

August 7, 1786: The Congress of the Confederation considered a motion offered by Charles Pinckney of South Carolina to amend the Articles of Confederation in order to give Congress more control over foreign affairs and interstate commerce. Because amendments to the Articles required the unanimous consent of the States, an unlikely eventuality, Congress declined to recommend the changes.

September 11–14, 1786: Annapolis Convention. New York, New Jersey, Delaware, Pennsylvania and Virginia sent a total of twelve delegates to the conference that had been proposed by Virginia in January to discuss commercial matters. (New Hampshire, Massachusetts, Rhode Island and North Carolina sent delegates, but they failed to arrive in time.) The small attendance made discussion of commercial matters fruitless. On September 14, the convention adopted a resolution drafted by Alexander Hamilton asking all the States to send representatives to a new convention to be held in Philadelphia in May of 1787. This meeting would not be limited to commercial matters but would address all issues necessary "to render the constitution of the Federal Government adequate to the exigencies of the Union."

February 4, 1787: The end of Shays' Rebellion. General Benjamin Lincoln, leading a contingent of 4,400 soldiers enlisted by the Massachusetts governor, routed the forces of Daniel Shays. A destitute farmer, Shays had organized a rebellion against the Massachusetts government, which had failed to take action to assist the State's depressed farm population. The uprisings, which had begun in the summer of 1786, were completely crushed by the end of February. The Massachusetts legislature, however, enacted some statutes to assist debt-ridden farmers.

February 21, 1787: The Congress of the Confederation cautiously endorsed the plan adopted at the Annapolis Convention for a new meeting of delegates from the States "for the sole and express purpose of revising the Articles of Confederation and reporting to Congress and the several legislatures such alterations and provisions therein."

May 25, 1787: Opening of the Constitutional Convention. On May 25, a quorum of delegates from seven States arrived in Philadelphia in response to the call from the Annapolis Convention, and the meeting convened. Ultimately, representatives from all the States but Rhode Island attended. The distinguished public figures included George Washington, James Madison, Benjamin Franklin, George Mason, Alexander Hamilton, Gouverneur Morris, James Wilson, Roger Sherman and Elbridge Gerry.

May 29, 1787: Virginia Plan proposed. On the fifth day of the meeting, Edmund Randolph, a delegate from Virginia, offered 15 resolutions comprising the "Virginia Plan" of Union. Rather than amending the Articles of Confederation, the proposal described a completely new organization of government including a bicameral legislature that represented the States proportionately, with the lower house elected by the people and the upper house chosen by the lower body from nominees proposed by the State legislatures; an executive chosen by the legislature; a judiciary branch; and a council comprising the executive and members of the judiciary branch with a veto over legislative enactments.

June 15, 1787: New Jersey Plan proposed. Displeased by Randolph's plan, which placed the smaller States in a disadvantaged position, William Patterson proposed instead only to modify the Articles of Confederation. The New Jersey plan would give Congress power to tax and to regulate foreign and interstate commerce, and would establish a plural executive (without veto power) and a supreme court.

June 19, 1787: After debating all the proposals, the convention decided not merely to amend the Articles of Confederation, but to conceive a new national government. The question of equal versus proportional representation by States in the legislature then became the focus of the debate.

June 21, 1787: The Convention adopted a two-year term for representatives.

June 26, 1787: The Convention adopted a six-year term for senators.

July 12, 1787: The Connecticut Compromise (I). Based upon a proposal made by Roger Sherman of Connecticut, the Constitutional Convention agreed that representation in the lower house should be proportional to a State's population (all of the white residents, and three-fifths of the blacks).

July 13, 1787: Northwest Ordinance. While the Constitutional Convention met in Philadelphia, the Congress of the Confederation crafted another governing instrument for the territory north of the Ohio River. The Northwest Ordinance, written largely by Nathan Dane of Massachusetts, provided for interim governance of the territory by Congressional appointees (a governor, secretary and three judges), creation of a bicameral legislature when there were 5,000 free males in the territory, and ultimate establishment of three to five States on an equal footing with the States already in existence. Freedom of worship, right to trial by jury, and public education were guaranteed, and slavery prohibited.

July 16, 1787: The Connecticut Compromise (II). The Convention agreed that each State should be represented equally in the upper chamber.

August 6, 1787: The five-man committee, appointed to draft a constitution based upon 23 "fundamental resolutions" drawn up by the convention between July 19 and July 26, submitted a document containing 23 articles.

August 6–September 10, 1787: The Great Debate. The Convention debated the draft constitution and agreed to prohibit Congress from banning the foreign slave trade for twenty years.

August 16, 1787: The Convention granted to Congress the right to regulate foreign trade and interstate commerce.

September 6, 1787: The Convention adopted a four-year term for the President.

September 8, 1787: A five-man committee, comprising William Samuel Johnson (chair), Alexander Hamilton, James Madison, Rufus King and Gouverneur Morris, was appointed to prepare the final draft.

September 12, 1787: The committee submitted the draft, written primarily by Gouverneur Morris, to the Convention.

September 13–15, 1787: The Convention examined the draft, clause by clause, and made a few changes.

September 17, 1787: All twelve State delegations voted approval of the document. Thirty-nine of the forty-two delegates present signed the engrossed copy, and a letter of transmittal to Congress was drafted. The Convention formally adjourned.

September 20, 1787: Congress received the proposed Constitution.

September 26–27, 1787: Some representatives sought to have Congress censure the Convention for failing to abide by Congress' instruction only to revise the Articles of Confederation.

September 28, 1787: Congress resolved to submit the Constitution to special State ratifying conventions. Article VII of the document stipulated that it would become effective when ratified by nine States.

October 27, 1787: The first "Federalist" paper appeared in New York City newspapers, one of 85 to argue in favor of the adoption of the new frame of government. Written by Alexander Hamilton, James Madison and John Jay, the essays attempted to counter the arguments of anti-Federalists, who feared a strong centralized national government.

December 7, 1787: Delaware ratified the Constitution, the first State to do so, by unanimous vote.

December 12, 1787: Pennsylvania ratified the Constitution in the face of considerable opposition. The vote in convention was 46 to 23.

December 18, 1787: New Jersey ratified unanimously.

January 2, 1788: Georgia ratified unanimously.

January 9, 1788: Connecticut ratified by a vote of 128 to 40.

February 6, 1788: The Massachusetts convention ratified by a close vote of 187 to 168, after vigorous debate. Many anti-Federalists, including Sam Adams, changed sides after Federalists proposed nine amendments, including one that would reserve to the States all powers not "expressly delegated" to the national government by the Constitution.

March 24, 1788: Rhode Island, which had refused to send delegates to the Constitutional Convention, declined to call a State convention and held a popular referendum instead. Federalists did not participate, and the voters rejected the Constitution, 2708 to 237.

April 28, 1788: Maryland ratified by a vote of 63 to 11.

May 23, 1788: South Carolina ratified by a vote of 149 to 73.

June 21, 1788: New Hampshire became the ninth State to ratify, by a vote of 57 to 47. The convention proposed twelve amendments.

June 25, 1788: Despite strong opposition led by Patrick Henry, Virginia ratified the Constitution by 89 to 79. James Madison led the fight in favor. The convention recommended a bill of rights comprising twenty articles, in addition to twenty further changes.

July 2, 1788: The President of Congress, Cyrus Griffin of Virginia, announced that the Constitution had been ratified by the requisite nine States. A committee was appointed to prepare for the change in government.

July 26, 1788: New York ratified by a vote of 30 to 27 after Alexander Hamilton delayed action, hoping that news of ratification from New Hampshire and Virginia would influence anti-Federalist sentiment.

August 2, 1788: North Carolina declined to ratify the Constitution until a bill of rights was added.

September 13, 1788. Congress selected New York as the site of the new government and chose dates for the appointment of and balloting by presidential electors, and for the meeting of the first Congress under the Constitution.

September 30, 1788: Pennsylvania chooses its two senators, the first state to do so. Elections of senators and representatives continue through August 31, 1790.

October 10, 1788: The Congress of the Confederation transacted its last official business.

January 7, 1789: Presidential electors were chosen by ten of the States that had ratified the Constitution (all but New York).

February 4, 1789: Presidential electors voted; George Washington was chosen President, and John Adams Vice-President.

March 4, 1789: The first Congress convened in New York, with eight senators and thirteen representatives in attendance, and the remainder en route.

April 1, 1789: The House of Representatives achieved a quorum, with 30 of its 59 members present, and elected Frederick A. Muhlenberg of Pennsylvania to be its speaker.

April 6, 1789: The Senate, with 12 of 22 senators in attendance, achieved a quorum and chose John Langdon of New Hampshire as temporary presiding officer.

April 30, 1789: George Washington was inaugurated as the nation's first President under the Constitution. The oath of office was administered by Robert R. Livingston, chancellor of the State of New York, on the balcony of Federal Hall, at the corner of Wall and Broad Streets.

July 27, 1789: Congress established the Department of Foreign Affairs (later changed to Department of State).

August 7, 1789: Congress established the War Department.

September 2, 1789: Congress established the Treasury Department.

September 22, 1789: Congress created the office of Postmaster General.

September 24, 1789: Congress passed the Federal Judiciary Act, which established a Supreme Court, 13 district courts and 3 circuit courts, and created the office of the Attorney General.

September 25, 1789: Congress submitted to the States twelve amendments to the Constitution, in response to the five State ratifying conventions that had emphasized the need for immediate changes.

November 20, 1789: New Jersey became the first State to ratify ten of the twelve amendments, the Bill of Rights.

November 21, 1789: As a result of Congressional action to amend the Constitution, North Carolina ratified the original document, by a vote of 194 to 77.

December 19, 1789: Maryland ratified the Bill of Rights.

December 22, 1789: North Carolina ratified the Bill of Rights.

January 25, 1790: New Hampshire ratified the Bill of Rights.

January 28, 1790: Delaware ratified the Bill of Rights.

February 24, 1790: New York ratified the Bill of Rights.

March 10, 1790: Pennsylvania ratified the Bill of Rights.

May 29, 1790: Rhode Island ratified the Constitution, by a vote of 34 to 32.

June 7, 1790: Rhode Island ratified the Bill of Rights.

January 10, 1791: Vermont ratified the Constitution.

March 4, 1791: Vermont was admitted to the Union as the fourteenth State.

November 3, 1791: Vermont ratified the Bill of Rights.

December 15, 1791: Virginia ratified the Bill of Rights, making it part of the United States Constitution.

Sources: Richard B. Morris, ed., *Encyclopaedia of American History,* 6th ed. New York: Harper & Row, 1982; Samuel Eliot Morison, *The Oxford History of the American People,* New York: Oxford University Press, 1965.

Reprinted from *This Constitution: A Bicentennial Chronicle,* Winter 1984, published by Project '87 of the American Historical Association and the American Political Science Association.

Citations

The following—by subject heading—are the principal citations of cases relevant to the text of this book. Only those cases considered important and/or mentioned in the text are included. However, they provide the core of study for anyone who wants to pursue additional research into specific areas. The cases are listed in the order in which they appear in the text.

Debates under wraps (page 31)
McCulloch v. Maryland, 17 U.S. 316 (1819)

Other sources of rights (page 42)
Reid v. Covert, 354 U.S. 1 (1957)
Whitney v. Robertson, 124 U.S. 190 (1888)

How Constitution is changed (page 44)
Dyer v. Blair, 390 F. Supp. 1291 (N.D. Ill. 1975)
Coleman v. Miller, 307 U.S. 433 (1939)
Griswold v. Connecticut, 381 U.S. 479 (1965)
McCulloch v. Maryland, 17 U.S. 316 (1819)
Dred Scott v. Sandford, 60 U.S. 393 (1857)
United States v. Nixon, 418 U.S. 683 (1974)

Changing the Constitution Frequently (page 50)
Chisholm v. Georgia, 2 U.S. 419 (1793)
Dred Scott v. Sandford, 60 U.S. 393 (1857)
Pollock v. Farmers' Loan & Trust Co., 157 U.S. 429, 158 U.S. 601 (1895)
Oregon v. Mitchell, 400 U.S. 112 (1970)

Bill of Rights and states (page 53)
Barron v. Baltimore, 32 U.S. 243 (1833)
Hurtado v. California, 110 U.S. 516 (1884)
Gitlow v. New York, 268 U.S. 652 (1925)
Powell v. Alabama, 287 U.S. 45 (1932)
Palko v. Connecticut, 302 U.S. 319 (1937)
Adamson v. California, 332 U.S. 46 (1947)
Mapp v. Ohio, 367 U.S. 643 (1961)

The Fourteenth Amendment's scope (page 56)
Twining v. New Jersey, 211 U.S. 78 (1908)
Lochner v. New York, 198 U.S. 45 (1905)

Adkins v. Children's Hospital, 261 U.S. 525 (1923)
West Coast Hotel Co. v. Parrish, 300 U.S. 379 (1937)
Griswold v. Connecticut, 381 U.S. 479 (1965)
Roe v. Wade, 410 U.S. 113 (1973)
Goldberg v. Kelly, 397 U.S. 254 (1970)
Loving v. Virginia, 388 U.S. 1 (1967)
Brown v. Board of Education, 347 U.S. 483 (1954)
Orr v. Orr, 440 U.S. 268 (1979)

All rights equal? (page 58)
United States v. Carolene Products Co., 304 U.S. 144 (1938)
Gannett Co. v. DePasquale, 443 U.S. 368 (1979)
United States v. Miller, 307 U.S. 174 (1939)
Engblom v. Carey, 677 F. 2d 957 (2d Cir. 1982)

Can amendment be repealed? (page 60)
Olmstead v. United States, 277 U.S. 438 (1928)
Katz v. United States, 389 U.S. 347 (1967)

Losing your congressional district (page 63)
Wesberry v. Sanders, 376 U.S. 1 (1964)
Baker v. Carr, 369 U.S. 186 (1962)
Reynolds v. Sims, 377 U.S. 533 (1964)
Gomillion v. Lightfoot, 364 U.S. 339 (1960)

Appropriations for army (page 72)
Swift v. Director of Selective Service, 448 F. 2d 1147 (D.C. Cir. 1971)

AT&T breakup (page 73)
United States v. E. C. Knight Co., 156 U.S. 1 (1895)
Northern Securities Co. v. United States, 193 U.S. 197 (1904)
United States v. American Telephone & Telegraph Co., 552 F. Supp. 131
    (D.D.C. 1982), aff'd, 460 U.S. 1001 (1983)

Congress and the environment (page 75)
Wickard v. Filburn, 317 U.S. 111 (1942)
Hodel v. Virginia Surface Mining Ass'n, 452 U.S. 264 (1981)

Bill of attainder (page 76)
Cummings v. Missouri, 71 U.S. 277 (1867)
Ex parte Garland, 71 U.S. 333 (1867)
United States v. Lovett, 328 U.S. 303 (1946)
United States v. Brown, 381 U.S. 437 (1965)
Nixon v. Administrator of General Services, 433 U.S. 425 (1977)

Ex post facto (page 77)
Calder v. Bull, 3 U.S. 386 (1798)
Carpenter v. Pennsylvania, 58 U.S. 456 (1855)
Hawker v. New York, 170 U.S. 189 (1898)

De Veau v. Braisted, 363 U.S. 144 (1960)
In re Yamashita, 327 U.S. 1 (1946)

President impeached (page 88)
United States v. Nixon, 418 U.S. 683 (1974)

Impeachment requiring crime (page 91)
Myers v. United States, 272 U.S. 52 (1926)

Why a Supreme Court? (page 95)
E. S. Bates, The Story of the Supreme Court, p. 15 (1936)
Marbury v. Madison, 5 U.S. 137 (1803)
Fletcher v. Peck, 10 U.S. 87 (1810)

Chief justice (page 99)
Chisholm v. Georgia, 2 U.S. 419 (1793)
Brown v. Board of Education, 347 U.S. 483 (1954)
Reynolds v. Sims, 377 U.S. 533 (1964)

Selection of justices (page 102)
Brown v. Board of Education, 347 U.S. 483 (1954)

Impeachment of justices (page 104)
Marbury v. Madison, 5 U.S. 137 (1803)
United States v. Isaacs, 493 F.2d 1124 (7th Cir. 1974)

Sessions of Court (page 108)
Brown v. Board of Education, 347 U.S. 483 (1954)
Arizona v. California, 373 U.S. 546 (1963)
Dred Scott v. Sandford, 60 U.S. 393 (1857)
Herbert v. Lando, 441 U.S. 153 (1979)

Anyone argue a case (page 111)
Matter of Admission of Rose, 71 L. Ed. 2d 862 (1982)
Dartmouth College v. Woodward, 17 U.S. 518 (1819)
Youngstown Sheet & Tube Co. v. Sawyer, 343 U.S. 579 (1952)
Brown v. Board of Education, 347 U.S. 483 (1954)
McCulloch v. Maryland, 17 U.S. 316 (1819)
Faretta v. California, 422 U.S. 806 (1975)
Keeton v. Hustler Magazine, Inc., 465 U.S. 770 (1984)

First federal law overturned (page 113)
Marbury v. Madison, 5 U.S. 137 (1803)
Dred Scott v. Sandford, 60 U.S. 393 (1857)

First state law overturned (page 115)
Fletcher v. Peck, 10 U.S. 87 (1810)

Invalidating laws often (page 117)
Marbury v. Madison, 5 U.S. 137 (1803)
Immigration & Naturalization Service v. Chadha, 462 U.S. 919 (1983)

Court changing its mind (page 119)
Gideon v. Wainwright, 372 U.S. 335 (1963)
Betts v. Brady, 316 U.S. 455 (1942)

National League of Cities v. Usery, 426 U.S. 833 (1976)
Garcia v. San Antonio Metropolitan Transit Authority, 105 S. Ct. 1005 (1985)
Plessy v. Ferguson, 163 U.S. 537 (1896)
Brown v. Board of Education, 347 U.S. 483 (1954)

Enforcing Court decisions (page 122)
Cherokee Nation v. Georgia, 30 U.S. 1 (1831)
Worcester v. Georgia, 31 U.S. 515 (1832)
Nixon v. United States, 418 U.S. 683 (1974)
Brown v. Board of Education, 347 U.S. 483 (1954)
Cooper v. Aaron, 358 U.S. 1 (1958)

Courts declaring laws unconstitutional (page 124)
Marbury v. Madison, 5 U.S. 137 (1803)
Roe v. Wade, 314 F. Supp. 1217 (N.D. Tex. 1972), aff'd, 410 U.S. 113 (1973)
Caldor, Inc. v. Thornton, 191 Conn. 336, 464 A.2d 785 (1983), aff'd, 105 S.
    Ct. 2914 (1985)
California v. Carney, 105 S. Ct. 2066 (1985)
State v. Long, 700 P.2d 153 (Mont. 1985)

New states (page 129)
Coyle v. Smith, 221 U.S. 559 (1911)

State seceding (page 132)
Texas v. White, 74 U.S. 700 (1869)

States' rights (page 134)
Dred Scott v. Sandford, 60 U.S. 393 (1857)

State boundaries (page 137)
Arizona v. San Carlos Apache Tribe, 463 U.S. 545 (1983)
California v. Nevada, 447 U.S. 125 (1980)

States suing (page 138)
Nevada v. Hall, 440 U. S. 410 (1979)
Marbury v. Madison, 5 U.S. 137 (1803)
Alabama v. Arizona, 291 U.S. 286 (1934)
Alabama v. Texas, 347 U.S. 272 (1954)

Taking (page 140)
Hawaii Housing Authority v. Midkiff, 104 S. Ct. 2321 (1984)
Pennsylvania Coal Co. v. Mahon, 260 U.S. 393 (1922)
Agins v. City of Tiburon, 447 U.S. 255 (1980)
Penn Central Transportation Co. v. City of New York, 438 U.S. 104 (1978)
Loretto v. Teleprompter Manhattan CATV Corp., 458 U.S. 419 (1982)
Ruckelshaus v. Monsanto Co., 104 S. Ct. 2862 (1984)

Sports team moving (page 143)
City of Oakland v. Oakland Raiders, 32 Cal. 3d 60, 646 P.2d 835, 183 Cal.
    Rptr. 673 (1982)

Eighteen-year-old vote (page 146)
Oregon v. Mitchell, 400 U.S. 112 (1970)

Women and voting (page 147)
Minor v. Happersett, 88 U.S. 162 (1875)
Oregon v. Mitchell, 400 U.S. 112 (1970)

Language requirement for voting (page 149)
Nixon v. Herndon, 273 U.S. 536 (1927)
Terry v. Adams, 345 U.S. 461 (1953)
Lassiter v. Northampton County Board of Elections, 360 U.S. 45 (1959)
Louisiana v. United States, 380 U.S. 145 (1965)
Oregon v. Mitchell, 400 U.S. 112 (1970)

Paying to vote (page 150)
Breedlove v. Suttles, 302 U.S. 277 (1937)
Harper v. Virginia State Board of Elections, 383 U.S. 663 (1966)
Cipriano v. City of Houma, 395 U.S. 701 (1969)
Salyer Land Co. v. Tulare Lake Basin Water Storage District, 410 U.S. 719 (1973)

Voting rights after moving to another state (page 151)
Lassiter v. Northampton County Board of Elections, 360 U.S. 45 (1959)
Evans v. Cornman, 398 U.S. 419 (1970)
Carrington v. Rash, 380 U.S. 89 (1965)
Dunn v. Blumstein, 405 U.S. 330 (1972)
Marston v. Lewis, 410 U.S. 679 (1973)
Burns v. Fortson, 410 U.S. 686 (1973)
Kusper v. Pontikes, 414 U.S. 51 (1973)
Rosario v. Rockefeller, 410 U.S. 752 (1973)
Sununu v. Stark, 383 F. Supp. 1287 (D.N.H. 1974), aff'd mem., 420 U.S. 958 (1975)

Political parties (page 153)
James MacGregor Burns, The Deadlock of Democracy: Four-Party Politics in America (1963)
Nixon v. Herndon, 273 U.S. 536 (1927)
Nixon v. Condon, 286 U.S. 73 (1932)
Smith v. Allwright, 321 U.S. 649 (1944)
Terry v. Adams, 345 U.S. 461 (1953)

National election day (page 155)
Ex parte Yarbrough, 110 U.S. 651 (1884)

Giving to a political candidate (page 157)
Buckley v. Valeo, 424 U.S. 1 (1976)

Campaign spending (page 159)
Buckley v. Valeo, 424 U.S. 1 (1976)
Federal Election Commission v. National Conservative Political Action Committee, 105 S. Ct. 1459 (1985)

Paid chaplain (page 162)
Marsh v. Chambers, 463 U.S. 783 (1983)

Nativity scenes (page 163)
Lynch v. Donnelly, 104 S. Ct. 1355 (1984)
McCreary v. Stone, 739 F.2d 716 (2d Cir. 1984), aff'd sub nom. Village of
Scarsdale v. McCreary, 105 S. Ct. 1859 (1985)

School prayer (page 165)
Engel v. Vitale, 370 U.S. 421 (1962)
Abington School District v. Schempp, 374 U.S. 203 (1963)
Wallace v. Jaffree, 105 S. Ct. 2479 (1985)
Widmar v. Vincent, 454 U.S. 263 (1981)
Brandon v. Board of Education, 635 F.2d 971 (2d Cir. 1980), cert. denied, 454
U.S. 1123 (1981)
Lubbock Civil Liberties Union v. Lubbock Independent School District, 669
F.2d 1038 (5th Cir. 1982), cert. denied, 459 U.S. 1155 (1983)
Nartowicz v. Clayton County School District, 736 F.2d 646 (11th Cir. 1984)
Bender v. Williamsport Area School District, 741 F.2d 538 (3d Cir. 1984)
Bell v. Little Axe Independent School District, 766 F.2d 1391 (10th Cir. 1985)

Forced to send a child to school contrary to religion (page 167)
Pierce v. Society of Sisters, 268 U.S. 510 (1925)
Wisconsin v. Yoder, 406 U.S. 205 (1972)

Religious tax exemptions (page 169)
Walz v. Tax Commission, 397 U.S. 664 (1970)

Tax break for private schooling (page 170)
Mueller v. Allen, 463 U.S. 388 (1983)

Doing anything religion mandates (page 171)
Reynolds v. United States, 98 U.S. 145 (1878)
State ex rel. Swann v. Pack, 527 S.W.2d 99 (Tenn. 1975), cert. denied, 424
U.S. 954 (1976)
United States v. Lee, 455 U.S. 252 (1982)

Medical treatment contrary to religion (page 172)
In re Brooks' Estate, 32 Ill. 2d 361, 205 N.E.2d 435 (1965)
Application of President & Directors of Georgetown College, Inc., 331 F.2d
1000, rehearing en banc denied, 331 F.2d 1010 (D.C. Cir.), cert. denied, 377
U.S. 978 (1964)
Crouse Irving Memorial Hospital, Inc. v. Paddock, 127 Misc. 2d 101, 485
N.Y.S.2d 443 (Sup. Ct. 1985)

Sunday store closings (page 173)
McGowan v. Maryland, 366 U.S. 420 (1961)
Braunfeld v. Brown, 366 U.S. 599 (1961)
People v. Abrahams, 40 N.Y.2d 277, 353 N.E.2d 574, 386 N.Y.S.2d 661 (1976)

Working on sabbath (page 175)
Tooley v. Martin-Marietta Corp., 648 F.2d 1239 (9th Cir.), cert. denied, 454
U.S. 1098 (1981)
Trans World Airlines, Inc. v. Hardison, 432 U.S. 63 (1977)
Redmond v. GAF Corp., 574 F.2d 897 (7th Cir. 1978)
Estate of Thornton v. Caldor, Inc., 105 S. Ct. 2914 (1985)

Conscientious-objector status (page 177)
Selective Draft Law Cases, 245 U.S. 366 (1918)
United States v. Seeger, 380 U.S. 163 (1965)
Welsh v. United States, 398 U.S. 333 (1970)
Gillette v. United States, 401 U.S. 437 (1971)

Freedom of speech (page 179)
Chaplinsky v. New Hampshire, 315 U.S. 568 (1942)
New York Times Co. v. Sullivan, 376 U.S. 254 (1964)
Whitney v. California, 274 U.S. 357 (1927)
Cohen v. California, 403 U.S. 15 (1971)

Saying anything against the government (page 181)
New York Times Co. v. Sullivan, 376 U.S. 254 (1964)

Saluting the flag (page 183)
Minersville School District v. Gobitis, 310 U.S. 586 (1940)
West Virginia State Board of Education v. Barnette, 319 U.S. 624 (1943)
Wooley v. Maynard, 430 U.S. 705 (1977)

Burning the flag (page 184)
United States v. Crosson, 462 F.2d 96 (9th Cir. 1972)
Street v. New York, 394 U.S. 576 (1969)
Spence v. Washington, 418 U.S. 405 (1974)

Government workers' rights (page 185)
United States Civil Service Commission v. National Ass'n of Letter Carriers, 413
   U.S. 548 (1973)
McAuliffe v. Mayor of New Bedford, 155 Mass. 216, 29 N.E. 517 (1892)
Pickering v. Board of Education, 391 U.S. 563 (1968)
Connick v. Myers, 461 U.S. 138 (1983)
Elfbrandt v. Russell, 384 U.S. 11 (1966)
Cole v. Richardson, 405 U.S. 676 (1972)

Freedom of the press (page 187)
Near v. Minnesota, 283 U.S. 697 (1931)
New York Times Co. v. United States, 403 U.S. 713 (1971)
United States v. Progressive, Inc., 467 F. Supp. 990 (W.D. Wis. 1979)

Reporters' sources (page 189)
United States v. Nixon, 418 U.S. 683 (1974)
Branzburg v. Hayes, 408 U.S. 665 (1972)
In re Farber, 78 N.J. 259, 394 A.2d 330 (1978)
Herbert v. Lando, 441 U.S. 153 (1979)

Barring reporters from court (page 190)
Sheppard v. Maxwell, 384 U.S. 333 (1966)
Nebraska Press Ass'n v. Stuart, 427 U.S. 539 (1976)
Gannett Co. v. DePasquale, 443 U.S. 368 (1979)
Richmond Newspapers, Inc. v. Virginia, 448 U.S. 555 (1980)
Globe Newspaper Co. v. Superior Court, 457 U.S. 596 (1982)
Press Enterprise Co. v. Superior Court, 464 U.S. 501 (1984)

Right to die *(page 194)*
In re Quinlan, 70 N.J. 10, 355 A.2d 647 (1976)
In re Conroy, 98 N.J. 321, 486 A.2d 1209 (1985)
Zant v. Prevatte, 248 Ga. 832, 286 S.E.2d 715 (1982)
In re Caulk, 480 A.2d 93 (N.H. 1984)

Right of remarriage *(page 196)*
Loving v. Virginia, 388 U.S. 1 (1967)
Zablocki v. Redhail, 434 U.S. 374 (1978)

Privacy in the bedroom *(page 198)*
Olmstead v. United States, 277 U.S. 438 (1928) (dissenting opinion)
Griswold v. Connecticut, 381 U.S. 479 (1965)
Doe v. Commonwealth's Attorney, 425 U.S. 901 (1976), aff'g 403 F. Supp. 1199
    (E.D. Va. 1975)
Hollenbaugh v. Carnegie Free Library, 439 U.S. 1052 (1978)
Andrews v. Drew Municipal Separate School District, 507 F.2d 611 (5th Cir.
    1975), cert. dismissed, 425 U.S. 559 (1976)
Drake v. Covington County Board of Education, 371 F. Supp. 974 (M.D. Ala.
    1974)

Abortion *(page 200)*
Roe v. Wade, 410 U.S. 113 (1973)
Akron v. Akron Center for Reproductive Health, Inc., 426 U.S. 416 (1983)
Bellotti v. Baird, 428 U.S. 132 (1976)
H.L. v. Matheson, 450 U.S. 398 (1981)

Paying for an abortion *(page 202)*
Roe v. Wade, 410 U.S. 113 (1973)
Maher v. Roe, 432 U.S. 464 (1977)
Harris v. McRae, 448 U.S. 297 (1980)

Contraceptives *(page 203)*
Skinner v. Oklahoma, 316 U.S. 535 (1942)
Griswold v. Connecticut, 381 U.S. 479 (1965)
Eisenstadt v. Baird, 405 U.S. 438 (1972)
Carey v. Population Services International, 431 U.S. 678 (1977)

Breaking into a home without a search warrant *(page 205)*
Camara v. Municipal Court, 387 U.S. 523 (1967)
Brinegar v. United States, 338 U.S. 160 (1949)
Illinois v. Gates, 462 U.S. 213 (1983)
Mapp v. Ohio, 367 U.S. 643 (1961)
Monroe v. Pape, 365 U.S. 167 (1961)
Bivens v. Six Unknown Named Agents of the Federal Bureau of Narcotics, 403
    U.S. 388 (1971)

Reading something obscene *(page 206)*
Roth v. United States, 354 U.S. 476 (1957)
Jacobellis v. Ohio, 378 U.S. 184 (1964)
Miller v. California, 413 U.S. 15 (1973)
Jenkins v. Georgia, 418 U.S. 153 (1974)

Stanley v. Georgia, 394 U.S. 557 (1969)
United States v. Reidel, 402 U.S. 351 (1971)

Right to bear arms (page 209)
Presser v. Illinois, 116 U.S. 252 (1886)
Quilici v. Village of Morton Grove, 695 F.2d 261 (7th Cir. 1982), aff'g 532 F.
    Supp. 1169 (N.D. Ill. 1981), cert. denied, 104 S. Ct. 194 (1983)
United States v. Miller, 307 U.S. 174 (1939)

Children's rights (page 210)
Craig v. Boren, 429 U.S. 190 (1976)
Planned Parenthood v. Danforth, 428 U.S. 52 (1976)
Tinker v. Des Moines Independent Community School District, 393 U.S. 503
    (1969)
West Virginia State Board of Education v. Barnette, 319 U.S. 624 (1943)
H.L. v. Matheson, 450 U.S. 398 (1981)

Treating different groups differently (page 212)
Brown v. Board of Education, 347 U.S. 483 (1954)
United States v. Carolene Products Co., 304 U.S. 144 (1938)
Craig v. Boren, 429 U.S. 190 (1976)

Separate-but-equal facilities (page 214)
Plessy v. Ferguson, 163 U.S. 537 (1896)
Roberts v. City of Boston, 59 Mass. 198 (1850)
Sweatt v. Painter, 339 U.S. 629 (1950)
Mclaurin v. Oklahoma State Regents for Higher Education, 339 U.S. 637 (1950)
Brown v. Board of Education, 347 U.S. 483 (1954)

School busing (page 216)
Brown v. Board of Education, 347 U.S. 483 (1954)
Brown v. Board of Education, 349 U.S. 294 (1955)
Cooper v. Aaron, 358 U.S. 1 (1958)
Swann v. Charlotte-Mecklenburg Board of Education, 402 U.S. 1 (1971)
North Carolina State Board of Education v. Swann, 402 U.S. 43 (1971)
Milliken v. Bradley, 418 U.S. 717 (1974)
Pasadena City Board of Education v. Spangler, 427 U.S. 424 (1976)
Washington v. Seattle School District No. 1, 458 U.S. 457 (1982)
Crawford v. Los Angeles Board of Education, 458 U.S. 527 (1982)

Affirmative-action programs (page 218)
Brown v. Board of Education, 347 U.S. 483 (1954)
Regents of the University of California v. Bakke, 438 U.S. 265 (1978)
United Steelworkers v. Weber, 443 U.S. 193 (1979)
Fullilove v. Klutznick, 448 U.S. 448 (1980)
Firefighters Local 1784 v. Stotts, 104 S. Ct. 2576 (1984)

Race as factor in college admissions (page 219)
Regents of the University of California v. Bakke, 438 U.S. 265 (1978)

Women's rights—1787 (page 221)
Bradwell v. Illinois, 83 U.S. 130 (1873)
Reed v. Reed, 404 U.S. 71 (1971)

The ERA and women's rights (page 223)
Craig v. Boren, 429 U.S. 190 (1976)
Stanton v. Stanton, 421 U.S. 7 (1975)
Orr v. Orr, 440 U.S. 268 (1979)
Kahn v. Shevin, 416 U.S. 351 (1974)
Rostker v. Goldberg, 453 U.S. 57 (1981)

Pregnancy benefits (page 224)
Geduldig v. Aiello, 417 U.S. 484 (1974)
General Electric Co. v. Gilbert, 429 U.S. 125 (1976)
Newport News Shipbuilding & Dry Dock Co. v. EEOC, 462 U.S. 669 (1983)

Discrimination against homosexuals (page 226)
Dronenberg v. Zech, 741 F.2d 1388 (D.C. Cir. 1984)

Alien rights (page 227)
Crane v. New York, 239 U.S. 195 (1915)
Patsone v. Pennsylvania, 232 U.S. 138 (1914)
Oyama v. California, 332 U.S. 633 (1948)
Graham v. Richardson, 403 U.S. 365 (1971)
Sugarman v. Dougall, 413 U.S. 634 (1973)
Examining Board v. Flores de Otero, 426 U.S. 572 (1976)
In re Griffiths, 413 U.S. 717 (1973)
Foley v. Connelie, 435 U.S. 291 (1978)
Ambach v. Norwick, 441 U.S. 68 (1979)
Bernal v. Fainter, 104 S. Ct. 2312 (1984)

Welfare and state residency (page 229)
Shapiro v. Thompson, 394 U.S. 618 (1969)
Memorial Hospital v. Maricopa County, 415 U.S. 250 (1974)
Starns v. Malkerson, 401 U.S. 985 (1971), aff'g mem. 326 F. Supp. 234 (D. Minn. 1970)
Sturgis v. Washington, 414 U.S. 1057, aff'g mem. 368 F. Supp. 38 (W.D. Wash. 1973)
Martinez v. Bynum, 461 U.S. 321 (1983)

Guilty entitled to a trial (page 231)
Duncan v. Louisiana, 391 U.S. 145 (1968)
Sheppard v. Maxwell, 384 U.S. 333 (1966)

Exclusionary rule (page 233)
Boyd v. United States, 116 U.S. 616 (1886)
Weeks v. United States, 232 U.S. 383 (1914)
Rochin v. California, 342 U.S. 165 (1952)
Mapp v. Ohio, 367 U.S. 643 (1961)
United States v. Leon, 104 S. Ct. 3405 (1984)
Massachusetts v. Sheppard, 104 S. Ct. 3424 (1984)

Affording a lawyer (page 235)
Gideon v. Wainwright, 372 U.S. 335 (1963)
Scott v. Illinois, 440 U.S. 367 (1979)
Fuller v. Oregon, 417 U.S. 40 (1974)
Ross v. Moffitt, 417 U.S. 600 (1974)

Defending yourself in court (page 236)
Faretta v. California, 422 U.S. 806 (1975)
McKaskle v. Wiggins, 465 U.S. 168 (1984)

Pleading the Fifth Amendment (page 239)
Miranda v. Arizona, 384 U.S. 436 (1966)
Schmerber v. California, 384 U.S. 757 (1966)

Double jeopardy (page 240)
United States v. Dinitz, 424 U.S. 600 (1976)
Burks v. United States, 437 U.S. 1 (1978)
Oregon v. Kennedy, 456 U.S. 667 (1982)

Cruel and unusual punishment (page 242)
Wilkerson v. Utah, 99 U.S. 134 (1879)
Francis v. Resweber, 329 U.S. 459 (1947)
In re Kemmler, 136 U.S. 436 (1890)
Furman v. Georgia, 408 U.S. 238 (1972)
Woodson v. North Carolina, 428 U.S. 280 (1976)
Gregg v. Georgia, 428 U.S. 153 (1976)
Rummel v. Estelle, 445 U.S. 263 (1980)
Hutto v. Davis, 454 U.S. 370 (1982)
Solem v. Helm, 463 U.S. 277 (1983)
Hutto v. Finney, 437 U.S. 678 (1978)
Estelle v. Gamble, 429 U.S. 97 (1976)

Child's free speech rights (page 245)
Tinker v. Des Moines Independent Community School District, 393 U.S. 503 (1969)
Burnside v. Byars, 366 F.2d 744 (5th Cir. 1966)

Suspending child without hearing (page 246)
Goss v. Lopez, 419 U.S. 565 (1975)
Pegram v. Nelson, 469 F. Supp. 1134 (M.D.N.C. 1979)
Dodd v. Rambis, 535 F. Supp. 23 (S.D. Ind. 1981)
Petrey v. Flaughter, 505 F. Supp. 1087 (E.D. Ky. 1981)
Boynton v. Casey, 543 F. Supp. 995 (D. Me. 1982)
Tarter v. Raybuck, 556 F. Supp. 625 (N.D. Ohio 1983)
Board of Education v. McCluskey, 458 U.S. 966 (1982)

Sex education (page 248)
Cornwell v. State Board of Education, 314 F. Supp. 340 (D. Md. 1969), aff'd, 428 F.2d 471 (4th Cir.), cert. denied, 400 U.S. 942 (1970)
Davis v. Page, 385 F. Supp. 395 (D.N.H. 1974)
Citizens for Parental Rights v. San Mateo County Board of Education, 51 Cal. App. 3d 1, 124 Cal. Rptr. 68 (1975), appeal dismissed, 425 U.S. 908 (1976)
Smith v. Ricci, 89 N.J. 514, 446 A.2d 501 (1982)

Removing books from school library (page 248)
Board of Education v. Pico, 457 U.S. 853 (1982)

Searching child's locker (page 250)
New Jersey v. T.L.O., 105 S. Ct. 733 (1985)

Can boss fire me? (page 252)
Elrod v. Burns, 427 U.S. 347 (1976)
Branti v. Finkel, 445 U.S. 507 (1980)
Gay v. Board of Trustees, 608 F.2d 127 (5th Cir. 1979)

Right to join union (page 253)
Commonwealth v. Hunt, 45 Mass. 111 (1842)

Political firing (page 254)
Elrod v. Burns, 427 U.S. 347 (1976)
Branti v. Finkel, 445 U.S. 507 (1980)
Mummau v. Ranck, 687 F.2d 9 (3d Cir.), aff'g 531 F. Supp. 402 (E.D. Pa. 1982)

Decision for war (page 256)
Bass v. Tingy, 4 U.S. 37 (1800)
Crockett v. Reagan, 720 F.2d 1355 (D.C. Cir. 1983), aff'g per curiam 558 F. Supp. 893 (D.D.C. 1982)

Draft (page 260)
Selective Service System v. Minnesota Public Interest Research Group, 104 S. Ct. 3348 (1984)
Rostker v. Goldberg, 453 U.S. 57 (1981)

Treason (page 262)
United States v. Cramer, 325 U.S. 1 (1945)
Haupt v. United States, 330 U.S. 631 (1947)
Kawakita v. United States, 343 U.S. 717 (1952)

Wartime rights (page 264)
Ex parte Milligan, 71 U.S. 2 (1866)
Schenck v. United States, 249 U.S. 47 (1919)
Debs v. United States, 249 U.S. 211 (1919)
Korematsu v. United States, 323 U.S. 214 (1944)
West Virginia State Board of Education v. Barnette, 319 U.S. 624 (1943)
Minersville School District v. Gobitis, 310 U.S. 586 (1940)

Rights of member of armed forces (page 267)
Dynes v. Hoover, 61 U.S. 65 (1858)
Parker v. Levy, 417 U.S. 733 (1974)
Carlson v. Schlesinger, 364 F. Supp. 626 (D.D.C. 1973)
United States v. Wolfson, 36 C.M.R. 722 (1965)
Toth v. Quarles, 350 U.S. 11 (1955)
Reid v. Covert, 354 U.S. 1 (1957)

Bibliography ====================

The following is a list of books on American constitutional history and American constitutional law that will prove helpful to the individual who wishes to delve further into the history and workings of our constitutional system. Where a paperback edition is available, the entry includes full bibliographical information, unless the paperback is published by the original publisher of the hardcover edition, in which case only the date of the paperback edition is included. This list is by no means exhaustive.

Abraham, Henry J. *Justices and Presidents.* Rev. ed. New York: Oxford University Press, 1985; paperback, 1985.

Bailyn, Bernard. *The Ideological Origins of the American Revolution.* Cambridge, Mass.: Harvard University Press, 1967; paperback, 1968.

Baker, Liva. *Miranda: Crime, Law, and Politics.* New York: Atheneum, 1983; paperback, 1985.

Berger, Raoul. *Impeachment: The Constitutional Problems.* Cambridge, Mass.: Harvard University Press, 1974; paperback, with new material, New York: Bantam, 1974.

Beveridge, Albert. *John Marshall.* 4 vols. Boston: Little, Brown, 1916–1919.

Black, Charles L., Jr. *Capital Punishment: The Inevitability of Caprice and Mistake.* New York: W. W. Norton, 1981; paperback, 1981.

Brant, Irving N. *The Bill of Rights: Its Origin and Meaning.* Indianapolis: Bobbs-Merrill, 1965; paperback, New York: Mentor/NAL, 1967.

Commager, Henry Steele. *The Empire of Reason: How Europe Imagined and America Realized the Enlightenment.* New York: Anchor Press/Doubleday, 1977; paperback, New York: Oxford University Press, 1981.

Corwin, Edward S. *John Marshall and the Constitution.* New Haven: Yale University Press, 1919.

Corwin, Edward S., and others. *The President: Office and Powers.* New York: New York University Press, 1984; paperback, 1984.

Cox, Archibald. *The Role of the Supreme Court in American Government.* New York: Oxford University Press, 1976; paperback, 1977.

———. *Freedom of Expression.* Cambridge, Mass.: Harvard University Press, 1981; paperback, 1981.

Dunne, Gerald T. *Justice Joseph Story and the Rise of the Supreme Court.* New York: Simon & Schuster, 1971.

———. *Hugo Black and the Judicial Revolution.* New York: Simon & Schuster, 1977; paperback, 1978.

Fisher, Louis. *Constitutional Controversies Between Congress and the President.* Princeton, N.J.: Princeton University Press, 1985; paperback, 1985.

Fehrenbacher, Don E. *The Dred Scott Case.* New York: Oxford University Press, 1978; paperback abridged edition under the title *Slavery, Law, and Politics,* New York: Oxford University Press, 1981.

Friendly, Fred W. *Minnesota Rag: The Story of Near v. Minnesota.* New York: Random House, 1981; paperback, New York: Vintage, 1982.

Hamilton, Alexander, James Madison, and John Jay. *The Federalist Papers.* Edited by Clinton L. Rossiter. New York: Mentor/NAL, 1961, paperback. (The best of the many editions.)

Hyman, Harold M., and William E. Wiecek. *Equal Justice Under Law: Constitutional Development, 1835–1875.* New York: Harper & Row, 1982; paperback, 1983.

Jensen, Merrill. *The New Nation: A History of the United States during the Confederation, 1781–1789.* New York: Alfred A. Knopf, 1950; paperback, Boston: Northeastern University Press, 1982.

Kelly, Alfred H., Winfred Harbison, and Herman Belz. *The American Constitution: Its Origin and Development.* 6th ed. New York: W. W. Norton, 1982.

Kluger, Richard. *Simple Justice.* New York: Alfred A. Knopf, 1975; paperback, New York: Vintage, 1977.

Levy, Leonard W. *The Law of the Commonwealth and Chief Justice Shaw.* Cambridge, Mass.: Harvard University Press, 1957.

———. *Origins of the Fifth Amendment.* New York: Oxford University Press, 1968; paperback, 1969.

———. *Emergence of a Free Press.* New York: Oxford University Press, 1985. (Revised edition of *Legacy of Suppression: Freedom of Speech and Press in Early America,* Cambridge, Mass.: Harvard University Press, 1960).

Lewis, Anthony. *Gideon's Trumpet.* New York: Random House, 1965; paperback, New York: Vintage, 1966.

Mason, Alpheus Thomas. *Brandeis: A Free Man's Life.* New York: Viking, 1946.

McCloskey, Robert G. *The American Supreme Court.* Chicago: University of Chicago Press, 1955; paperback, 1960.

Morris, Richard B. *Fair Trial: Fourteen Who Stood Accused, from Anne Hutchinson to Alger Hiss.* Rev. ed., paperback, New York: Harper & Row, 1963.

———. *Seven Who Shaped Our Destiny: The Founding Fathers and Revolutionaries.* New York: Harper & Row, 1973; paperback, 1976.

———. *Witnesses at the Creation: Hamilton, Madison, Jay, and the Constitution.* New York: Holt, Rinehart & Winston, 1985.

Murphy, Paul L. *The Constitution in Crisis Times, 1918–1969.* New York: Harper & Row, 1971; paperback, 1972.

Nevins, Allan. *The American States During and After the Revolution.* New York: Macmillan, 1927.

Rossiter, Clinton L. *The American Presidency.* Rev. ed. New York: Harcourt, Brace, 1960; paperback, New York: Mentor/NAL, 1961.

———. *1787: The Grand Convention.* New York: Macmillan, 1966.

Rutland, Robert Allen. *The Birth of the Bill of Rights, 1776–1791.* Chapel Hill, N.C.: University of North Carolina Press, 1981; paperback, Boston: Northeastern University Press, 1983.

————. *The Ordeal of the Constitution: The Antifederalists and the Ratification Struggle of 1787–1788.* Norman, Oklahoma: University of Oklahoma Press, 1966; paperback, Boston: Northeastern University Press, 1983.

Simon, James. *Independent Journey: The Life of William O. Douglas.* New York: Harper & Row, 1980; paperback, New York: Penguin, 1981.

Smith, James Morton. *Freedom's Fetters: The Alien and Sedition Acts and American Civil Liberties.* Ithaca, N.Y.: Cornell University Press, 1955; paperback revised edition, 1962.

Storing, Herbert J., with the assistance of Murray Dry. *What the Anti-Federalists Were For: The Political Thought of the Opponents of the Constitution.* Chicago: University of Chicago Press, 1981, paperback. (A reprint of *The Complete Anti-Federalist,* vol. 1. Edited by Herbert J. Storing and Murray Dry. 7 vols. Chicago: University of Chicago Press, 1981).

Tribe, Laurence H. *American Constitutional Law.* Mineola, N.Y.: Foundation Press, 1978.

Warren, Charles. *The Making of the Constitution.* Boston: Little, Brown, 1926, 1937, and 1946.

White, G. Edward. *The American Judicial Tradition.* New York: Oxford University Press, 1975; paperback, 1976.

————. *Earl Warren: A Public Life.* New York: Oxford University Press, 1982.

Wood, Gordon S. *The Creation of the American Republic, 1776–1787.* Chapel Hill, N.C.: University of North Carolina Press, 1969; paperback, New York: W. W. Norton, 1971.

Anyone interested in the history of the Constitution should examine the various contemporary diaries and records of the Federal Convention of 1787. The best compilation is Max Farrand, editor, *The Records of the Federal Convention of 1787,* 4 vols; New Haven: Yale University Press, 1911, 1937; a new edition of the fourth volume is being prepared by James H. Hutson of the Library of Congress. A convenient one-volume edition is Charles C. Tansill, ed., *Documents Illustrative of the Formation of the Union of the American States,* Washington, D.C.: Government Printing Office, 1927 and later reprints. James Madison's notes, the best single record of the Convention's work, are published separately: James Madison, *Notes of Debates in the Federal Convention of 1787,* Athens, Ohio: Ohio University Press, 1969; paperback, 1985.

Index

How free are we?

DATE DUE			
5/7/87			
NOV 1 2 1991			
5/6/94			